BEHIND THE THE BADGE

ANDREW FAULL

BEHIND THE BADGE

THE UNTOLD STORIES OF SOUTH AFRICA'S POLICE SERVICE MEMBERS

Published by Zebra Press
an imprint of Random House Struik (Pty) Ltd
Reg. No. 1966/003153/07
80 McKenzie Street, Cape Town, 8001
PO Box 1144, Cape Town, 8000 South Africa

www.zebrapress.co.za

First published 2010

1 3 5 7 9 10 8 6 4 2

Publication © Zebra Press 2010
Text © Andrew Faull 2010

Cover photographs © Getty Images/Hamish Blair

PUBLISHER: Marlene Fryer
MANAGING EDITOR: Robert Plummer
EDITOR: Shelly Dall
PROOFREADER: Beth Housdon
COVER DESIGNER: Michiel Botha
TEXT DESIGNER: Monique Oberholzer
PRODUCTION MANAGER: Valerie Kömmer

Set in 11 pt on 15.5 pt Adobe Garamond

Printed and bound by CTP Book Printers, Boompies Street, Parow, 7500

ISBN 978 1 77022 055 3

For the men and women of the South African Police Service

CONTENTS

CONTENTS

ACKNOWLEDGEMENTS

This book is the product of ideas, support, energy, time and love shared freely with me by dozens of people, all of whom I am indebted to.

Firstly, to the twenty-eight current and former policemen and -women who told me their stories at no benefit to themselves – thank you. It is your words and your lives that make up the pages of this book. Special thanks to those members who went on to help me connect with other respondents, and who have continued to offer support to me in my work. Extra-special thanks to Johan Boning for his early contacts, and to Stef Grobler for his willingness to answer even the silliest of questions throughout the re-search process.

This book had its genesis in 2004 when Elrena van der Spuy at the University of Cape Town introduced me to the concept of 'police culture'. In lending me her private copy of Mark Baker's *Cops: Their Lives in Their Own Words*, she awakened in me a longing for a book in which I could hear the voices of South Africa's Police Service (SAPS) members. I knew that if it wasn't already out there for me to read, I'd want to put it together. Thank you, Elrena.

I am grateful to *Servamus* and the *SAPS Journal*, both of which published letters I'd written inviting SAPS members to contact me to participate in the book.

I was assisted by numerous people in making contact with potential respondents. Among others, my thanks go to Tracy Meyjes, Irvin Kinnes, Jannie du Toit, Nathi Mjenxane, Craig Mitchell, Caty May and Lillian Mashele for their considerable help in this regard.

I am grateful to my colleagues in the Crime & Justice Programme at the Institute for Security Studies who have helped me in numerous ways: to Johan Burger for the tip-off about *Servamus* and for clarifying the rank structure; to Tizina Ramagaga for the Sunday-afternoon name changes; to Thokozile Mtsolongo for help with a transcript; to Bilkis Omar for her helpful comments on a draft; and to Chandré Gould for a bed, for recommending Zebra Press, for her police contacts and for her overall encouragement. I am also grateful to Judy and Bastian Smith-Höhn for their accommodation and transport assistance in Pretoria.

I am indebted to a number of others who gave feedback on a draft: Norman Faull, Caroll Faull, Mia Faull, Simon Hareb, Kristin Anderson (thanks also for the contact!) and Deryck Sheriffs (thanks also for the timeline tip!). I am further grateful to my family, Norman, Caroll, Mia, Wendy and Jonathan (to whom I am also grateful for the timeline help!), for their love, support and sundry assistance throughout this journey.

I am grateful to Marlene Fryer and Robert Plummer at Zebra Press for their enthusiasm, encouragement and support, and for providing me with the necessary push to finally get things going. Thanks to Shelly Dall for her careful edit and suggestions around the final manuscript, and to Robert for his substantial help in improving the structure. Marlene Swanepoel at the SAPS Museum in Pretoria came to the rescue at the last minute and helped me with the timeline.

I am indebted to all the permanent SAPS members and reservists who, over the years, have shared their insights, time and energy with me while I was performing reservist duties.

Thank you to all the SAPS reservists who contacted me with a willingness to participate, as well as those permanent members who volunteered but with whom I was unable to meet. If there are any others who I have forgotten, I apologise – I am thankful to everyone who has supported me along the way.

Finally, to all members of the South African Police Service, thank you for the inspiration.

ANDREW FAULL
MARCH 2010

INTRODUCTION

If asked, almost all South Africans have something to say about *The Police* – that amorphous, nondescript, all-encompassing blur of blue so central to our lives. More often than not our views are less than flattering: '*The Police* are lazy', '*The Police* are corrupt', '*The Police* always come too late'… But who or what is *The Police*?

If it were a machine, *The Police* would be made up of almost two hundred thousand parts, each unique, but connected, and working with those around them to produce a steady, deep baritone purr. Tens of thousands of other parts would, over the decades, have been replaced by newer, younger models, while others would have fallen victim to the perils of a moving mass of metal. But the South African Police Service (SAPS) is not a machine and it is not made up of parts. It is a massive organisation that has, since its founding as the South African Police force (SAP) in 1913, employed hundreds of thousands of South Africans from all walks of South African life.

Of course it is easy and convenient for us to refer to these individuals simply as *The Police*, but labels such as 'policeman', 'member' and 'officer' are only some of many with which these hundreds of thousands identify. Before they joined *The Police*, and long after they retire, they will identify as black and white, African and South African, rich (though rarely) and poor, men and women, brothers and sons, mothers and cousins. They are gay and straight, young and old, healthy and frail, able and injured. They are motor mechanics and IT experts, sharpshooters and negotiators, dog handlers and pilots, musicians and divers. They are managers, mentors, detectives and sector heads, chairpersons and committee members. They are midfielders and wings, outdoor enthusiasts and movie freaks, surfers and sprinters, intellectuals, doctors and students, extroverts and introverts. They are all these things and many more. Some are motivated, some have lost their fire. All of them are people with hopes and dreams, who laugh and cry just like the rest of us. They are South African men and women who, when they go to work, happen to be affiliated with a national police body, a uniform and a badge. For this reason we too often see them only as *The Police*.

It is true that some serving members should not have been hired into the SAPS. It is not an organisation for just anyone. But there are many, many more for whom it represents a vessel through which they can live their dreams and make a positive contribution to society. Sometimes exactly the right people are hired into the organisation, but the circumstances in which they find themselves can end up crushing their spirits.

The SAP/S has a long, complicated and sometimes violent history. For most of its existence it was a tool used by the minority elite to protect an illegitimate state and implement its laws. This elite minority used it to put down uprisings and detain political opponents. They were liberal in their use of force and were implicated in assassinations. Then over a relatively short period a switch was flipped, the rules changed and a new era began. Members were expected to adapt and get on with things. From the early to mid-nineties, there was a conscious move away from a police *force* to a community-centric police *service*. At the same time, the country experienced a dramatic rise in violent crime. Everyone looked to the SAPS to quell it until, in 2009, political leaders began calling for a shift *back* to a police force, as if, once again, the organisation were a ball of clay to be moulded to fit a transient political vision.

Histories such as these leave their marks on the individuals caught up in their making.

For outsiders, the notion of what police *should* do and how they *should* behave is shaped by a mostly limited understanding of the law, by their own personal desires and by fiction. In reality, the actions and behaviour patterns of the men and women of the SAPS are formed by navigating the space between what the law *requires* and *allows* them to do, and what society *expects* them to do. In South Africa the expectations placed on the everyday cop are enormous, often bordering on the impossible, while a progressive constitutional framework is interpreted as overly limiting police powers to act. In order to survive the weight of these competing forces, police develop their own informal rules, codes and systems to deliver on their mandate. These can be as inconsequential as paying house calls to members of the neighbourhood to improve public perception, or as sinister as manipulating crime statistics in the hope of pleasing management. These informal systems are not taught at police college but rather learnt on the job, where a member's real socialisation takes place. Because these systems are generally informal and unofficial, it becomes difficult for outsiders to access, engage with and understand them. Even to the new student entering the SAPS, familiarity with the informal culture at their post develops over time, through experience, observation and storytelling.

Storytelling is a central part of police culture. The bulk of an operational police official's work is conducted in public spaces, far beyond the gaze of his or her colleagues. An occupational by-product of this environment is that police officials inevitably become storytellers. Whether in writing arrest statements, giving evidence in court, illustrating a lesson to a student or through old-fashioned exchanges to pass quiet hours of a night shift, storytelling is central to police life.

However, in general these stories are not meant for the ears of anyone outside the organisation. Indeed, often they are not trusted with fellow SAPS members who are not part of the same shift, unit or station as the storyteller. What the public is given are sound bites of places, numbers and official outcomes – sanitised truth. Meanwhile the full stories remain locked within the wall of police group solidarity.

As a national police body the SAP/S has been central to South Africa's history. It has been seen as the embodiment of state oppression and violence, presented as a solution to pervasive crime and held up as a symbol of hope for a better future. Ultimately the SAPS is a product of the society out of which it has grown. In this sense when we look into it we find a grainy mirror reflecting the fragmented health of a nation, reminding us who we really are. There are voices in this book that ask readers to remember that police are human too. But by virtue of the work we ask police to do, their humanity does not always emerge shining. Is this because they are bad people, or is it the nature of the organisation and the society out of which it has grown – a patchwork of light and darkness?

Through this book I have tried to offer readers a glimpse of the space between the official and the expected in which members of the SAPS exist. In so doing, I hope readers will begin to see beyond the blur of blue that is *The Police*, to see the individuals behind the badge and the tangled world they inhabit on our behalf.

Method and structure

This book is the product of interviews with twenty-eight current and former members of the SAPS conducted between late 2008 and September 2009. It is structured thematically and is intended to be read from beginning to end. However, some readers may prefer to dip in and out as they see fit. Readers may also choose to follow individual contributors through the book by referring to the page numbers listed next to the names in the About the Contributors section on pages 275–282.

Chapters 1 and 2 – covering childhood, joining the police and police college – serve to introduce the various contributors and are the only chapters in which all of them feature. Thereafter they appear only in chapters relevant to their personal experience of the police.

Some of the earlier chapters are ordered chronologically, to give readers a sense of SAPS history and provide a background to the contributors. Other chapters follow a more thematic structure.

Throughout the book, where possible and relevant, years are displayed at the end of excerpts to indicate approximately when the event(s) recounted occurred. Readers should note that neither these years, nor facts claimed by respondents, have been verified. Characters' imperfect memories, beliefs and perceptions make up their understanding of SAPS reality and in this sense have real-world ramifications as they feed into the organisational paradigm.

In the SAPS, when a woman's name is written, her gender is indicated by the placement of an 'F' in brackets after the rank designation, e.g.

Constable (F) Dlamini. Men are not given a marker. While some might take issue with the system, because it is an official method I have used it in this book. In doing so, I mean no offence.

The timeline at the back of the book is intended as a simple guide to locating some of the events referred to by respondents, or events which I believed pertinent to the stories and to the SAP/S.

Where characters have mentioned other people in their stories, these names have been changed.

We always say there are things that happened that you laugh about and talk about at a braai, but there are things that you never talk about. What happens on the shift stays on the shift; what happens in the station stays in the station. It always stays inside with the police or on the shift. It's got nothing to do with outside. Nothing, nothing, nothing. — **Inspector Marais**

BECOMING A COP

There are three types of people who become cops. There are people who become cops because they live for it. It's their passion. Call it a 'cop gene', maybe some DNA thing that just programmes him to be a cop. Five hundred years ago he would have been in armour on horseback, slaying dragons and rescuing maidens. There are people who just have this need to serve and help others. I like to think I'm in this category.

Then you get those people that are glorified bullies. They like the power, they like the authority and they like to bully people. Again that goes back through time.

Then I think you get the third type of people who are just there because it's a job; it's not a calling. So long as I'm getting paid I'm not going to kill myself; I'm going to do what I have to do not to get fired. I think it's not just in South Africa; I think it's like this all over the world.

— **Sergeant Jordaan**

I grew up in Pretoria. My father was a member of the police band and my mother was a nurse. My earliest memories are of accompanying my dad when the band gave performances during parades. My father was never a police officer; he was a musician. But there was the lure of the uniform and joining the South African Police. It seemed to be a vibrant, dynamic organisation, sort of a romantic thing to do, to become a policeman. The whole idea was to become a detective. A friend of my parents was a detective, a senior guy. When he spoke of the cases that he investigated and the things that he was involved in, that grabbed my imagination.

I said to myself, 'I'd love to unravel a case and be an investigator!' I joined on 15 January 1963. My dad, being in the police himself, was stationed at the police college. I'd gone in early. We were standing in a queue there and a sergeant came along and he said to me in Afrikaans, 'Excuse me, sir, have you been sworn in yet?' I said, 'No, I haven't,' and he said, 'If you'll just stand here, the coffee will be ready just now.' So it carried on and I was then sworn in. I was still standing around when along came the same sergeant who said, 'Excuse me, have you been sworn in?' and I said, 'Yes, I've been sworn in,' and he shouted, 'What the hell are you doing standing around here? Get your hair cut!' I said to myself, 'Oh my goodness, what have I done?' – **Director Grobler (joined 1963)**

I was born in Middelfontein in Limpopo province, on the farms, in 1955.

On the farm there were so few of us. We didn't meet people who asked us what we wanted to be one day. But when I moved from the farm to the village, people at school would ask what you wanted to be when you grew up. I would tell them that when I grew up I wanted to join the police force. People in the township said the police were bad, but people in the village respected the police. Even if a policeman was alone he could control them; they would do what he said.

I joined because I wanted to serve the public. I could see that most of my age group were involved in crime, so to pull myself out of that, I thought, let me join the police and serve the community. I was appointed on 10 November 1975 at John Vorster Square in Johannesburg.

 – **Inspector Mampuru (joined 1975)**

I had a passion to be a policeman. Since I was a youngster and I saw policemen walking about, I just wanted to be one. I joined the police in 1977. When you arrive at the station you've got a dream that you want to fulfil. But you don't necessarily get to that dream, to the branch you want to go to. I only got to that dream at a later stage, when I joined SANAB. After college I was transferred to Ermelo. It took me from 1978 to 1986 to reach my dream. – **Captain de Beer (joined 1977)**

I grew up in the countryside, in Stellenbosch, renowned for its vineyards and wine farms. As a young child growing up in a predominantly white area, my parents (who were farm workers) only saw the town's business area once a month, usually transported by the white farm owner. It was also the only time of the month when the mainly coloured labour force was allowed to go into the predominantly white town.

During this visit to the town for purchases of clothing and life necessities, most of the farm workers would become heavily intoxicated because of the availability of alcohol. As a little child I was always accompanied by an adult male or my father, a drinker at the time. The white police officers would rock up there with the van; the poor farm labourer is sitting there on the side of the road because he doesn't know the town – he's tired because he worked that morning before the trip to the town. He's waiting for the wives or other people, but by sitting down on the pavement the whites would presume that he was already drunk. Instead of asking the man, 'What is your name, sir?', 'What can I do for you?', 'How can we help you?', 'What is your reason for sitting down in the road?', they would simply open the back of the van, grab him by the scruff of the neck, boost him physically into the back of the van, lock him up and give him a R30 fine. As a young person, I renounced that; I rebelled against the police. I even physically intervened by fighting and holding on to the old brown cross-straps that the police used to wear on the brown uniforms before the blue uniforms were brought into use.

As a child I grew up with the belief that one day, when I grew up, I would join the police in order to change the way they dealt with the public.

Entry into the police wasn't easy sailing. It wasn't just having an interview and completing a job application form. You had the physical examination, the doctor's examination … and because the police at the time were predominantly white, they used to be big, rough guys. New recruits were measured against their physiques. They used a tape measure – they took your full length from your shoes to your head and they measured your chest and waist. If you did not meet the prescribed criteria as far as body build, height and mass were concerned, you were summarily discarded as no good for the police. Intelligence, capacity, people skills, integrity, knowledge were never considered for an interview. I dread to know what would happen today if we applied the same philosophy. Needless to say, I waited two years after my application to hear from the police. Then I was suddenly asked, 'Do you still wish to be a policeman?' and the answer was, 'Yes.' I was employed by the University of Stellenbosch at the time, where I was earning good money. I took a three hundred per cent reduction in pay to join the police. — **Inspector Khan (joined 1981)**

My father and grandfather were police officers – so I grew up in a police environment. When I was in Standard 9 and 10 my interest in studying was not that good. I was more involved in motorcycling, so I didn't achieve very good marks.

I wanted to go and study education but I decided that due to my 'excellent' achievement in matric that option was not available to me. I didn't have university admission, so that also limited my options. I wanted to join the police to make a difference in people's lives, but also for the adventure. I was of the opinion that the South African Police at that stage was a very adventurous working environment. There were a lot of good things about the police, especially then.

— **Senior Superintendent Boning (joined 1982)**

I was born in Johannesburg, but I moved to Limpopo when I was very young. I attended school there and then went back to Johannesburg to work at a factory. We manufactured TV aerials. Then my uncle said, 'No, no, no, no, no! You are going to become a criminal! This lifestyle of yours isn't good. Tomorrow morning I'm taking you to the police.' He was a cop at the time, working in the security branch. In 1981 he took me to John Vorster Square and signed me up. John Vorster Square was the headquarters of the security police. If you tried to run away from there, you 'fell'.*

---

*　Reference to Ahmed Timol and Matthews Mabelane, whom police claimed had jumped and fallen from the tenth floor of the building in 1971 and 1977 respectively. Six others allegedly hung themselves. It is believed that they were tortured and killed by security police.

I didn't choose to join the police; it was pressure from the family. If I hadn't joined the police maybe I *would* have become a criminal, because that was a hard life. If you didn't succeed, you thought of being a criminal. Crime paid. There was less crime then. At that time the criminal stole from the white man, not from the black man. We named it 'repossession'.

– Inspector Rameama (joined 1982)

I was born in Lady Selborne, the location. It was demolished and we were forcibly removed to Mamelodi and Atteridgeville around the Pretoria area. I grew up and was schooled in Mamelodi Primary until 1976, when we rioted. We were doing it against Afrikaans. I was sixteen or seventeen. From June nothing happened at school because we were burning cars, hijacking delivery trucks, taking the goods, burning the trucks. As a crowd of schoolchildren we would stop them; we would throw stones at the windscreens so the drivers had to brake.

It was no work, no school until the Afrikaans-only education policy changed. We were doing agriculture in Afrikaans; Bantu Education – every subject was in Afrikaans except Sepedi and English. Our parents decided that their children should be educated, so I went to Pietersburg and completed my matric in '78 and '79. Then I came back home and started selling beer, running a shebeen. I smuggled in dagga from Lesotho in 1979, '80, '81 and '82. I was supporting my parents. I don't remember a day when my mother went to work. My father worked for the railway, building the railway lines. He wore leather all over because he worked at the foundry building the rails, carrying them, cooling them. At the end of every month I went there to take his pay to my mother.

So I thought, no man, these policemen are busy taking *tsho-tsho* from my shebeen. They would take my beers and take bribes from me. They were always arresting me but never put me in jail. They came, arrested me, I paid, they brought me back. I wanted to be like them; I wanted to get *tsho-tsho* just like they did. So I thought, I'm going to join them. That's when I decided I was going to the police force. When they hired me, they sent the security branch to interview me. They asked me where I was in 1976. I told a lie. I said I was in Pietersburg, schooling there.

'Were you not in the riots?' they asked. I said, 'No, no, no!' That is when I was hired.

Before I joined the SAP, I nearly crossed the border to Botswana to join MK. Then the management of the ANC said, 'No, we want you inside. Go forward.' I was a youth-club member of the church and a community member organising toyi-toyis. We never slept at home because the security branch would always come and look for us at night. So we slept on the roof of the toilets at my parents' home. When the police came, we would see them before they saw us. Then we would *spring* and leave but the parents would be assaulted. They wanted me. So I had to lie when I joined the police.

On my first day, my first job was washing bakkies – in brand-new clothes! I thought it was a punishment. Within two days they took me to the detectives. Within three months they told me I was wanted at the college.

It was just about working. The only company that was hiring black people was the SAP.   **– Inspector Moji (joined 1983)**

When I joined the police it was about serving my community. I was encouraged by a friend of mine from school who joined before me. Also, I couldn't go further after matric because of financial restrictions. I thought the police would be the best thing for me. I joined straight after high school.

There was an old man who I was working for on Saturdays. He was a brigadier in the SAP, but I didn't know that. I went to him and asked, 'If a person wants to be a police officer, what must he do?' I thought every white man knew these things. He said, 'If you complete your matric, just tell me.' When I finished matric I showed him the statement of my results and he said, 'Shit, very clever!'

The following week we went to head office, he took me through the whole process – the medical examination ... then we went to my mother to get consent. I was eighteen when I joined, so they needed to get consent from my mother to make sure she agreed that I could join the police. In '87, many police, especially blacks, were being killed in the townships because they were seen as sell-outs, so it was a very dangerous career to choose. They just wanted to make sure that everyone agreed and was satisfied. We then went to the school to get some background information. About a month later I got a call and started.

At the time I was not politically minded. For me it was just to go and serve and to arrest criminals. To me a criminal didn't have a colour. It was only when I entered the SAP that I learnt I wasn't allowed to arrest a white man; I could only arrest black people. But then, to me it was all about service. I still loved the career.   – **Captain Mthembu (joined 1987)**

I grew up in Potgietersrus (now it's called Mokopane). I was not like the other children. I did almost every naughty thing that one could do. I never thought I would become a police officer. Nobody could ever believe it.

When I was about to finish matric, I was in a study group of about five. We agreed that we had an interest in public health administration. We thought we would register to be public health inspectors.

In 1984, the struggle came into our area, especially on 16 June. That's when we started burning things. We ran around breaking everything – shops and company delivery cars. My parents were very strict, so they sent me to Kwena Moloto College in Pietersburg for two weeks of winter school. When I returned, my mother met me in town and told me that I could not go home because all of my friends had been arrested. I had to go to Pretoria. I stayed there for about three months without going to school. Then everything subsided and I went back home and went to school.

In 1986, I passed my matric. My results were not satisfactory to go into health administration, so I was just lingering around Pretoria visiting my father. As I was walking around one day I saw people at the city council offices queuing for a job. I went and gave my details. On 1 May 1987 I started work as a municipal police officer. It was just a coincidence.

I was about twenty-one, so the naughtiness was still there. When your commander told you to do something, you felt you were being oppressed. At that time it was hard; you could be fired on the spot. If they said, 'Just go and wash my car,' and you said no, you could get fired.

When I went home to Potgietersrus and told people I was a policeman, they couldn't believe it, because they saw the way we had been spearheading the struggle and how naughty we had been, how the community had not trusted us much when we were growing up. Until 1989 – when we municipal police were employed in the SAP – they did not believe I was a policeman.

There were only black municipal police. The whites were in the top ranks. There were no whites in the lower ranks. We had to enforce the by-laws. The garbage men drove around on tractors and trailers at three o'clock in the morning and they were being attacked, so we had to go and guard them while they moved around. We escorted the Mamelodi mayor too. At that time Mamelodi was run by itself, by the mayor. Even the councillors' houses we guarded. People who urinated on the street – we arrested them.

In those days, they would put two of you at a very big place like a mall to guard it. I would ask myself, 'Do those people put me here thinking that nothing will happen?' I would just leave and go to the hostel where I was living and I would sleep. I was unruly. I felt I was wasting time just sitting there.

From 1987, as a recruit I was earning about R340, then after college I was earning R430-something. Things changed when we were amalgamated with the SAP. That's when the salary went up to R900 and the ranks came and the political situation changed.

The municipal police were part of the South African Municipal Workers' Union. So when the municipal offices were on strike, we were supposed to be on strike. It became a burden for the SAP. We had guns; when we were on strike we could use our guns to fire back. So there was a discussion and we were amalgamated with the SAP in 1989.

– **Inspector Kekane (joined 1987, municipal police; 1989, SAP)**

I grew up in George. I wanted to do something for the country, either the police or the defence force. But the defence force wasn't for me. I didn't join the defence force because there was too much training beforehand; it would have taken too long to get into the action. It seemed more enjoyable to join the police. – **Inspector Burger (joined 1988)**

I grew up in Mokopane in the North West. When I was in middle school there was a police officer who was transporting his child to school every day. He was a colonel. His daughter was at the same school as me. That's when I started to develop a liking for the police. The way he was dressed – clean-shaven, neat uniform – the police car he was driving, with the long aerial … I liked it.

At school I was a disciplined person. In most of middle school I was a monitor. Then in Standard 7 I was a chief prefect. One of the teachers used to tell me that with the way I was disciplined I could work in the police force. I liked the idea of being a policeman but I wanted to become a lawyer or a prosecutor.

When I was in middle school, 1986, it was bad times. I checked both sides and I realised that the police were doing what they were supposed to be doing. I was not exposed to much politics, but I could understand that the police were trying to restore order. I was not so exposed to the other side, to the killing.

When I was doing Standard 10 in Atteridgeville, I had a friend. He also liked the police. I told him, 'Man, let's join the police.' He said, 'No, look what's happening now in our area – I'm afraid they will attack my family's home.' I joined in 1989 and the following year I went to the college. In 1991 my friend also joined the police.

– **Superintendent Molebatsi (joined 1989)**

I joined accidently. A friend of mine had wanted to join the police her whole life. I told her she was crazy – women don't join the police! In my matric year she went to write her entry tests. I drove with her and her mom and I sat there outside the door waiting for her. The sergeant came out and said, 'What are you doing here?' I said, 'I'm just waiting for a friend.' He said, 'Well, write the tests and then I'll tear them up. They're interesting; it's nice to write.' So I wrote the test.

I went on my matric holiday to Margate. When I came back my mom and dad said, 'The police are looking for you.' I said, 'Margate's police?' I couldn't imagine how they could have traced me back to Pretoria! They said, 'No, Pretoria's police.'

The police invited me for an interview. I got the job and thought I'd do it for a year while I decided what I wanted to go and study. I got hooked on the adrenalin and liked it. My year became twelve years. I was taken in that direction; I didn't choose it.

– **Inspector (F) van Niekerk (joined 1990)**

I was born in the Free State. I was an active little boy; I loved army and police stuff. I had lots of police and army toys. I used to play a lot in my room and I would take photos of the little plastic soldiers.

I've always wanted to protect this country. Always. People used to see that as a racial thing and that irritated me immensely, because when I served in the national defence force, as a serviceman – I was in the intelligence unit in the South African Army – I had a lot of African soldiers that worked with me. I had a desire to protect this country. I didn't have a desire to protect it from any race; I had a desire to protect it from a communist threat – which whether the people joke about it now or not was a real threat pre-1990. It definitely was a threat. I don't care who says what; I don't care about any of these hyper-liberals telling me it was just a bullshit story. It wasn't. There was a threat. I know – I saw it. The threat was six, seven, eight, nine thousand Cubans on the Angolan border wanting to come into South West Africa. And if they got in there, they weren't going to stop there, that's for sure. If they got to South Africa they would have destroyed it, made it a banana republic – a communist republic where you've got to stand in queues for food.

My great-grandfather and my grandfather both served in the South African Defence Force. My grandfather was in the air force; he was a well-honoured South African pilot. There are records of him in books. My grandfather fought against Nazi Germany when Hitler was executing people in gas chambers, millions of people. He showed me photographs that he got when he was in the war. It shocked me. It shocked me to see what a dictator could do to a country and a people – to annihilate another race because he disagreed with their religion. It's wrong, absolutely. I applied the same principle to the ANC threat and the MK threat.

Right after school, in 1988, I went to do my national service. Six months after I klaared out, I joined the SAP. I had a very strong desire to become a detective, to investigate things and try to catch criminals. I signed up in June 1990.

I worked at the court as a student constable for a couple of months and then I went to college in Pretoria. My first payslip was R640.

– Inspector Stevens (joined 1991)

I was born in Ladysmith. My father passed away early. We were seven in my family, and we were a very poor family. My brother first joined the force and I joined later. I was inspired by him. Through him I started liking the police force. **– Inspector (F) Dlamini (joined 1991)**

I was born and grew up in Rhodesia, which was for all intents and purposes an active war zone – a bit different to the average South African kid. We moved to the Transkei; my father set up a business there. He had been ripped off by his business partners and that whole sense of injustice stuck with me for quite a while. My dad never really recovered from that. He died when I was sixteen.

Around sixteen I got into computers, being one of the original 'nerdy geek' kind of guys. That just stuck with me. I got into hacking because in those days that's how you got to learn how to use a computer. It wasn't something criminal per se; it wasn't anything malicious. It was exploring and seeing what was out there.

I had to take a fairly responsible role at sixteen, with my dad dying. He pretty much left my mom destitute. So it was a difficult upbringing from that point of view, but an interesting upbringing. I had very strong relations with my mom and my sister. My relationship with my dad was somewhat strained but I can almost attribute that to his serving in the defence force in Rhodesia and the things that he'd experienced. We had many friends who had been killed. So as a kid you were seeing things that you shouldn't have seen.

I've always just had a strong sense of justice. As a kid I was always the knight in shining armour, the cop in cops and robbers, the good guy. I think that just became ingrained in my personality.

I didn't initially want to be a cop. I had always wanted to be a scientist. The whole science issue and the forensic stuff really intrigued me. Law enforcement was always there in the background, especially forensics and investigation. I enjoyed the original Arthur Conan Doyle stories: the Sherlock Holmes stories about detectives solving cases using science and logic. So I don't think I ever gravitated towards the idea of becoming a uniformed cop, a traditional law enforcement officer. But the idea of a detective or investigative scientist was always in the back of my mind. And fate has a strange way of playing itself out.

I wanted to study after school, but with my dad having died, my mom wasn't in a financial position to pay for my varsity studies. At that stage affirmative action was already starting to hit so I was applying for bursaries and being told, 'Sorry, we don't give bursaries to white people any more.' So in '89 already the country had started to change significantly. With my computer interest I wanted to do something and the only universities I could probably have gone to were Rhodes in Grahamstown or UPE down in PE, but that just wasn't an option financially. The technical college in East London offered an electronic engineering course so I thought, electronics, that's got to be similar. I ended up enrolling, working in the evenings at the Spur and paying my way for my studies. But after two semesters I just thought, this is not for me.

Then unfortunately that dreaded brown envelope came from the defence force with my draft papers, so I was in a position where if I didn't study I would have to join the defence force. Then a friend of mine who was a cop at the time said, 'Why don't you go and join the police?' I think at that stage the defence force was a year and if you joined the police for two years they would pay for your studies. This was sounding more and more like an attractive thing, and then of course the investigation thing came back to mind and I decided to join the cops in lieu of the defence force. Eighteen years later, I'm still in law enforcement – no longer the police, but I've never looked back since!   – **Sergeant Jordaan (joined 1991)**

I grew up in Durban. We moved to the Transvaal, where I went to school at Belfast High School. I earned provincial colours in athletics and hockey at school. I played senior hockey once I left school. I was in boarding school most of my school career.

In the beginning, I joined the police because there was nothing else that I wanted to do. What happened was that I had a bursary to study law. Then a friend of mine committed suicide when I was in matric. The two of us had planned to do more or less the same thing. I just decided that I didn't have the courage to do it on my own. I had a mentor at school. I stayed at his house during the holidays when I was studying for my matric prelims. His brother arrived and said, 'Why don't you join the police?' And I said, 'Well, why not?' So that's how it started. I had never thought of it before then. It was just a spur-of-the-moment thing.

– **Inspector (F) Kemp (joined 1991)**

I left the army in 1990 and went to live in Plettenberg Bay. I joined the police to join the reserves. When joining the reserves there was an old guy who said, 'If you haven't got work and you join the police you'll only do three months in the college because you've already got three years in the army.' So I joined the police and planned to go back to Plettenberg Bay, but after college I went to Potchefstroom for two years and from there I just took it further – it was just the adventure of it. – **Inspector Marais (joined 1991)**

I was one of those that joined because there was nothing else to do. I couldn't find anything else. I actually wanted to be a beauty therapist, but I registered too late for college. There was an ad on TV: I think that was the only time the police advertised on TV for recruitment.

I took the train from Ottery to Athlone. I came from the back of the police station, entered the building and joined the queue. When I finished filling in the forms, I left out the front. Then I saw that the queue was coming in from the front of the station. The actual queue was much, much longer – I had pushed in! To me it was fate, because if I'd come from the front I would have seen the queue and turned around. I think it was meant to be.

It took about a month or two for them to call me after signing up. I was tested on 25 June; I was eighteen or nineteen. They don't really take eighteen-year-olds these days. Back then they went to recruit at schools.

It was going to be temporary work so that I could get some money to study, but then I enjoyed it. That's why I say it was fate; it was meant to be. — **Superintendent (F) January (joined 1991)**

I joined the police because I loved the organisation and I wanted to contribute towards the reduction of crime. I was about twenty-six. Before I joined, I'd been at school. I was staying at a farm so I started school when I was eleven years old. That is why I finished late. I finished school at about the age of twenty-three. Then I worked temporarily and I joined the police. — **Captain Ndlovu (joined 1991)**

I'm from a family of three: one brother and one sister. My mother was divorced and got married again, so my brother is from the second marriage. I'm the eldest. Growing up was a struggle. My mother was a factory worker. We had to make ends meet after the divorce. My mother moved out with me and my sister. We slept wherever we could find place – at other people's houses, sometimes in the bush. My mother moved around with us, then she would go to the factory. I would take my sister to crèche and I would go to school.

At the end of the day it made me a better person, because I could understand why she didn't leave us. She was still young and that was her choice. She was supportive of us and until today we are still supportive of her. I will support her until the end of her life if she should go before me.

At school I wanted to be a policeman, but because of what my mother was going through I had to go and work for her sister. I had to leave school at an early age and my dreams of becoming a policeman were shattered.

I grew up in the struggle days. I saw lots of things going on, how policemen treated people. I was at Modderdam High, a school that was very active in the struggle. I attended meetings with comrades like Ashley Kriel and Anton Franz. In 1982, I went to the army to go and experience for myself what life was about on the Border, because they talked about guerrillas. I wanted to experience things for myself; not to hear things, but to go out there and see it.

In 1992, they took assistant constables. They had to have Standard 8 so that's where I saw my way in the door. At the time I was working at County Fair as a supervisor, earning R325 a week. I left that job. To my surprise my first salary cheque in the police was R325 *per month*! But I went through it for two years, then I went back to college and became a permanent police official in 1994.

There were two kinds of special constables – those with the blue overalls, and the assistant constables. In the beginning we were supposed to do gate duties, but then they started using us in the charge office. That's when they saw that they could use us because we could read and write. When we started it was not that bad but you were the 'boy' in the picture, you were the labourer. You would do all the gate work, all the cleaning. But it depended on you. If you accept being labelled, people will label you.

I still don't have matric, so I don't think I'll be promoted any further than inspector. But I do my job with a passion and I think that's what keeps me going.

– Inspector Lakay (joined 1992, special constable; 1994, SAP)

I was born in Prieska and grew up in Groblershoop in the Northern Cape. Groblershoop itself is a small town. In the town there are about a hundred houses, but we have seven other informal settlements around the town.

When I was a little girl I was raped by a relative. From Grade 5 I was afraid that I would fall pregnant. I didn't realise that you couldn't become pregnant later on because of being raped once, many years ago. So I had this thing inside myself that I would become pregnant, even though I wasn't sexually active.

I did my school career in Groblershoop. We lived near the town on a farm settlement. When I was a little girl it was my dream to join the police. My father worked at Water Affairs and my mother worked as an operator at Telkom, so we weren't very rich. They couldn't send me to university or anything like that. It was always a dream of mine to join the police but it was also easier than getting another job because my mom and dad didn't have money.

I think the rape experience was one of the things that pushed me to become a police official – to help other women protect themselves in a situation like that and to come forward to the police. I'm not going to come forward any more but it's not too late for other ladies and girls, and also for my children. Parents must talk to their children and tell them about the dangers of playing in places where their parents cannot look after them. I also want to help the senior women, to inform them not to walk on the streets and drink. This is another reason why I joined the police. **– Inspector (F) Basson (joined 1994)**

Policing just looked lekker to me. I liked the people, the field uniform that they wore, the action … It was against my parents' wishes – my mother didn't like it – but I just told her I was going to the police. There was nothing else I wanted to do. I went straight from school. In January 1994, I started at Bishop Lavis College. We were the second intake that included whites. It had always been a college for coloureds before then.

– Inspector Kotze (joined 1994)

I joined the police because I had this thing in my heart that I wanted to serve the public and protect them from harm, protect their property. I was very concerned about the welfare of people. I didn't join the South African Police Service because I was hungry for power; I joined it for the love of the profession. I think from my side I have made some changes.

– Inspector Ramela (joined 1995)

I grew up in Nelspruit, Mpumalanga. It was a small town then, but now it's big. We call it Mbombela township, near Nelspruit. But the township was removed, so in 1978 we were relocated to Kanyamazane. I was schooled there until matric. Then I came to Cape Town where I attended UCT until third year. I was studying social sciences. In 1993 I went to work for the City of Cape Town in the income branch.

I became a reservist in 1995 because I wanted to contribute positively towards the changes and the transformation that was taking place in our country, specifically the fight against crime. I believe there will never be any liberation if people are not liberated in their own streets. I was using a train to go to work and I would notice people getting robbed in the trains. I used to get off at Philippi and walk through the bushes to my place. It was horrible, because there would be people lying in the bushes, people attacked while coming from work. So I decided to join the police to participate in crime reduction from 1995. I became permanent in 2002.

There were some forms of discrimination in the police between the reservists and the permanent members. There was a problem whereby the permanent members were not of much support to the reservists at the time. People would always say, 'Don't worry about this one, he is a reservist.' So it always seemed like the police was more for a particular group of people who were regarded as *the* people while the reservists should not be taken notice of. I wanted to prove a point that in the police if you apply your mind nothing is impossible.

    – Inspector Lukhele (joined 1995, reserves; 2002, permanent)

I was born in Limpopo province in 1976. It is a rural area. Unfortunately, I never met my parents; I only heard about them. I was brought up by my granny. I was told that my mother was killed by my dad due to domestic violence. He killed my mom and was arrested. Then while he was in jail he was killed by other inmates. That's all I know about my parents.

I only learnt that I didn't have a mom when I was about ten years old. When I learnt it, I started feeling bad and it affected my schoolwork and everything. My mom's younger sister took me to stay with her until I accepted that I didn't have parents, then I started to get back on track.

When I was in Grade 9 my big brother, the firstborn of my parents, was killed as well. In Limpopo there is this thing of muti killing. He was killed for that. At the time it was a homeland, and in our homeland, the Venda homeland, muti killings were accepted. There was a season, October and November, where the chief would call a meeting and warn all the parents to look after their children because it was time for killing for muti. The police would arrest you, but in the community itself it was accepted. That's how my brother was killed. His killers were known but were never arrested due to their status in the community.

My brother was the breadwinner; I was staying with him. He was about twenty-five when he was killed. I felt devastated; I had to drop out of school. I didn't write exams that year because I had to move back to my aunt and the school was too far. I asked a lot of questions: 'Why is this happening to me? Why is everyone close to me dying?' I was very worried. It changed my life a lot. I became very aggressive and I started to like fighting.

The next year I went back to school. I passed matric in 1995. I wanted to go to varsity but due to my financial conditions I couldn't afford it. I wanted to study a BSc because I was good at maths and science. But instead I enrolled at a teachers' training college for '96, '97, and in '98 I finished my diploma. Then I got a post, but I only taught for a year.

While I was still in college, I decided I wanted to do something that would control my worries. When I thought about my parents and my brother, I would become worried. I wanted to do something that would prevent somebody else from losing their family members in such a negligent way. I wanted to do something to protect the community. So, while I was teaching in 1999, I applied for the police. The first time I didn't make it. The second time I made it, in May 2000.

– **Constable Sibuyi (joined 2000)**

I was born at seven in the morning on 30 May 1983 in Hendrik van der Bijl Hospital to my divorced mother. Since my mother was divorced, I got her surname. At four years old, I got a sister from a different father.

I was a big boy: not fat and not thin. Children used to be scared of me, and since I was an introvert, I did not have a lot of friends at pre-school. I went to Laerskool Totius from Grade 1 to Standard 1. The children used to test my patience a lot and made fun of me because of my funny surname. I went to Laerskool DF Malherbe for Standard 2 up until Standard 5. I had more friends there but we used to call ourselves 'the reject squad' since we were all generally a bunch of weirdoes and f-ups. We used to get ourselves in a lot of trouble. In Standard 5, myself and two friends became media prefects. The lady prefects thought it would be nice to collect money to buy the teacher a present for her birthday. Me and my friends thought it would be even better if we stole the money to buy porn. It didn't stop there: we plundered the teacher's purse and paid a matric to buy us porn magazines. We obviously got caught out. Thankfully the teacher was a psychology student and did not get us expelled. She decided to 'counsel' us instead.

There were lots of similar incidents. Even though I was relatively big and children were scared of me, I was a 'pissy'. After Standard 5, I went to Hoërskool Driehoek because my best friend went there. I should have gone to a technical school instead since my aptitude tests advised this, but I was a pissy and scared of going to a new place alone. I never really enjoyed myself there. I ended up changing my surname at the end of Grade 11 and going over to Hoërskool Transvalia because the girls were hotter there and a lot of the students there did not know me.

After school I went to the air force, and after Basics I managed to get myself into the SAPS. It was basically three months' SANDF Basics, two weeks off and then three months' SAPS Basics. I was a sucker for punishment.

My uncle was a member of Koevoet. He was killed in the same month and year that my sister was born, two months before he would have been finished with the war. I cannot remember him. I can, however, remember the family sitting in my grandmother's bedroom when my grandmother received the call about my uncle's death. I also cannot remember the funeral, but something must have stuck. I have always wanted to be in the SAPS. It is actually disturbing. I didn't want to be in the SAPS for the pride and glory and all that crap; I actually just wanted to die on duty and get a state funeral. Maybe my subconscious remembers something about my uncle's funeral. Maybe it was nice.

I recently discovered a photo album with a report card inside. I was three years and six months old at the time. It said in Afrikaans, 'Gert wants to be a policeman. He always wears hats and guns and plays with mobile apparatus. He also plays with police cars.' In Standard 4 we had a media project on what you wanted to be when you grew up. I went to Vanderbijlpark police station and met a constable. He made me do a complete docket: from complainant statement to photo album, arrest statement, pointing-out statement, recovery-of-property statement – everything. It took me the whole day and the constable was really patient. He also made a file with a picture of Sherlock Holmes on the front and a SAP – not SAPS – badge on the front with all the steps and procedures of becoming a police official up until detective. I got 98 per cent for that assignment. Everybody was very impressed with my project. I never got to thank him for his help. I think he might have changed my wants from dying on duty to actually surviving and retiring one day.   – **Constable van der Merwe (2003)**

I was born in Cape Town. At the age of seven we moved to Ravensmead on the Cape Flats and from there to Elsies River. At the age of fourteen I started to play tennis. I always wanted to play tennis but there was never the finance or facilities. I wanted to be a professional tennis player; I never thought about anything else. I never made it because of the money.

I grew up confused about my sexuality. My mother and father were very religious – my dad especially was very homophobic. One day I was sitting in front of the TV and there was a gay march going on on-screen. My dad said something like, 'These bloody people will all go to hell for what they're doing.' I got upset with him and said, 'You're judging people and you don't know what they are going through.' I went upstairs and slammed my door closed but as I was going up I saw my mom give my dad a look as if to say, 'I told you he was gay!'

At the age of nineteen my dad was trying to get me a girlfriend, but I wasn't interested. She was very beautiful, but what was I going to do with her, comb her hair?

In matric, I went to go and stay with my aunt. While I was staying there I got a casual job at Mr Price. When I finished matric in 1996 I was offered a permanent position, but the money still wasn't enough. My passion was still to become a professional tennis player.

Then I saw this ad in the newspaper; I thought it was surgical massage. I always wanted to massage. My mom was a domestic worker and always used to come home and complain about her feet being sore, and I would massage them. But I saw 'M2M' next to the ad. I thought, let me just try this out and phone these folks.

I phoned and the first question this oke asked me was if I was gay or bisexual or straight. I thought, what an odd question and I put the phone down. I was confused at the time. I phoned another agency and this time I sort of knew what was going on. It doesn't take a scientist to know. So the oke asked me the question and I said, 'bisexual' and he said, 'Do you want to come in for an interview?' So I went to the premises and when I got there I was surprised to find that the office was in a house. When I went into the room for the interview I saw all these porn magazines. For the first time in my life I saw gay porn! I thought, okay, this is it.

When I read 'M2M' I knew it must be 'man to man' or 'male to male' and it was a whorehouse. I was so desperate to become a professional tennis player, I would have done anything to reach my goal. I thought I'd just do it and get it over and done with. He trained me on a pillow on the first day and the next day he said, 'Are you ready for this?' and I said, 'I probably don't have a choice, do I? I want to make money.'

That's the day that my now ex-boyfriend came there. He was friends with the guy who had the massage parlour. He had just got divorced and we became friends. That's how we decided to hook up. The next day I said to him, 'Tell your friend I can't do this, because it's not my type of work and it's a bit embarrassing. And if my parents found out what I was doing, they would kill me!'

We were together for ten years. I joined the police while I was with him. It was his idea. He had been in the police in 1975. He said I wasn't disciplined enough, so why didn't I go and join the police? I didn't have a job at the time, so I went to join.   – **Constable Louw (joined 2004)**

I grew up in a rural area, Ladysmith, in KZN. I came to Gauteng when I was about nine years old, and I resided in Sebokeng. I grew up with the hatred of apartheid. I hated the police because they had shot my brother. I hated them a lot.

My brother was in the movement of the African National Congress. The police used to come to our house, kick the door down and look for my brother. They would find he was not there and then they would beat us.

That was in the eighties. I think I was five years old. It only stopped in 1993 when he was shot. On the day he was shot, the police came and took him and this friend of his. His friend escaped while the police car was in motion. After a few days he came and told us that my brother had been shot. We don't know what happened to him; we are still looking for him.

When I grew up it was a simple life. I would go to school; I would come back. I was drinking when I was in high school. I drank a lot. There was once a function at my school. I was drunk with my friends. Then police officers arrived at the school and assaulted me and my friends. From that day onwards I was curious about the police and what made them do that. I wanted to get into the police to understand why they are so unhappy. Out of my anger there was a little bit of curiosity. So I joined the police in 2007. — **Constable Shabangu (joined 2007)**

2

COLLEGE

I remember calling our PT instructor 'Sir'. He said, '"Sir"? I'm not "Sir"; I'm "Sergeant"!' And then going through the socialisation process … First they break you down, then they rebuild you to get you into a cohesive group – that was traumatic. Having to go from unfit to very fit was a painful experience, physically painful. There was no mercy.

The college was a good experience. All the times when we were drilled to near-exhaustion because somebody had done something that the sergeant didn't like, and then the feeling of pride during the passing-out parade … In those days the police cap had a band around it in the police colours, gold and blue, and you had an epaulette saying 'College'. This denoted the fact that you were a student. Just before you passed out you could remove that. Then you walk on air – absolutely the most magical day of your life. 'Now I'm a constable; I'm no longer a student!'

– **Director Grobler (1963)**

I spent six months at the police station before going to college. That's how it worked then. In 1975 I was posted to Newlands in Johannesburg, at Sophiatown police station. I was a student constable there until June 1976. At the time of the riots, I was still a student. I hadn't gone to college.

The riot was in Soweto on 16 June. We were posted to Dube, where there was a municipal police training college. Our duty was to collect the corpses of the people who had been killed by the police when they were striking for black power.

When the people scattered, we had to collect those corpses and load them into the police vehicle. It was not easy for the mortuary car to get into the location as it was so tense. They were burning any car, it didn't matter what it was. We were there with an escort, the Hippos and the soldiers to cover us so that we wouldn't get harmed. I don't know how many dead bodies there were. When you come to that situation as a student you will never remember anything. That thing was so traumatic.

Some of our people were saying, 'Why don't you leave the force?' My family said I should leave but I told them, 'A person can die at any time; let me do this.' I thought this job was a call from God: let me serve until God says it's enough.

From 30 June 1976, I attended the college at Hammanskraal. While at the college the streets were still tense. We were always on standby. We didn't have any weekends off. We only got a weekend off when we were preparing to go to Transkei for its independence. We were deployed to work there as part of the SAP – the Transkei didn't yet have their own police. We left Pretoria on 14 October and arrived there on 16 October. We stayed at the old training college of the South African Police Service. The first colleges for black people were in the Transkei before they moved to Benoni and then to Hammanskraal. We stayed there.

We were there until the coming of independence on 26 October 1976. There were so many people; they slaughtered lots of cattle and were so happy enjoying themselves. We were there to make sure there was order. It was very nice. We arrived back at Hammanskraal on 30 October. We travelled on a special train.

Everyone at the college was black. The only white people were the commanders, like the head of the college. Most were blacks there, and the highest rank for blacks was a lieutenant. In those days they had more ranks – they have combined them now.

There was no enjoyment at the college; it was difficult. The slightest mistake and you knew you were going to feel it. Everywhere you went you had to run, even if you were going to the mess to eat. When you were changing for physical training you had to run to your bungalow to change and then run back to the parade ground. If they found you running, they punished you. They would make us do push-ups on our fists, or tell us to go and pack all our things, take that bag and a dustbin, and run around the ground until they let us stop. But that thing taught members to be disciplined.

As time passed, I enjoyed myself because I was fit. We had our pass-out parade on 3 December 1976. I was posted straight to the riot unit from college.   **– Inspector Mampuru (1976)**

College was not a place you wanted to be, but afterwards you think back and realise it was awesome. All the breaking down and building up, it makes a better person out of you. In those days it made a better person out of you. We still had PT and all that stuff. These days they've got floor polishers. We had to clean the floors with our hands; we called it 'taxis'.

When you're in Standard 5, you're the big guy in the small village. When you're in matric, you're the big frog in the small pond. Then after school you go to the police and you get there and they explain to you that, actually, you're nothing. But in a good way … because once they've built you up, you are a man; you're capable of handling yourself.

At college they deducted from our salaries fifty cents for movies and one rand for haircuts. Even if you didn't want a haircut they gave you one.

You were in a platoon and if somebody did something wrong, everybody had to do the PT. It taught you camaraderie; you're there to support each other. In those days you learnt how to do police work. These days they teach you human rights and electric lights and Big Korn Bites.

– Captain de Beer (1977)

Other policemen, when they sign up, go to training college. I didn't do that because I went to intelligence. Any person who's been trained has a preconceived notion of what he's going to do. So if you want someone to do intelligence you don't train them; you don't go according to a prescribed norm: you improvise.

I spent five years doing intelligence in the then Transvaal – in the heart of Soweto, Brixton, Hillbrow, Pretoria. Eventually I took a transfer to Cape Town in June 1986. Arriving there, I went to college for the first time in my five-year career as a police officer.

My college experience was nice. It was racialised at the time: whites-only, blacks-only, coloureds-only and Indians-only. Coloureds were at Bishop Lavis – I attended Bishop Lavis College. It was a nice experience – empowering, thought-provoking, inspiring.

– Inspector Khan (1981–1986)

College was six months and it was very strict. I was in Charlie company, which was said to be one of the stricter companies, but I presume every police officer will say that his company was stricter than others. We had a full sergeant. Some of the others had lance sergeants. You had respect for that person. When he talks, you don't argue with him – you do as he says.

At first it was an eye-opener because as a teenager there is some kind of rebellious thing in you. Suddenly you're in this very disciplined environment. When that person says, 'Run there,' you run! It was strict. The focus was on operational things. It was tough for me, but as things progressed I could see the change. I became fit and a bit more knowledgeable.

– Senior Superintendent Boning (1982)

From John Vorster, where I signed up, I went to Sandton police station. It was a nice job. I was working at the detective branch. But then I had to go to the college. At that time it was military training. There was no time for books. At that time you enter the college as a Christian, but within two weeks you change completely. Your Christian life is over!

– Inspector Rameama (1982)

You had to put your forehead on the ground and stand on your head on the gravel. Then you start singing, head down, bottom up. That's what they made us do. It was training. Bleeding, on your forehead …

On the uniforms there is a lanyard with a whistle attached to it. In the past it was leather. The instructor would whip you with that on top of your shaved head. They did it to make you strong and to make you angry. Both the black instructors and the white ones whipped us. Our white instructor was Satan.

We got paid at the end of the month, but before you got paid you had to go to the tuck shop. We were forced to buy a suit – we didn't usually wear suits. And they had photos of firearms. They forced us to buy them, to buy pictures of guns. Taking our money …

The slogan at the college was, 'We shit with one hole' – *Sinya ngo-one*: 'an injury to one is an injury to all'. One mistake and we punish the whole college. If my platoon leader made a mistake then they said, 'These boys don't have respect.' Then at two o'clock in the morning in winter, in PT shorts and vests, with those white takkies, they made us sing and do exercises.

If they say they want to re-educate us because we were apartheid policemen then I will say no. They don't train them like that today. Today they are fatties. They can tell their instructor they are tired. They go home every weekend.   **– Inspector Moji (1983)**

We trained in Hammanskraal. It was Hammanskraal for blacks, Pretoria College for whites, Cape Town for coloureds and Chatsworth, Durban for Indians. Our training was intense in terms of physical training; discipline was maintained. But we were beaten. It was abuse. They hit us. We did training where we would ask ourselves what it was for. Especially on the last day, when you had to stand on your head. They would say you were earning your police badge. That was the culture. You had to stand on your head on a tar road for about ten to fifteen minutes. Some people when they got up had blood coming out of their forehead. Before you could wear the cap with the police badge you had to stand on your head and if you were injured on your forehead it was a sign that you'd earned your badge.

They really beat us. I was a platoon leader. There were thirty-six in the platoon. If they found that one of the rooms wasn't clean enough, then everyone would have to take a beating. They would say *Sinya ngo-one* – 'you all die because of one person'. That was the punishment we had to take. The tall ones would lift you up, stretched out, holding your hands and your feet. The instructor would stand with a broomstick and hit us very hard, each person. Maybe they decide they'll hit you six times, then everyone would get six. Some people even decided, 'No, man, this is not the place for me.' They would run away, or their parents would come and fetch them. For me, I liked the position I was in and I liked everything about the police, so there was never a time when I said this beating was too hard and I must go home.

Our trainers were black, but the supervisors were white. Most seniors were white. Then when you go down the ranks, the captains, warrant officers and sergeants were black. When we were beaten, it was the junior guys who did it but it was an instruction from the senior guys to instil discipline. When they came to parade they expected a certain discipline. If there was one guy who did something wrong, then he blamed the instructors. Then they would hit us again and tell us, 'This is the discipline we want!'

For me it was racist. It didn't happen in the white colleges. I was recruited at a white college so I saw the difference. It was very, very different there.

– **Captain Mthembu (1987)**

I went to college for three months. It was a special municipal police college. After three months, you went to the job. When I compare the training to the training today, it was very hard; it was some kind of labour. They did not emphasise the academic side of the training. What they made sure was that you could handle a gun, you could shoot and you were physically fit.

We were training in Joburg. In May, June, July it's very, very cold. They would wake us up at 4 a.m. There was frost on the ground and they made us pick up leaves and papers. Your fingers burned. All the time you had to be on the run. If a sergeant saw you walking, you would be in for it. I realised that since they were not emphasising academic achievements, it simply meant it was up to me to learn what was in the book. They just give you the book, then what? Nobody failed tests – which is impossible. So it was up to me as an individual to learn.   – **Inspector Kekane (1987)**

I was first a student at Wierdabrug police station for six months. Then when I went to college we had to go for another six months. That was the first year they had that many women. They didn't have enough, so our intake had double the amount of women than they usually trained.

On the third day, they called us in and said they had good and bad news. The bad news was that we were going to work very hard. The good news was that we were only going to train for three months, because they needed to train a lot more women. It was so bad at the time that they didn't even have uniforms for us, so we had very big or very small men's clothes and women's clothes – whatever they could put on us.

I was at Pretoria College. Everything we did was only with women, although there were men being trained at the same time in the same college. In 1990, it was still whites-only at Pretoria West. Nothing was strange about it, because everything was still like that.

We all got fat! You had to eat very quickly – you only had half an hour and if you were at the back of the row, sometimes you wouldn't get there in time. They feed you three starches in one meal. Your mom doesn't think you get fed enough, so she brings you three Kentucky Rounders and a chocolate cake on the weekend. So we all got fat, and we all got acne from the bad food, but we survived. — **Inspector (F) van Niekerk (1990)**

I came out of a white environment – a white army – and I went into a white police college. College was quite interesting, different to the army. I remember in the army it was a bit more serious in the sense that you couldn't choose who you wanted to be with, whereas in the police the guy who was sitting next to you was of relatively good morals; he had a standing. In the army the guy next to you could have been a dope smoker. Because of conscription, you had to be there, so you couldn't say, 'I don't want to serve with you.' So the army taught a brotherhood that the police never did – that you should give everybody a chance.

With all respect, I think it was more dangerous joining the police than joining the army. By then the Angola threat was over. We withdrew from South West Africa in 1989 and 1990 was like a holiday up there. In 1990 the townships were burning. Alexandra and Sharpeville, those were war zones.

— **Inspector Stevens (1991)**

I went to Bishop Lavis College in Cape Town in July 1991. It was my first time outside Ladysmith, seeing other people. There were those who went first in January – they were the first women. I was in the second group. We were very proud to be policewomen – very proud! We told ourselves that we were brave because we were among the men.

It was tough. We were short of English materials. They were teaching lots of subjects in Afrikaans but after two months it was English. It was hard because I didn't know Afrikaans.   **– Inspector (F) Dlamini (1991)**

College was difficult. It was still whites-only then. It was a big intake; the college was literally packed. With a surname like 'Jordaan' everyone assumed I was Afrikaans, but I'm so far removed from my Afrikaans roots that they're a nonentity. They slotted me into an Afrikaans platoon as the only English-speaking guy.

I got a very rude awakening to some of the realities of the social dynamics of South Africa. I spent most of my high school in East London, which is a very English community – that was my norm. Suddenly to be taken out of that environment and thrust into Pretoria and a police culture where being English was not a good thing – I was given an incredibly rough time. You were looked down on; you were treated as a second-class citizen. The fact that I did well at college didn't seem to help.

But college was interesting; it was like a rite of passage, cutting your apron strings from home and going into the big world out there where you didn't know anybody. To a large extent it was a hostile world. You were out there on your own. I was a bit of a loner, primarily being an English-speaker. The irony was that even though I was an English-speaker I didn't associate with the English platoon. Because I wasn't in their platoon, I wasn't part of their little clique. I spent a lot of time by myself, threw myself into the actual work. It probably helped with my focus and discipline. My marks were fairly good and I think that helped to get me into the commercial branch later.

Our post-college placements were made for us. Because I'd previously done electronic engineering, they posted me to a radio technical unit. What I know about fixing radios is dangerous and dodgy at the best of times. I thought, no, this isn't for me. But when I saw that my friends were going to Unit 19 – the riot unit – fixing radios didn't sound like a bad idea!

Three or four weeks after that, these guys from the commercial branch came around looking for recruits. About six or seven hundred people applied – mostly those from Unit 19 who didn't want to go!

It was quite a lengthy process. We did psychometric tests and interviews and an exam. It was three of the most gruelling days of my career. After that we didn't hear anything, and after college I was posted in Bloemfontein to the radio and technical unit for a month or two. The guys I worked with were big jokers; they knew I wanted to go to the commercial branch.

Then I got this phone call out of the blue from a colonel. The guy said, 'Are you still interested in being in the commercial branch?' I looked on the switchboard and I saw that my commander's light was on. The guy sounded so similar to him. I said, 'Ja, you're talking shit, stop joking around!' – not realising that it actually *was* the commander of the commercial branch in the Free State! Afterwards I went to my commander and said, 'That's a bloody nasty joke to play on someone,' and he said, 'No, I was on the phone to someone else.' I phoned the commercial branch up and begged and pleaded. I went down to see the commander at his offices. He took one look at me and said, 'You're not going to survive in the Free State. Where do you come from?' I said, 'I come from East London.' He said, 'We've got posts there; I'll send you back home.' That was it. That moment was the start of my police career.

– **Sergeant Jordaan (1991)**

I matriculated and started in the police on 3 January 1991. We were the largest intake of women that had ever been at the police college. We were kept away from the men. You were only allowed to talk and sit next to men during certain periods. You weren't allowed to 'familiarise' yourself with them. They were very strict on stuff like guys visiting after hours.

College was tough. The PT and stuff like that was really tough. The discipline was very strict. Every morning we stood inspection. I slept on a steel *trommel* the night before inspection because I didn't want to mess up the bed, which I'd ironed. It was like that – you don't sleep on the bed because you've spent two hours preparing it for an inspection and you'd rather sleep on the floor or on something else.

In front of each barracks the street had to be swept; the door handles had to be polished; the fire extinguisher in front of the building had to be polished. Each person had to polish the piece of floor next to his bed. We spent hours shining that piece of floor and if someone stood on it, you would scream. After polishing, we would walk around in our socks. But it was amazing. It taught you a culture.

My fondest memories: I remember us walking behind the students' band on the way to the parade ground, hoisting the flag and playing the national anthem. It was, *wow*; it was really great. If you were to say to me, would you choose to go to college *now* or choose to go back *then*, I would go back then, any day.

Today they're not as strict as they used to be. Discipline is a part of saving your life outside. If you don't have that discipline, you can't serve a community and save your life. I think it's impossible. So they get away with murder today.   **– Inspector (F) Kemp (1991)**

I went to college in January 1992 and there were girls that had just left school, seventeen-year-olds. They were recruited in school. Even before they wrote matric they had filled out the forms.

In 1991 they took in a lot of women to try to balance the genders. As a result, the ladies that went before us only did three months at college because they were trying to push people through. We were the first multi-racial group, so that was very interesting for me. It was just after Nelson Mandela had been released. At that time they also started taking older women. Before, there had been an age limit.

At school we had been segregated. This was actually the first time I had spoken to other race groups, apart from having a black domestic worker. It was very interesting for me. We were curious. We were equal, so we were asking each other about home and how our upbringings were. Besides the race thing, there was class as well. Some of us came from a poor background; some of us came from better backgrounds.

There were definitely some white people who still thought they were better. Because I went to Bishop Lavis it was still mostly coloureds, so I was in a comfort zone. There were some that you could see didn't feel easy and kept to one side.

College was tough. Punishment was there. If your room wasn't clean, there was punishment. But overall, mentally, what kept me strong was that I was being paid for being there. I was getting a free bed, free meals, free everything … so I tried to look at the positive.

When you look back at the end of the day, you see that you have to be disciplined; there have to be set ways of doing things. Even by folding your sweater in a certain way – the set way – they were teaching us about structure, uniformity and discipline. I enjoyed it.

The one day I was so proud: the floor was polished, my bed was made, I had measured everything. From the top of your mattress to where the sheet folded had to be measured, and they gave you a ruler to measure it. My room was cleaned, my clothes were packed – but I left my bag of dirt behind the door! My drill instructor hung it around my neck and I had to run around the parade ground. But while I was running, I was laughing.

When we graduated I stayed at the college and walked into the barracks and we all had some drinks together. The lady who was my drill instructor and platoon commander said it was very hard for her to keep a straight face because every time she punished me, I would laugh about it. She told me there were no hard feelings.

There were only women in our section of the college. We were separated from the men until the last month. I was chosen to be a detective and in that month when we were training with specialists, we mixed with the guys.

I think it was good to be only women; there were no distractions. Women and men think differently, and it wasn't men competing against women, so in that way it was good.

– **Superintendent (F) January (1992)**

When we joined, the colleges were mixed. They had just started this multi-racial thing. It was a bit hard because we were used to the apartheid system, so we were getting to know each other, always stepping on each other's toes. The relationships between black and white were not good. We were doing the same job, but the one was feeling superior to the other one. I trained at Bishop Lavis in Cape Town. It was mostly coloureds. Most of the tension was between whites and blacks. The whites did things like just push in at the front of a queue. Then if you asked why, they would just say, 'Who are you? You can't tell me that.' It made me feel bad … But you want to work – you are there to make a living – so you let it go. I thought, I will get to the front eventually. **– Captain Ndlovu (1992)**

At the beginning of 1994 I went to college. It was all right. We did a lot of shooting and a lot of theory. The one thing I didn't like very much was the lady I was sharing a room with – she didn't like the experience very much, so she made it difficult for me sometimes. It was 1994, after the election, when Mr Mandela was starting as the new president. I think that was the first intake that was mixed. That wasn't a problem for me – it was good. At school it was only white. I don't think anyone in my platoon had a problem with it; we all handled it very well.

Men and ladies were in one college, but the platoons were not mixed. So we didn't know a lot about the men. We ate together and at the end of the day we could mix. **– Inspector (F) Basson (1994)**

College was easy for me, but for some of my friends it was difficult. In 1993, my school was still nearly all white – there were one or two non-whites with the new changes. But when I got to college my room-mate was coloured, in the two rooms next to me were two coloured guys, the room on the other side had two coloured guys, and the room opposite mine had two coloured guys. There were lots of white people too – it was lekker for me. Growing up, we had not had a chance to mix.

I had thought there would be tension, but there wasn't any. There were a few black people. It was a bit more difficult to understand them because they had a very different culture. They did things differently, like spoke loudly. But college was easy. I enjoyed it because we worked with guns every day; it was lekker to go and shoot and get fit.

When I was still at college they had found one or two of the *laaities* killed by the station strangler in the bushes. They took the whole college to the bush to search for more bodies. We found six children that day. Some of them were all right; some were a bit decomposed. Two of them were brothers. All of them had been sodomised. They got a counsellor to come and talk to us at the college afterwards. **– Inspector Kotze (1994)**

The time when I joined was the time when the then president Nelson Mandela was just inaugurated and he introduced this thing of 'service'. In the college they were lecturing us about the change. We were the first group at the time. The police had been doing things that were very inhumane. Previously they were training policemen as if they were in the military. During my training we concentrated on books. We learnt about human rights and the purpose of the policeman. That's when I began realising that police are not there to enforce the law but to render a service to the community. That's what I got from the college.

When we were being trained, they said that the police needed to change, because policemen were viewed as enemies. White people didn't view it like that, because they were being served – only black people were overlooked. So they told us that we must try to change and try to teach the old policemen, and that they would try to introduce some training and education to the old policemen.

There was no harsh treatment – the instructors did not mistreat the students. The atmosphere was very good. We could socialise, speak our minds, come up with suggestions. What I liked about the students was that they were all matriculants and they liked books. I saw that the South African Police Service was going in the right direction.

– **Inspector Ramela (1995)**

I went to Pretoria College. It was previously used by white police officers, but now everyone is using it. At the college I didn't expect things to be hard for me. But the treatment that they give you there – it's like you are under arrest. If you do anything without their permission, you are punished. That was hard for me. But the physical training was lekker: I liked it because I used to play soccer and run, so it was easy for me. I was there for six months. – **Constable Sibuyi (2000)**

I had just come from air force Basics: I was super fit and disciplined. SAPS Basics was a complete jol. I was in the *berede* bungalow, just across from the instructors' quarters. I immediately made friends with two coloured guys, Angelo and Mark. I didn't want to mix with the whites since they all had huge egos and it pissed me off.

I used to finish my inspection stuff in no time and would use the rest of the time to go and shag my girlfriend. I loved it when the students were forced to do guard duty. I would put on my uniform and sneak to my girl's bungalow and spend the night there. When I sneaked out again and the other guards saw me, I would shine my Maglite into a dark corner and say, 'There he goes!' I would then run in that direction for a while and return to my bungalow when it was safe.

We used to give the coloured instructors phone numbers of female students and in return they would give us booze.

Mark really looked like a darky, but he spoke Afrikaans like a professor. One night we got pissed and wanted to sneak off campus to get more booze. We chose a side entrance to sneak out. As we approached the gate we saw that the security guard was asleep. We were about to sneak out when we saw head-lights approaching us from the rear. Even though the car was far away, we decided to hide in some nearby bushes just in case it came in our direction. Unfortunately the driver, an inspector, had already seen us. He stopped next to the security guard, kakked him out and started throwing stones and bricks into the bushes. One of the bricks struck Mark and he shouted in pain.

The inspector then instructed us to get into his bakkie. He told us that we were going to be kicked out of college and arrested for drunkenness. Around the corner from the duty room, he stopped the car and told us that he liked it that we were mixing races and could see that we were good friends. He told us that if we gave him twenty rand, he'd let us go. Mark with his big mouth told the inspector, 'Ja, sure. But our mixer is also fin-ished; could you get us some more?' I thought, *ag nee, nog dieper in die kak*. To my surprise, the inspector agreed. A few minutes later, he stopped at our bungalow and gave us our Coke. When I looked in the bakkie, there was a bottle of brandy and a two-litre Coke on the floor of the passenger side.

– **Constable van der Merwe (2003)**

Two months into my training I became the platoon leader of my unit because the guy that they had chosen was nineteen years old and couldn't handle the pressure. They had a democratic vote and voted me in. I was very strict in the work that I did. You change when you become a leader. They didn't like that about me.

As we were nearing our passing-out parade, while we were busy showering, one of the guys asked me if I was gay. I said to him, 'Why would you ask me something like that?' and he said, 'I'm just asking!' I said, 'No, why would you ask me something like that?' And he said, 'Because you're a bitch, that's why!' So I said, 'If you honestly want to know – yes, I am.' He said he admired the fact that I was gay and that I'd taken up all the responsibility with the guys.

Obviously the news reached the other platoon members and they said to me, 'Why didn't you tell us you were gay?' I said to them, 'What does it matter if I'm gay?' They said, 'We showered with you!' So I said, 'Man, your penises are so small I couldn't even see them!'

— **Constable Louw** (2004)

I went to Pretoria for training. They were very rude to us there. They were shouting at us: you must do push-ups, you must run. They swear at you …

At college, I almost got kicked out of the police. I challenged one of the captains. I asked him why we had to run every single day. He told me, 'You have to run.' I told him, 'No, you run yourself. I am sick and tired of running! I've been running since the day I arrived at this college!' The captain told me to go to the dormitory to pack my things, and that he was firing me. I went to my dormitory but I didn't go back to the captain and he didn't see me again that day until parade. Standing on the parade he was calling, 'Hey! The student constable that I was talking with: come and talk to me before I come and find you!' I didn't go; I kept quiet. He was standing there shouting, giving me a last chance and whatnot. The parade was dismissed and I went to the dormitory.

Then there was another incident on 16 December, before the passing-out parade. I visited this inspector of mine. We were not allowed to visit our instructors, but I thought I would just go. He said, 'What are you doing here? You know the director doesn't want you to come and visit us. The duty officer is going to kill you!' I told him, 'Forget about the duty officer.' I sat down with that instructor and we talked. He gave me three bottles of Castle Lite. It had been a long time since I'd drunk beer. By the third beer I couldn't walk, because my system was no longer used to that amount of alcohol.

When I came out of the instructors' dormitory, I couldn't walk properly. I bumped into a senior superintendent. He asked me, 'Are you a student here or do you work here?' I told him, 'No, Senior Supt., I am a student here.' Then he said, 'But you are fucking drunk!' I said, 'No, Senior Supt., don't swear at me, *bra*.' He was so angry! He told me to pack my bags, then he took me to the director. He asked me why I was drunk. I said, 'Director, it was the meat that I ate. I went out the college to the place where people are braaiing. I went there to buy myself some food and there was this guy who was pouring a bottle of alcohol over the meat. I bought that meat, I ate that meat and now here I am not even walking properly.' The director said, 'Get out of my office; you are making me sick!' Then the senior supt. told me to go back to my bungalow and to go to the afternoon parade in full uniform. He said I was going to do guard duty. That night I went to the parade in full uniform. From the 16th until the passing-out parade, I worked night-guard duty.

I passed out of the college and came to Sebokeng police station, where I was trained as a student constable.   – **Constable Shabangu (2007)**

People say the police are stupid; they say the police are fat. Not all policemen are stupid and fat. The senior officials should get blamed for that. It's their problem we're fat. It's their problem we're ignorant and not taught properly in our work. I do not think the law of the police can be taught in six months. If I have to go to university for three years to study something, how can they teach somebody the law for six months and then expect them to go and rule people's lives and tell them what is right and wrong? How – when they don't even know themselves what is right and what is wrong?   – **Constable Louw**

3

POLITICS AND POLICING

I've never questioned my role as a policeman in terms of criminal behaviour – for example if we went to arrest a suspect and he tried to shoot at us and we shot him in self-defence. But I've questioned it regarding laws such as the pass law. If you found a person on the street after a certain hour and he didn't have a pass, you had to lock him up. That was very unfair and inhumane.

At the time we believed it was the right thing to do. You were trained that the law says you have to have a pass; if you don't then you are out of line and you need to be arrested. You were enforcing the law, so if the law was wrong then obviously the enforcement was also wrong. But in terms of that time, it was legitimate for you. We were very young. I think it was very difficult for the black police officers, especially in the areas of the riots, because they had to go back to the very same environment where the riots were. If I can criticise the apartheid police for one thing – and it wasn't everywhere: it depended on the commander, because in a lot of cases the commanders stood up for their black colleagues – it would be that there were cases where this policeman was just left to go back home, where he then received threats from people saying that they knew he was a police officer and he was driving in a Casspir and shooting at the people. Maybe he hadn't shot at the people, but he had been involved, and a lot of their houses were thrown with petrol bombs and their belongings destroyed. I think it was unfair that the police didn't have a support base for those people. **– Senior Superintendent Boning (early 1980s)**

The pass laws were so cruel. If somebody from Limpopo was working in Joburg or Pretoria, they would arrest him for the pass law – he was not allowed to be there. That was something which I didn't understand. I sometimes had to arrest people for that. I was working with my superiors in crime prevention, in a group. If we stopped to check people and their ID was not right, they had to stand aside. But sometimes you could see this man was all right; this person was a father.

The 'special permit' was a stamp stating the period from when until when he could work. If I checked the person and I saw his special had expired but he was a father – he was a man supporting a family – if my superior couldn't hear what I was saying, I would say to him, 'Hey man, you must go and fix your special.' Sometimes I would let him go if my superior wasn't watching, but if he was watching I had no powers. But I feel that the thing I was doing was not right for those people. I was depriving them of their rights. They were trying to do something to support their families. When I think back I feel very bad. I regret what I've done, but I can't reverse the situation. If I've done wrong, I ask an apology of everyone I have done something wrong to. If I came across them I would say, 'Please forgive me for what I've done.'   **– Inspector Mampuru (late 1970s–early 1980s)**

It was a question of internalisation. They had the pass laws and then they had the curfew laws, which meant that black people were not allowed to be on the street between twelve o'clock and four or five o'clock – 'night pass' they called it. If you saw a black guy on the street at that time, he was arrested immediately. Forget about the reason. Nobody was allowed on the streets. In those days that was one of the issues. A lot of genuine black guys were arrested. A lot of crooks were also arrested in the process and I think, to a degree, it kept crime down. I won't say it kept it down entirely. You always had the white crooks, the white housebreakers. And you also had the criminal element in the black community. They were out and about and busy at night and they evaded the police; they made sure they didn't use the street.

Look at the pass laws – you could arrest a guy for not having his pass book, his identity document. If he did have his identity document with him, you could have a look and see: had he paid his tax? If he hadn't paid his tax, you arrested him. If you put that into today's context and you walk down the street, here's a white guy and you say, 'Where's your ID document?' and he hasn't got it and you arrest him – think of the outcry there would be!

So there were a lot of inequalities that took place – I'm not going to say they didn't; I'm not going to justify them either – but in those days it was the done thing. Why? Because that is the way the work was done. You arrived at your station and that is how it was done. You didn't question it. Exactly the same thing happens today – this is the process, this is the procedure, this is how it's done. You conform. Either you adapt – you take it – or you leave it. If you don't adapt, you can leave, thank you very much; find yourself another job. There wasn't a question of forcing you to do it; it was accepted that this was how you would do it. I wouldn't be surprised to learn that there were people who weren't very happy with the way things were done.

I think black police were also so indoctrinated by the ideology of the day that they never questioned the laws, although they were also subject to those same discriminatory laws, like carrying their pass books. But they did it because it was the done thing. We were supposed to enforce the laws – they didn't question it. We were probably all misled: maybe the politicians were lying to us. They most certainly were, looking back over the years. If apartheid had never happened, South Africa would be a totally different country today.   – **Director Grobler (1960s–1980s)**

Being a police officer you are not a politician. We did not question it. If they find out you're questioning it you will be arrested. They will check if you are working with one of the organisations fighting the government; they will think you are a terrorist. The security branch will deal with you.

The terrorists were trying to destroy the country. Those people were fighting for their rights, but if you came across them you had to arrest them. I saw them as freedom fighters because they were fighting for their rights; they were trying to free themselves. But sometimes I thought it was the wrong thing because innocent people were killed. If somebody comes and plants a bomb at a mall, innocent people will die. That person only looks for a soft target. It was the wrong thing. All of those people who were killed were innocent. But they were trying to fight for their freedom.

– **Inspector Mampuru (1977–early 1980s)**

I was also in the riots. It was happening across the whole of South Africa in 1984, the national riots. People can riot for valid reasons. That was the problem. I knew what a riot was – I had been rioting in 1976. Now I was the person who was supposed to stop the riot in 1984. It was difficult. You had to shoot your brother. – **Inspector Rameama**

In the riot squad we used teargas, stoppers and rubber bullets. Sometimes you felt some police were doing things that were not necessary but you could not say anything. People could be doing something peacefully and then the police would come and provoke them. If you provoke people, they will react and then the police shoot rubber bullets and they will run; some will be injured. Sometimes you felt a little depressed. You thought, if it was me what would happen?

When your commander gives a command you have to act. If you don't act you will be in a helluva lot of trouble. But if we hadn't worked for the apartheid police, who would have served our own people when they came with a complaint? As a black police officer they had to come to me; they had to talk with me; I had to interpret for the white person. I had to interpret because if I were not there, there would have been no communication between a white person and a black person. We had to serve because without us those people would never have got help. But not all whites were the same. Some cared for the black people and tried to help them in a good manner. But some were so harsh. Even our own black brothers and sisters were harsh. – **Inspector Mampuru (1980s)**

I didn't want to go to the Border. I said to myself, 'Why? It's a bloody political thing. Why don't you get the politics sorted out? Let's stick to what we're supposed to do. Let's fight crime – we're not fighting terrorists!'

I never questioned the reason for being a policeman, but I questioned a lot of things that I had to do. At one stage they started this counter-insurgency thing. I was still a uniformed bloke, a constable. We had to go to what is now called the Asiatic Bazaar. In those days it was called Marabastad. They had a police station, a mobile unit, large trucks and things like that, and they would mobilise for riots. We had to go there on Saturdays – on your off-day – and they would give you a tin hat and you'd do what they'd call 'anti-guerrilla warfare'. They would take you to Atteridgeville, a black township west of Pretoria. There was an army area there, and there you would run around the bushes. I didn't appreciate that. I said to myself, 'Why the hell must I do this? It's got nothing to do with policing!' That was a military responsibility.

I was on the Border for four months, only one stint. It was a traumatic thing. I was very scared of going. I had a dream before I went. In it, I was lying behind some kind of protection and looking through the riflescope. We didn't have scopes on our rifles on the Border but I remember looking through it in the dream and seeing a guy on the other side pointing a gun at me. The next moment I was lying on my back and the guys were looking at me and saying, 'Shame.' That scared the living daylights out of me, and that was with me all the time. I said to myself, 'I'm going to the Border, I've had this dream and I think it's a premonition. I'm going to be shot.'

But when we were involved in a firefight, that was the last thing on my mind. It's a funny thing that when the adrenalin starts pumping, you forget about a lot of things. You don't think, 'I must hide behind something.' I'm not a hero; I've never been one. As a matter of fact, I think I'm a bit of a sissy – but I certainly didn't have a self-preservation urge. It's only afterwards when the whole thing's being mopped up that you think, 'Well look what *could* have happened.'   **– Director Grobler (1984/85)**

I went to Ovamboland twice – Border duty. That was a time which nobody can buy. If you weren't there, you weren't there, sorry. I didn't have very much contact, but I saw things happen; I saw death. At that stage in a person's life you just say, 'Another one bites the dust.' If you think back, it was traumatic stuff and you realise it wasn't the fun you thought it was. At the time we thought the shoot-outs were fun. Not for years afterwards did any of it affect me.

I was in Ovamboland in '82 and '83. In those days Koevoet was operating there. Stuff happened. I was with the COIN unit doing special duties, not with Koevoet – they were permanent. But we saw the things they did. It was like a trophy when they brought in a body.

The local population, the Ovambos, they had a difficult time. The army gets there; they want information from them. Then the police get there; they want information out of them. Then the terrorists get there and they want information from the other side. So they had a difficult time. They were driving Ford bakkies and we were driving Casspirs and Buffels. They were using the same roads. If they walked over a landmine – *boom!* – everything goes up in the air. I saw Casspirs there get blown up in the air!

The worst I got there was malaria. I prayed to die. It gets up to forty-two degrees there in the summer. I was lying in a tent, in a sleeping bag, under three blankets, shivering.   – **Captain de Beer (1982/83)**

From college I went to Maleoskop. It was part of the training, but extended to counterterrorism. It was harsh, tough. In the basic training the focus was on equipping you to be a police officer in the police station. At Maleoskop you were trained to do guerrilla warfare. It was clear who the enemy was. You had to defend the country; it was war. The aim in the police college was minimum force, working with the community, apprehending criminals. At Maleoskop, there's no minimum force: you defend your life – yours and your buddy's. The other guy's not going to ask you what's happening. He's going to shoot at you and you have to shoot back.

After college I went to the station. At that stage they just sent a letter to the station to say we need X number of people for the Border. Then the station commissioner must nominate people. Most of the time, the married people would try not to go. Sometimes they would tell you, 'You *will* go,' but on two occasions I volunteered because I wasn't married and I had previous experience, so I knew what it was like. For people who didn't know, it was more about fearing the unknown.

Every time before you went to the Border, you did a refresher course. You go back to Maleoskop for a week before you are placed at the Border. At Maleoskop you were trained that this is the enemy, you need to defend the country and you need to act against the threat. Even today I don't think that it was wrong. I think that the whole war situation should not have happened because there should have been better negotiations. But people were coming to South Africa with the intention to plant bombs, with the intention to kill people – not only white people. So if I question those things I question why there was war and not why we acted in a certain way. There's nothing else you can do. These people are coming and there's a conflict situation; you need to act otherwise you're going to be buried. The whole process before should have been handled differently.

– **Senior Superintendent Boning (1985; 1987–1990)**

So many policemen get social problems: guys threatening to kill their family because they just go nuts. You found that especially coming back from the Border. This was something I could never deal with properly. The organisation sends you to a border to fight a border war for whatever reason. There it teaches you one thing only, and that is to kill other people. Now you come back into a sane society, but that killing machine doesn't have an off switch. That guy comes back into society and he can't adapt; he becomes *bossies* – completely disorientated. They never had a mechanism to destress or demobilise people. You were sent home and you were given seven rest days and then you were expected to go back to your office like nothing had happened. Many things went wrong as a result of that.

– **Director Grobler**

On 8 November 1989 I transferred back to riot squad again. I worked there until 2006. My only duty was going to work at the riots. Sometimes they would take us to KwaNdebele where there were so many people killing each other, burning houses and so on. The people were against the government of the homeland, their own people. They were fighting against each other. We tried to stabilise the place. Sometimes we worked three or four days without any time off; day and night, no water to wipe our bodies, nothing.

In 1990, I was posted at Beit Bridge border gate. There, my duty was just to control the access of people coming in and going out from Zimbabwe.

I worked there, then came back to my riot squad in Pretoria and Joburg. Sometimes I was sent to Bophuthatswana before it became the North West, and Limpopo. We went on many courses, including an internal security course so we could know what to look for on the Border. The course took six weeks. It was tough, not nice. A lot of the time you had all your luggage on your shoulders. Even if it's one hundred kilometres, we had to walk that hundred kilometres. When we went to the shooting range, we would walk, and get there at two o'clock in the morning. When we were finished, we had to walk back to the base. No transport, nothing. But white police travelled by bus. We were separated, even in 1991. If the whites stayed at Alpha Camp, we would be based at Foxtrot Camp.

The time was tense in Thokoza in 1992 and '93, when the ANC and IFP were attacking each other with their own forces, MK and the Defence Unit. It was so tough. We worked there. Sometimes your duty for the day was just to drive in a Casspir with a trailer and collect all the corpses – collect them and put them at the base so the mortuary could collect them. At that time you didn't want to eat meat. We saw terrible things. People had been burnt. When I saw meat, I felt like I was eating those people. It took me a year before I could eat meat again. The problem was that they didn't arrange any counselling for us. People were dying like flies. Even our colleagues died. When we knocked off, people took chances – they went outside to buy two beers and never came back. They killed them because they were police.

That was my saddest time in the police. It was so terrible. Any moment you could be told to go to a section to collect a corpse. The whole day: you book on duty at six o'clock in the morning, and until six o'clock in the evening, you're collecting corpses.

It was my duty to maintain law and order. Even if I said I wanted to resign, they could still have killed me. They were killing everybody. In my heart I just said, 'God knows what His plan is.' It was terrible. It was frustrating to see people killing each other and not knowing why. They were used by these organisations. So people were dying until 1994.

Before the election in 1994, we were working day and night. I was working around Thokoza, Sebokeng, Vaal, Rand and Soweto, still with the riot squad. We worked hard until after the election, when things tried to change. Then we could apply for promotions because black and white were now equal. But whites were still dominating; they were still having the last say. Blacks were being promoted, but some of them did not know how to run the police force.

I just thought to myself, let me work, as long as my children have something to eat.   **– Inspector Mampuru (1989–1994)**

From '91 to '96, I was basically involved in political violence the whole time.

In the early nineties – 1991, 1992 – there were big riots in the East Rand. I was deployed in Thembisa: it was a war zone. There were some big fights between the ANC and Inkatha, big fights, and it was difficult for the police. We were patrolling these areas where the migrant labourers lived in their hostels and the people would be there on the fourth floor. We would drive the Casspir and they would throw petrol bombs into the Casspir. Some people got serious burns there.

Even in the eighties it was very hostile. One thing that I don't think the general public knows is that the police weren't seen as the threat and the enemy. It wasn't like that. We were protecting everyone. There might have been some instances where the police sided with Inkatha more, but we were protecting people. We needed to keep them apart. We were attacked from both sides, by Inkatha and the ANC.

What the people don't know is that the police didn't kill so many people. The very same African black people killed each other: they killed their own people with necklace murders, or by shooting them. I attended numerous scenes in this riot-related crime where people were burnt to death by their own people, if I can put it like that, and not by the police.

So the police were actually acting against criminals from both sides, protecting the lives of a lot of people who may have considered the police to be their enemy.

– Senior Superintendent Boning (mid-1980s–early 1990s)

After college, I came back to Ladysmith and was posted at Ladysmith police station.

There was too much violence in KZN at the time. We were all fit and ready for action. It was scary, because they were burning the houses and burning the people. But you just enjoyed going out there and seeing what was happening.

They were burning the houses, killing the people, toyi-toying. People were leaving their homes, moving from their houses in the middle of the night. There was this raping of the children. If you were ANC in an Inkatha place, they would come and molest your children, rape your children in front of you, things like that.

It was very sad. People were crying. When they came to report that, you felt their pain. The debriefings we have now are new – at that time there was nothing. You just went back home and waited for the next day.

– Inspector (F) Dlamini (1991)

A week out of college I went to Ventersdorp. There was that thing with F.W. de Klerk – the AWB tried to break up his meeting. It was a big thing: we had to fly in with a helicopter. Then all the unrest started. I worked in that area in Potchefstroom, then the mines, then I ended in Alexandra and Boipatong. My last thing was the Boipatong slaughter. The hostels came together in Vereeniging and they went into the Boipatong residential area and they just started hitting and killing people.

Then just after that Winnie Mandela came. We drove down to the sports centre where she was supposed to speak, to check that everything was okay. We drove down and there was nothing; it was clear. So we turned around and went back. But when Winnie arrived, there were four bodies lying in the road. All the bodies were old, like planks – you couldn't even bend the arms. The people who put them there waited for us to leave and just before her motorcade came, they put the bodies down. Then the car stopped and she climbed out. There were cameras every-where: 'Look what happened! Look what happened!' But we'd just driven there in the Nyala five minutes before that and there was nothing. That was part of life.

It was then that I got my transfer to Plettenberg Bay. That was my part in Gauteng. I never went back.   – **Inspector Marais (1992–1995)**

I was first posted in Witbank. People were starting to change because Mandela had been out for two years. It was that period when there was tension. There was violence. Everyone was on their toes in case there was violence. But we were on the whites' side because we were part of the police and the whites were in power.

If there was a riot at the police station, the police would go and shoot at the blacks at the location. Then the riots are finished. You as a black policeman go to the police station, then you knock off and must go back to those people you were shooting. Your white colleagues are left in town. If there were riots in the township we would go to the township – shoot-shoot-shoot-shoot, harass-harass-harass, teargas-teargas. Then you'd go back to the police station and knock off, take a taxi and go back to those people you were teargassing.

I felt like they were rioting for the right reason, but I was on the other side. We couldn't all be fighting. They were fighting for our rights; they were fighting against apartheid. But I felt my actions were justified – it was right to shoot them. It wasn't a problem because they should have found other ways to solve these things, not shooting or burning other people. I didn't think toyi-toying was the solution. I thought my job was justified. There were other ways they could have settled those things.

– **Captain Ndlovu (1992)**

When I joined the security branch, I didn't know it was so unpopular. I just thought it was about working undercover. Later, in 1995, I thought, shit, I was in the wrong place! Those people I was working with, they were the people doing all those funny things. I still remember Joe Mamasela and all those people. I was frightened.

At the security branch, we were called 'fieldworkers'. We went around gathering information, mostly about political organisations of the time. When people came to join the police we did some vetting, but mostly verbally, just to understand the person. We would talk to their neighbours and their friends. We wanted to gather information about his political background. If he was involved in politics then we would monitor him.

We didn't understand what we were busy with. We would gather the information, but you didn't see the file where your information went. You would just tell your supervisor. You had to call him 'Sergeant' because he was white, even though they were all constables. He was the one who wrote down the information that you gave him. He was also the one who arranged for payment of the *impimpi* if you had one.

Only now that I understand the role that we played am I angry. But at the time we enjoyed it. We had a car, we went around, so I didn't mind. To me it was more relevant to what the police did. We gathered information about the political organisations. We were given this mindset that these people were very, very dangerous, because they were called 'terrorists'. We would read in the newspapers about the bombs and how they killed people. We thought that one day we would be killed, so the best thing to do was to work against them. They brainwashed us very strongly, but it's only now that I understand that. We would have meetings and they would tell us a lot of negative things. We would believe it because we saw it in the newspapers.

Because of this brainwashing, I stayed far away from the people who were talking politics. For me they were very dangerous: something was wrong in their heads. Because of the brainwashing and because we liked what we did, I don't know what was happening in our minds, but we were very dedicated.

When I look back I realise it tainted me. I think at the time it was more about serving the government of the day than anything else. Like now – if there's something wrong with this government and you are part of it, you are tainted.

At the time we were part of it, we played the role. Sometimes they would bring people into the office, we would be given an instruction to beat this guy and we would beat him. Because you wanted to please these people, you would beat him. You didn't want to be seen as someone who was negative, who didn't want to do his job. We were more dependent on our superiors than on the person in front of us. We were dependent on them for a raise, for a promotion. You had a whole lot of generals who had this same idea: terrorists are terrorists and we need to kill them. So who were we to say, 'No, why are you beating these people?' At the time you had no say. You did your part and made sure you did what they wanted, otherwise you would be on the news. It was bad.

They made me beat people to get information out of them, for them to find out who the terrorists were. Especially the trade unions. If there was a strike and people were burning the place, we would get a few suspects and bring them to the office and we would have to beat them up to find out who was responsible for the burning. Then we would give that information to the detectives who were investigating the case.

We would put a sack over his head, beat him up and pour water over it so he couldn't breathe easily. Sometimes we would put him inside a big sack with a cat. When the cat finds him there, there's a whole lot of fighting. Because the cat is inside a confined space, it fights with the person; its claws can be very cruel. When the guy comes out, he will talk, because he doesn't want to go back in there. But it was more about beating them with our fists. Sometimes we used sjamboks. But that was mostly in the office, the seniors. They didn't want us to see the things they were doing in case it came out and we talked, so we were not part of that. They would use sjamboks and choking and electric shocks, but we were not part of that. We did our beatings in the bush.

We went to Vlakplaas when there were braais and things. We went to visit there, just to see the place. But at the time we didn't know it was a place of torture. It was only after the TRC that I thought to myself, ai, the places that I visited unwittingly, not knowing that it was very dangerous. In fact I should have lost my job because I was part of these things. But, to me, it was just work. I met Eugene de Kock, but we couldn't talk to them because they were more senior.

Some of the people I braaied with were involved in the killings, but we didn't know that then. They didn't come and tell us that this was what they were doing. We noticed that afterwards when people started talking. It was shocking because we called those people our colleagues.

When I look back, sometimes I wish I could turn back the clock, but you can't. Those are your footprints, something you can't deny. But it was part of work, serving the government of the day. I don't regret it, because that's what I was getting paid to do.

I was in the security branch until 1995, when I moved to the Kameeldrift police station. That's when I started to work in uniform.

After the transition – looking back, being involved in the security branch and doing very notorious things – I was very disappointed to have worked, talked, laughed, partied with people who would go home and do a lot of things that were out of line. You ask yourself if ever, one day without knowing it, you did something wrong. Maybe it was just God's grace that protected me.   **– Captain Mthembu (1989–1994)**

From college I went straight to the security branch, which was my dream. I'd read a lot about it. It was an efficient unit: highly motivated and well trained.

I used to think to myself that I would be scared if I was an MK trying to come into this country. I would be a bit nervous, pre-1990, even 1991. But obviously when the transition took place it was a different story.

I'm not a politician: I was a soldier and a policeman and I served the government of the day. So whatever their laws were, I would implement them. When the ANC was unbanned, when F.W. de Klerk made that decision, we had a huge right-wing threat.

There was a weapons cache that we lifted right near the N1, and that was before 1994. So the loyalty from the security branch to want a democratic South Africa is absolutely not debatable. We arrested more white people than black people from the time of the release of Mandela up until the first election in April. More whites were arrested for trying to cause anarchy and destruction than blacks. So anybody telling you that the security branch was a racist, SS-type, report-only-to-the-government-of-the-day structure – absolute nonsense. Why then would we pick up weapons that the right wing had stolen and hand them in? Surely we would overlook that? That kind of stuff used to hurt.   **– Inspector Stevens (early to mid-1990s)**

After 1994, we realised that we had been on the wrong side. We had been used to achieve the political motives of the time. It was more about supporting the ideology of the government that said a black person is a terrorist, a black person cannot govern South Africa. So when you think of that and you think of some of the incidents of racism that you experienced, that's when you realise that the organisation was, in fact, bad.

– **Captain Mthembu**

Section 29 was quite a harsh law. You could keep a guy for an undetermined amount of time. The law changed in 1994.

I enjoyed using it sometimes, but at other times it wasn't right. There were guys in custody for two years who hadn't done anything, which is not right. It made me sad. In a way I felt shit. The guy's arrested for six months and then you let him go; you didn't charge him. I feel a little bit of guilt about that.

It's easy to say it wasn't my fault, but it really *wasn't* my fault. Whether I liked it or not, I couldn't do anything about it anyway. I hadn't made the arrests. I just knew about them because I'd go down to correctional services and the guy would say, 'Listen, do you still want to keep this guy?' And I'd say, 'Oh fuck, no, sorry. No, fuck, he can go!' Or I'd say, 'Let me find out for you. Does anyone want to keep this guy? No? Okay, let him go!'

– **Inspector Stevens (early 1990s)**

Looking back, the SAP was basically the machine that kept apartheid going, but I never thought about it at the time. It was a politicised organisation then – but not overtly politicised as it is today. What happened in the South African Police *Service* – they changed the name in '94 – was that it went totally to the other side. Instead of saying, 'We are depoliticising the South African Police Service. It is no longer an organ that is following the dictates of the National Party but it's a service-orientated organisation that looks at the people' – which it should be – what they've done with black empowerment is, unfortunately, that a lot of incompetent people have been appointed to senior ranks with no, or very little, background. It's led to a heck of a lot of frustration. Not only among whites, but also among blacks.

– **Director Grobler**

4

SEGREGATION

There was a power hierarchy between white and black. In the sixties there was a time when the rank structure between the black members and the white members was different. The most senior rank that a black member could attain was that of what they called a 'head sergeant'.

They were called 'bantu' – 'bantu constable', 'bantu sergeant', 'bantu senior sergeant'. There was a force order out that irrespective of a black man's rank, his rank was lower than that of any white member.

They had a brown uniform and they wore pith helmets. Then, later on, they started issuing them with the same blue uniform that the whites had, and with firearms. Before, they never had firearms; they were issued with an assegai. So there was for such a very long time this absolute unfair treatment. But, strangely enough, everybody accepted it. There was no question of unions and stuff like that; those came years later.

It didn't interfere with relations because it was a whole social system that existed. Not only did it exist in the SAP but it existed in the community – that was just the accepted way.

There was a subtle shift. I think it started way back when the rank structure was integrated in the early seventies. The first thing that happened was the rank structure was integrated with that of the white members. The only difference was that the badges of rank differed. If you were a white commissioned officer, your pips were gold. But those of black members were silver. Why they did it, I don't know, but the rank was still the same – if you were a sergeant you were a sergeant.

— **Director Grobler (1960s–early 1970s)**

After we passed out I went to Protea in Soweto as a riot-squad member. The riot squad was mixed black and white. At the time, whites were always superior. They were the ones who were giving us instructions. Even if you had ten years' experience, here comes a new white constable from the college; he is a superior to you. As a black you had to listen to what he said, even if he was wrong. We didn't have any choice. We worked in that situation because it would not help to complain.

You felt frustrated, but because it was the law at the time there was nothing you could do. They would tell you the force order and you had to comply. You could feel the law was wrong, but if something was written down as a law you couldn't do anything until the law was amended. Even though you felt bad, you had no powers to do anything. Sometimes you would be taken to be the car guard at the river, or the dam. That car had been stolen and dumped there and the police would just leave the car there for three weeks. Every day somebody must be there to guard that car. White people just left the car. Even though they took fingerprints you must just sit there; you mustn't touch that car. If you are at a dam in winter you are freezing, but it was part of the job. Only blacks were posted as guards.

– Inspector Mampuru (late 1970s)

It was helluva different in the past. You didn't go and sit with a white man socially. He was your enemy, even in the same organisation. They could dismiss you at any time. They could say, 'Sign this form' and you would have no rights. '*Ek sal jou pak uit die mag uit*': I will default you out of the force. We had to say, 'Sorry, boss! Sorry, boss! Sorry, boss!' You would choose: 'Do I whip you or do I default you?' They would whip us with a leather belt.

I remember a friend of mine, he just quit, left the job – no resignation or anything. He said, 'That man is going to whip me. I'm not going to work here.' They whipped us with sjamboks too, whatever was nearest. The officers carried a cane covered in leather. They would hit us on the head, ten times. You couldn't complain. I stayed because of my wife, my children. My parents were not working – I was a breadwinner.

– Inspector Rameama (1980s)

After my training, my van crew was an African man. He was the person who trained me in practical, writing up the OB – what we know now as the 'community service commander'. Later I became the driver and he was my van crew. We ate together; we slept together; we did everything together. But at that stage people were not treated equally. There were a lot of people with attitudes, who would differentiate between white and black.

When I came to the police in 1982/83, I was placed at the station. I was never a person doing what they called 'gate duty' – you had to stand at the gate to open it. At that stage that was meant to be for the African people. It happened that whites did that too, but then it was as a type of punishment. When a person did something wrong he was placed on gate duties.

When I started out, black people became our friends because they were our buddies. For an eight-hour shift we were working together, sometimes for twelve hours, sometimes for longer. When I went to the Border and even to the riots, we spent days, months together. There was no way that I ever said that I'm on a higher level than him because I'm white and he's black, no ways. We covered for each other; we helped each other; we went to arrest people together; we searched houses together.

— **Senior Superintendent Boning** (early 1980s)

It was hard; it was tough. I was working at Wonderboompoort. Sometimes the station commander and warrant officers would tell me to go and make tea for them. Even students would tell me to go to the shops to buy things for them. I would say no. The white student who hadn't even been to college would want me to go to the shop for him. I would tell him I had been posted as a charge-office clerk: I would do the things I was supposed to do. I would not do what I was not supposed to do.

Those people had their own tricks, the white majority. Sometimes I would knock off early in the morning at six o'clock and get home at eleven o'clock. Then they say they want you at the station lecture at two o'clock. They didn't give us transport. So how was I going to get there? So I slept, because I had to go back to work in the evening. When I got to work, they said that, because I was not at the lecture, they were going to default me by taking one of my rest days. This warrant officer told me to come on my off-day with my private clothes so he could give me some jobs to do. When I got there, he gave me a lawnmower and told me to cut the grass. When I was cutting, I found a rock in the grass. I pushed the machine over it and the machine was damaged. They went and got another one, and I just rode it over the stone again. That day three lawnmowers were damaged. I did it because they were trying to frustrate me. After that I just sat down until four o'clock, when I knocked off and went home.

— **Inspector Mampuru (early 1980s)**

Black police officers were being assaulted under the instruction of the station commander. You couldn't tell your family. You couldn't tell your wife, 'My boss whipped me,' because she would have laughed. It would have made the situation worse.

In Witbank, a sergeant of mine was making me mad, so I stole his .38 from the safe and I sold it in KwaNdebele. He was a *boer*. A *boer*, *boer*, *boer*. He was the commander, so he was responsible for that firearm. I didn't book it out, I just gave it to someone and took the money. I stayed at home for six days.

On the seventh day they were supposed to open a docket of desertion against me. I went to the office of the station commander. He said to me, 'I can arrest you or whip you.' I said, 'Whip me.' He whipped me and told me to go home and come back after two weeks. Since then I've never defaulted. I knew what I had done. This job is about working for the community and that's good. But these commanders come with attitudes and these attitudes make us act. — **Inspector Moji (1986)**

The police only paid me R150 a month as a constable. The white constables were given a higher rate and privileged duties like driving a patrol van. Non-whites weren't allowed to drive a patrol van – whether for attending to complaints or for crime prevention patrols.

Whites didn't earn much more money but they were always seen as higher than the non-white of the same rank. Non-white police officers weren't allowed behind the counter in the CSC unless they did the filing. We seldom engaged with the community in the community service centre.

As a young student my first station was Stanford: a very quiet holiday resort town, ten kilometres outside Hermanus. Most of the coloured inhabitants were migrant workers who worked outside Stanford. On Fridays, the buses and trucks would come in and that was when our troubles would start.

My focus was to change the police, including the white officers – not only my people – so I constantly focused on their shortcomings. The white station commissioner didn't allow me to enter my place of work through the white door, but referred me to the non-white entrance. This was my first encounter with my *stasiebevelvoerder* as we called them at the time. I left it like that: I didn't whinge, because I knew that along the line I would teach him a lesson or two.

In Stanford there was a whites-only bar and a coloureds-only bar. The mistake that the developers made was to put the white bar on the wrong side of the main road. The white bar was the last bar between the white residences and the non-white residences. So it meant that when the non-white residents came out of their bar, they had to walk past the whites-only bar, which always led to conflict and fights.

One night we had a fight at the bar. I was accompanying the white warrant officer as a passenger. It was at the white bar and the suspects were three young white males, fighting with coloured bartenders who – because of the location of the township – had to walk past the white bar.

In such incidences the warrant officer would very politely say to the young white man, '*Boet*, please listen now, don't do this,' and he would then drive off. In contrast, if the suspect was a coloured person he would summarily be arrested, thrown into the back of the van and taken to the cell. No questions asked, no mercy shown. This was my experience, and this was what I wanted to change.

When the warrant officer decided to execute an arrest that night he was bumped over and landed on his back in the road. He was flung with one blow, by his own so-called white resident, the suspect that he'd warned. I intervened, arrested all three white suspects, put them in the back of the van, closed the door, helped the warrant officer to his feet and shook off the dust. I said, 'Don't worry, sir, I arrested the suspects. Are you all right?'

He said, 'Thank you very much.' From that day his attitude changed to such an extent that he even trusted me with his own family and private car.

— Inspector Khan (late 1980s)

Since I started in the SAPS, the relations between the races where I was were okay – everything was smooth. We played rugby together, we played cricket together. Maybe I was just a lucky one. At that stage I couldn't understand why people were complaining. Everyone was getting the same salary. I understand that before my time the one was getting paid more than the other one, but I couldn't understand why people were complaining. Maybe it was different in small towns where it was only white and coloured and Afrikaans-speaking – where there wasn't even a language difference.

— Inspector Burger (1988 onwards)

The SAP looked down at us as municipal police officers when we joined. They would give us the old dockets. They also employed the *kitskonstabels*. There was this stigma between the municipal police officers, the *kitskonstabels*, and the ordinary SAP members. But gradually things changed.

In the late eighties, the promotions were a matter of when they tell you to wash their car, you don't complain, you wash it; then you're promoted. They didn't consider any academic achievements. But then with the political changes things began to change. They started seeing us as one of them, giving us some respect. Before that, when they posted us, we could not be in a patrol car; we could only guard the gate or guard a suspect in hospital.

— Inspector Kekane (1989–early 1990s)

When I left college I went to head office. We were called 'messengers'. We would be given an office number, and when you got there a white lady would say, 'Go and buy me a cooldrink.' You'd just take the money, go and buy it, come back and give her the cooldrink and some change. If she wanted to she would give you two rand. That was our duty – only for black members. We didn't wear uniforms, we wore a white coat, like a doctor's coat.

I complained after I'd worked there for a year. The brigadier who'd assisted me to enlist was also working at head office. I went to him one

Saturday, because I was still working for him on Saturdays, and I told him that I had trained to be a cop and now I was doing messenger work. He said, 'So, you're not satisfied?' I said, 'No. When I made a decision to become a policeman, I didn't think I would do this kind of work.' He said we would talk on the Monday.

On the Monday he made some arrangements for me to go and work in the canteen where they served wine to SAP members. There were a lot of orders from members who wanted wine delivered to their houses. I worked very hard there; I was the only black. This general who was in charge of the canteen would look at a pile of boxes and say, 'These boxes are not meant to be here.' I had to pack them here, pack them there. Then the following day he would say, 'These boxes are not meant to be here, I want you to move them.' So I worked very hard. Whenever I knocked off I was very tired. It was only manual labour in the canteen – nothing that I had trained for at college.

I was afraid to complain again so I worked there for a year and then decided to make a transfer on my own, without telling the brigadier. That's when I moved to the security branch.

– **Captain Mthembu (1988–1989)**

In my time before '94, a black sergeant didn't have a say over a white constable and a black warrant officer didn't have a say over a white constable. To me this wasn't right, because rank would have been my philosophy for respect, not colour, but then, only rank that's deserved. Then you say to me, 'Salute that captain,' and I say, 'I can't,' because he's a bit of an idiot. I would have respected the rank had it been earned properly, had it not been dished out like Smarties.

We didn't have to salute black rank, but I saluted them out of respect. I showed them respect. I used to stand roadblocks in the township. I would be the only white on that roadblock and I would say to the black officer, 'Captain, would you like me to do anything for you?' They would look at me, amazed, and eventually realise that I was actually being sincere. I'd say, 'Captain, can you please excuse me? My time is up,' and they would look at me in shock and think, but you could've left anyway.

– **Inspector Stevens (1991–1993)**

I sensed a subtle resentment towards English-speaking members of the police. I think a lot of other English-speaking guys that I know felt the same thing. We weren't considered to be at the bottom of the rung, but we weren't close to the top either. We were almost viewed as foreigners. A colleague of mine in another specialised unit overheard a conversation with a senior member where they were discussing promotions. His exact words were, '*Daar sal nooit 'n Engelsman in bevel wees van die eenheid solank ek lewe nie.*' It was a lot worse when you were outside of East London. In Pretoria at that stage you just *didn't* speak English.

The police as a culture was discriminatory in a lot of respects. It was bad for non-whites. That being said, there were a damn lot of good cops out there who were not discriminatory, who weren't the bullyboys that everybody made them out to be. They weren't racist. But it was a weird time in South Africa's history. The country was literally changing, and the organisation that you worked for was changing at the same time.

– Sergeant Jordaan (early 1990s)

When I was a student I was at a suburban station that was a white station. The segregation was apparent there because if a coloured person had done something wrong the punishment was different. The white person's punishment was softer.

A coloured colleague of mine arrested a white officer for drunk driving, and my friend was moved from a white station to Mitchell's Plain. I felt that was unfair because in those days if you were at a white station and you behaved yourself you stayed there. If you misbehaved they sent you to a coloured station. If you misbehaved again they sent you to a black station. Black and coloured people were punished more in this way. That's why if you found a white person at Nyanga you knew they were *really* bad: it was a punishment station. It's not like that today. Now they are trying to get the stronger people to those stations, which is good because it's really tough in there. – Superintendent (F) January (1991–1994)

It was dangerous with regard to the community. It wasn't as hectic as it was in '76, '77, '78, '79 and '80. We joined in '87 when it was much better, although people were still looking at the police as though they were their enemies and their abusers. You had to be very careful when you went into your township.

When you came back from Hammanskraal, your white colleagues were taken to government houses in town and we were taken to Mamelodi. It was a hostel, but it was called a barracks. You had to share a bedroom. It was very shocking. Not a nice place to live in. But we were paying R30 a month, so what could you expect? The less you pay, the less you can expect. But it wasn't nice.

The white colleagues were taken to houses which are now being occupied by SAPS members. We only saw them after the transition, when apartheid was no longer practised. When we were told that there were quarters in town, a flat that belonged to the SAP, we couldn't believe it. We'd been taken to stay in Mamelodi where it was dangerous and filthy. SAP management and the government didn't care about black members – where you stayed was your problem. As long as you could pay and contribute, they were happy.

They didn't provide transport; we used the train to get to work. When you were in uniform, you didn't pay. But it was a risk, wearing a uniform without a gun. You take a train used by the public – that's where criminals hide themselves. So it was a risk. Even your salary was not equal to your white counterparts'. We were not getting paid like them. After '94 they tried to balance things. You could see people were angry because they balanced it. I think it started in '93, '94; that's when we started to earn a better salary.

When I was a constable in '87, a black constable compared to a white constable – it wasn't the same. I still remember the first cash that I got was R657,43c per month. We didn't understand this scale thing and your salary per annum; we just understood what we got each month and that's what we were interested in. For me it was a lot, because we were coming from school with no debt. — **Captain Mthembu (1987–1994)**

Before 1994 it was dark. In Witbank I was a police-station guard. As a black man you were given a pump-action shotgun. There's no fence, no gate – it's just open. But you must always be standing at attention at the side of the road with the cars driving past, standing like a statue.

Then a white man comes into the SAP via his father. He is a student but I am forced to call him '*Baas* Constable'. I had to teach him. Then after he had learnt the OB, he worked in the charge office. Now it's called the client service centre. You stood outside and he worked in the office with the heater, kettle and tea. You – as a black member – worked outside six-to-six, night shift and day shift. You couldn't leave the post; you would be defaulted. It changed in 1990, when the old man came out of prison.

– **Inspector Moji (1980s)**

5

TRANSFORMATION

Most of the officers were white when we left college and went to the station. In 1993 there was a promotion phase. Democracy was coming, and there would most likely be the election where all parties could register and everyone could vote. So they promoted a lot of white inspectors to captains before the shift to democracy.

– **Superintendent (F) January (1993)**

After the elections, over a period of about six months, maybe a year, the MKs and APLAs came into the army and the police. 'Morning, Constable; evening, General' – it was that kind of thing. They came in as constables, left as senior superintendents; it was a free-for-all. I realised then already that that was the end of my career: 1995, '96. I couldn't leave then, but I knew in my heart that I was done. My connection to the security branch was obviously not a good point on my CV. The guys in positions of power were shifting; it was becoming more ANC, MK, APLA – in my opinion the *black* man for the job, not the *best* man for the job.

I never stopped being an honest and proud policeman. I just knew that I couldn't expect to be promoted above the rank of inspector. I knew that would never happen.

I stayed for ten more years but I went to an undercover unit, so it was different.

When people became aware of the transition, a lot of guys resigned. The older guys, the over-fifties, called it a day. They knew it was over. I also knew. Unfortunately I was only twenty-eight or twenty-nine years old. I was scared.

I was scared to leave, scared not to leave. I didn't know what to do. I was convinced by some of the superior officers and a lot of my friends. They said, 'No, stay! Everyone's going to sign amnesty and get amnesty, and everyone's going to confess and love one another afterwards and have a group hug.'

It was a confusing time. For me it was difficult. Coming from where I did, going to where we went and doing what we did. I wasn't arresting black terrorists any more, I was arresting white terrorists. I was much busier in 1994, stopping people from disrupting the election that was going to sink my career. It's ironic: I actually protected the system that was going to sink me, that was going to discriminate against me. And I did it for one reason: because of my loyalty to the police, not the government. I was a policeman and I would honour the government of the day. I wasn't loyal to them; I was loyal to the police and they were implementing the government's laws.

When I started arresting white guys they used to call me a 'white kaffir', a 'kaffir lover', told me they were going to kill my family. It was rough.

I knew I wanted peace in this country. At the end of the day, we all want peace. At the end of the day every South African, whether he's black or white, catholic or protestant, he wants to braai on a Saturday, watch a bit of sport and spend the day with his family. He doesn't want to bomb places. Every South African inherently wants peace and that's what made it easy for me. I knew that by arresting those whities, I was helping make that happen.

Amalgamation was probably my most difficult time in the police because it was the absolute proof that unfairness was going to take place, that sanity was not going to prevail and that laws were going to be implemented irrespective of whether it was for the good of the country or not. I would have an officer that couldn't write, who was basically illiterate. It was going to happen – that was proof of it. You had the FIFO philosophy – fit in or fuck off.

The merger was an absolute disaster. Having a guy in a unit who can't fill in an SAP5; he doesn't have the ability to write an investigation diary; he doesn't have the ability to inspect an investigation because he's illiterate; he cannot read what you've written. Everybody says, 'Oh, it wasn't that bad.' It was. I saw it. I saw African guys from the homeland police that couldn't write, they couldn't spell, they didn't know what a monthly return on a vehicle was and they didn't know how to fill in an SAP135 logbook – they'd never used it. Now they're telling me it wasn't that bad. It was. I'm telling you it was.   **– Inspector Stevens (early to mid-1990s)**

There was a lot of talking during the transition. My white colleagues were very afraid, some even resigned. They were saying, 'This terrorist government is going to take our pensions, take our medical aid.' Some decided to leave and form companies. There were a lot of uncertainties. Our work shifted. We had to gather information on crime, not politics. That brought uncertainties for some people. They thought, what is all this now? In the security branch we were focused on relevant and very serious issues before: politics and terrorism. Now we had to gather information on crime, which for some was much less important. So uncertainty was there. But for me, I didn't have any other place I could go for employment. That was my home. So I welcomed the changes as long as they weren't taking away my job. I wasn't frightened. People were talking a lot but I believe in seeing, not hearing.

The white members couldn't take it when the ranks were made equal and things changed. Before, there was never a black officer in a police station in a white suburb. Once you became an officer, if you were black, you were taken to the township. You couldn't be an officer in a suburban station because your white juniors could not salute you. So every time you qualified to become an officer you were taken to Soshanguve, taken to Mamelodi, taken to Soweto. When the transition started it was more difficult for our white colleagues to look at us as equals. There was a lot of fighting over that.

When the homelands merged, there was some dissatisfaction among ourselves and our white colleagues because these homeland police were coming with their high ranks. I was worried about their qualifications and their ability to act responsibly as officers. Some of the officers coming from the homelands were very incompetent. It was more from their being close to a prime minister that they got their promotions, so we didn't have respect for them. There were those who were very capable, but there were those that were incompetent.

When I was in crime intelligence in Mpumalanga we had this one guy; he was an MK – he couldn't even write. He was a captain and when I left he was promoted to superintendent. He would go and gather information and then come to you: 'You write, because you went to school. I'll tell you what to write.' You had to learn to accept it. This is the new government that has taken over: maybe it's payback time for them.

– **Captain Mthembu (1990s)**

Coming out of college in 1990, we took pride in working as policemen. We learnt from the older policemen who still had a lot of pride in what they were doing. That encouraged us to do the same. There was a big difference after that with the people coming in at higher ranks – especially from different cultures – who didn't have that pride in their work. They just came to get their salary and they were placed in positions as seniors. I don't think they gave any of their juniors anything to look up to. It was just about what they had on their shoulders. The knowledge they had, the way they did their work, the pride in what they were doing started going down.

The people coming in at higher ranks were from the homelands, as well as some people already in the SAP. Some of them couldn't even write, but the next minute they became your superior. If they needed to write a report, you would write it for them.

I was fine with the political changes. I've never had a racial issue towards anyone. What started bothering me was the unfair promotion of people who didn't have abilities. It wasn't because they were black. If a white person who couldn't write became my superior, I would not have been happy with that either.   – **Inspector (F) van Niekerk (early 1990s)**

These ranks just came about because of some kind of affirmative action back then. They did not need anyone's academic record or service history. They just said, 'Oh, you are thirty-five years old and you have ten years' service in the SAP. You go to inspector.' Before 1990, promotions were only for whites or for those who complied with whatever they were requested to do. The new government realised that and said, 'Okay, let's give people promotions.' There would be someone who was forty years old but was never promoted. They wanted to speed that up. That's how I got the promotion. Otherwise I could have got nothing because I didn't comply with anything. **– Inspector Kekane (early 1990s)**

When the transformation started to happen there was almost this laager mentality, an encircling of wagons: people in senior positions started to look after themselves and their little groups. Everybody else was just left to the wind. That's unfortunately how it felt. This was post-'94 with the transition from SAP to SAPS. It literally felt like you were being thrown out into the wilderness and people were just looking after themselves. There were people promoting or benefiting certain racial groups so that they could look good in the eyes of everybody else. The culture shifted from 'We're all going to watch each other's backs' to 'I'm going to do what I need to do to look after myself.'

People from previously disadvantaged groups also started looking after themselves – 'I've been deprived for so long, so now I'm going to make the most of what I've got.' It was a tough time, a significantly tough time. Being involved in the commercial branch and investigating corruption cases against police officers, you got to see that. It was a very chaotic time, a time of a lot of distrust and a lot of fear. People didn't know what to expect. It still wasn't a unified service by any means. At that stage, we amalgamated with the different policing agencies from the homelands. In the Eastern Cape we had two homelands, so the cultural dynamic and shift there was significantly bigger than, say, in Pretoria, where not much had really changed. For us it was a massive change. Within our unit we had people brought in from other police forces that had different standards, different ways of working. A classic example was that, if we needed to do work and there were no cars available, you got in your own car and you drove to do the investigation. But the guys coming from the homelands would say, 'Okay, we've got no cars. We just won't work.' It was a clash of organisational cultures. It was tough. **– Sergeant Jordaan (1995–1997)**

Around '93, '94, after the release of Mandela, the mood in the country changed. I had the feeling that the place had changed, the laws had changed, the country had changed.

Someone came into the police station and wanted to lay a charge. Because they had said we now had eleven official languages I wrote the statement in Pedi. I was just testing what it felt like and what they would say. But I was in for it for that. The problem came when they allocated the docket to a detective who was a Shangaan. He could not read the statement, so he took it back to the captain, and the captain took it back to the commander. Then I was summoned to the police station. 'Why did you write this?' I said, 'Yesterday they just passed the laws that we can use eleven languages.' This was strange to them. Those people at the top were still powerful. For people to change back then, it was difficult.

I nearly got fired for that. They charged me the one day; the next day I went to the hearing. They wanted it to be quick so that I could be fired. Fortunately I was a member of the unions so I was rescued.

The change was difficult for those guys. What surprised me was that the people who reacted to the writing of the statement in Pedi, they were black people. They are the ones who drafted the charge against me.

– Inspector Kekane (early 1990s)

In the riot unit, there was definitely respect across the races. Working in Plettenberg Bay at the time – '93, '94, '95 – we were four, at the most six, guys on a shift. At that time it was mostly whites and coloureds in the unit. I worked on a vehicle with the one coloured guy. We worked on the vehicle together for a year, two years. So you get respect for each other. You play rugby together, and when you get a complaint forty kilometres from the station, you must be able to handle each other. If you can't handle the guy in the vehicle you mustn't climb in the vehicle with him. You had to look after each other. – Inspector Marais (mid-1990s)

At college in 1995 the relationship between white students and black students was marvellous! We could understand each other, we swam together, we used the gym together, we played soccer together, we played rugby together, we watched movies together, we stayed in the same bungalows, we used the same canteen. Everything was perfect in the college.

When I went to the station I found they still kept to the old way of separating people. When I arrived, there were certain posts that were only for certain race groups. I realised that most white people don't want to work in the client service centre. The shifts were handled by white people. When you came to change shifts, white people didn't even wait for the parade to be posted. When one went off duty and booked off the vehicle, he gave the keys to his friend and said, 'Take this vehicle; give it back to me tomorrow.'

I realised at the station that white people didn't want to work in the cells. White people didn't have respect for the black shift commanders because they were shy to post people. I realised that there was fear in those old black people. They just wanted a job.

I was posted with a white person. What they did during the night was that they went to the drive-in screens, where you park your vehicle, switch on your radio and watch movies. Then they just ignored the police radio. That's why the community was complaining.

There was a Superintendent de Waal. He was a white person, an old policeman, but he wanted to bring in changes. I respect him even now. He brought discipline. He stated that he didn't want to see white and white in one vehicle. He wanted to see black and white in one vehicle. Superintendent de Waal didn't even last three months. His white, *white* colleagues – top management – went behind his back. They came up with a proposal whereby they asked people to sign that they didn't need him. We didn't understand, and we signed that document. After that another station commissioner came and we realised that we had done wrong by signing that document. Then we went back to that old system and worked the way they wanted to work.   – Inspector Ramela (1995–1996)

How the members engage with one another has changed; it's fantastic. Shared trust, shared interests and even shared time after work. Personally I can't recall very bad racial interaction in my experience. But we are more perceptive to one another now. There is a greater understanding of the different race groups, the different needs and the different cultural backgrounds. — **Inspector Khan**

Everybody – black, white, Indian, coloured – if you entered for the exams, you had a fair chance to get promoted, just like the others. The ranks were equal between races in the early eighties, for sure. There was respect for that rank. When I came out of college – and even later in '86, '87, '88 – when a sergeant entered the charge office and there was a constable he would stand up and stretch. If a black officer saluted me, I would salute him the same way as I'd salute a white officer. There weren't black and white issues at that stage. The black and white issues started after '94. Racism came after '94.

I worked with blacks all my life, never a problem. We checked each other's backs, we worked together, we were in the field together, we braaied together next to a car. Sometimes we stayed there for a week on the road: we sat there and we drank a bottle of brandy together, we laughed together, we sang together, we cried together, we went on these dagga raids in Swaziland for five weeks twice a year, and we were all together there.

They brought the politics into the police too much. The police is not about crime any more. It's about politics, about the system. The biggest enemy for a policeman these days is the system, not the crooks. They don't get to the crooks; there's too much red tape: meetings and meetings and meetings. Every meeting the same problem is mentioned. It's like a circus – but the problem is they don't have tents any more.

You're promoted on colour these days. The people in charge are incompetent. Not everybody, but most of them. For a black guy as well – if you're not really into the unions and the politics you're also trapped; you sit where you sit. The former KwaNdebele, when they were amalgamated with the SAP – you can look at the old SAP members – they're still sitting as inspectors. But those guys with the politics behind them are all promoted; they're all superintendents and senior superintendents. That is a pity. You haven't got competent people on the management side.

It wasn't because of the equal rights. Everybody had equal rights before. They're making an issue of something that wasn't there. There were people, and there are still people, who are into the right wing and left wing. These days it's reverse racism, in my opinion. I had a colleague who worked with me for many years, Dr Selebalo. He died in a car crash. He watched my back, I watched his. If I was away on a course and my wife had a problem, she could have phoned him and he would have come and helped her. We worked side by side. We worked in Amsterdam, outside Swaziland. We were doing observation and he would sit next to me in the bakkie and we would drink brandy all the time.

If I gave somebody an order then he would just say, 'You're a racist.' But I had the authority as an officer to tell somebody what to do. The force changed to a service, but there's no service. When it was the force it was like the army – you could instruct somebody to do his job. These days you can't talk to anybody, or you're considered a racist and they transfer you.

– **Captain de Beer**

In the transition period what we found was that the comrades stood up to bring change. Before, the police were looking after the interests of the government. Then post-apartheid we started looking after the interests of the community – all the inhabitants of the Republic of South Africa. Before they used to enforce the law, but afterwards they became a service.

For a long time a lot of the old policemen – even now there are some – they couldn't adapt to the change. They were used to the old style for too long, so they chose to take the package rather than adapt.

– **Inspector Lakay**

I didn't notice a big change in our work with the introduction of human rights. We came, we did our work, irrespective of whether human rights were there or not. We still went out and did our jobs. We tried to do things according to the book, always. It's not like we were bad policemen before 1994, doing the wrong things, and suddenly there were human rights and we couldn't do the wrong things any more.

After 1994, we operated according to the new rules. Now you have to fire a warning shot; you are not allowed to shoot. And that Article 49, when that was changed, you didn't shoot so easily because you could have been arrested and you put yourself and your promotion on the line. But in a life-or-death situation, you just reacted the same way. You didn't now go and put on hand gloves to interact with people out there because they've got human rights. I was treating them with human rights before, although it wasn't a written rule, so afterwards I just carried on doing the same as I did before.   **– Inspector (F) van Niekerk (1994 onwards)**

Moving from a force to a service, they did all those courses with us: human rights policing. But to talk about it is one thing. In reality you still use the force when you need to. I was in court three times for assault: all work-related situations. I was guilty, but the court said not guilty; not enough evidence. That's the thing with the law – you've got the right to an attorney. I'll get you not guilty in anything.

The one assault was a normal complaint. We had a fight with the guy, and it got worse. The guy made an assault complaint: he had a blue eye and his finger was broken. For every assault case against you, you are involved in one or two others that never get reported. But this went further. It happened twice when I was in housebreaking cases. You work too hard with the suspects. That was part of life.   **– Inspector Marais (1990s)**

When I was a detective in Witbank there was a lot of fighting. That was after the transition, so you had to arrest some white people. They couldn't take it when you said, 'I'm arresting you for assault GBH.' They'd tell you, 'No, I'll follow you to the police station,' and it wasn't a request; they were *telling you* you couldn't arrest them because you were black. So you had to prove it to them. That happened a lot after the transition.

When I was a detective on standby, I had to attend some housebreaking scenes on the farms. When you went there and tried to interview the owner, they would say, 'I'm not talking to you. Your people, your friends – they are the ones who did this. So you might be one of them; maybe they sent you.' They would refuse to be interviewed by me. There was a lot of resistance at the time.   **– Captain Mthembu (mid-1990s)**

I was booked off for a while. I had what they call 'major depression'. According to the reports the depression was a result of my work. What happened in '97 when the MKs came in: some of them were actually quite nice guys; some of them weren't the devil personified. Some of them were idiots, but some of them were quite nice guys. Then I sat back and reflected and thought, *sjoe*, okay, hold on, we could have actually worked together many years ago.

The system was also changing. I knew I wasn't being promoted; I knew I was going to be discriminated against because I'm a white male. I knew all those things and I think it just hit me.

I probably would not have had these troubles without the transformation because I would have had my promotion and everything would have happened as it always did. Now we had to make place for ten thousand new guys of a new race. We had to make new ranks in order to accommodate the political structure. We couldn't be a police *force*, we had to be a police *service*. We couldn't be captains and majors, we had to be inspectors and superintendents. The whole thing changed. You couldn't have a yellow police Nyala, you had to have a white one. You couldn't have a camouflaged riot policeman, they had to wear blue uniforms. Those things obviously had a big impact. The guys that wore those camo uniforms were proud of them. Now you take them away, make them wear blue uniforms and tell them, 'You were bad then. Now you're still bad, but you're good if you wear a blue uniform.' How confusing is that?

I remember one of the politicians said, 'The security branch should be compared to pigs in a pigsty.' Those were his words. Two years later he's a minister. It makes you wonder, what's my position now? Because I'm one of those pigs in the pigsty. I'm one of those pigs that he's talking about. I'm one of those pigs that arrested those white people that got him into the position he's in; I'm one of those pigs. I'm one of the pigs that picked up the weapons cache that was going to be used against him. But that's politics. Politicians are like nappies; they've got to be changed frequently.

– **Inspector Stevens (1990s)**

Obviously there were many white guys who left, because they told themselves there was no chance of promotion. The SAPS chose to promote the designated groups. There are many absolutely competent, wonderful black investigators and commanders. But there are a few who are not. And those are the people that cause all the problems. This unequal treatment of equals cannot carry on forever; there must be some sanity. If you've had fifteen years and you haven't done anything to improve yourself, then you're not going to.

The South African Police force was an organisation that was serving the government of the day. It enforced very unpopular and very unfair laws. Today, thinking about it, I cannot believe it happened, but it did. That there should be some form of redress, yes. But it shouldn't carry on forever.

In the pre-'94 period the South African Police was a force and it dealt with things in a forcible manner. Post-'94, it became a community-orientated organisation that took the community into consideration. It hadn't done that before. Pre-'94 the community was just there; it was regarded as being the enemy. Policemen always regarded members of the public as being the enemy, whether they were white or black. They regarded them as being a different species – it was us against them. Not in a hostile way. But we referred to them as *hase* – 'rabbits'. Always against us, our enemy.

The biggest change since the transition has been the disappearance of discipline in the South African Police Service. Commitment too. There are very few guys who are committed to their jobs. They have the type of attitude: I've got a job, but I don't want to work. Having said that, there are magic guys among serving members now. They are dedicated, they work hard, they work overtime – hours and hours of overtime without being paid – doing a thankless job for an unthankful people.

– Director Grobler

I don't remember anything about the transformation at college. When I came to the police station we started receiving letters about how to handle certain things. The letters were about the Employment Equity Act, saying that certain things must be in place by a certain period. I think it was from 1996 that the equity started.

Before 1998, there weren't many problems. But then they started bringing in black people from other provinces, from the Eastern Cape and from Gauteng. The police officials from those places came to Groblershoop, but most of them couldn't speak Afrikaans; they only spoke English. This language issue sometimes caused a problem. It's still a problem. They recently sent five new students and three of them cannot speak Afrikaans.

– **Inspector (F) Basson (1996–2009)**

The police were still a police force then. When I started as a constable working in the unrest unit, even being white I sat at the back of the bakkie because I was a *blougat*. The sergeant and the inspector sat in front. Today you look at the police constables and they want to be behind the steering wheel from the beginning.

When I started at Plett I had to be in the charge office for four months doing the books, giving the prisoners their food, cleaning the cells. Then I became a passenger in the vehicle – we still had the old Toyota bakkies. After three months in the bakkie, I could begin driving. My commanding officer at the time was a coloured guy. You, as a young white guy, listened to this guy. From there I went to crime prevention. When I became a detective, they called you a *leerling bestuurder*. You started with finger-prints. If your fingerprints were not right they tore them up. Then you started with shoplifting, common assault, things like that.

Now they send the guy to college; he learns to be a detective there. That's what it says on paper. He comes to Thembalethu; his first standby weekend, he gets a murder. The whole statement is one folio. When that gets to court it gets taken and thrown out. It's not that guy's fault. They didn't start with him from the bottom. – **Inspector Marais (early 1990s)**

Human rights policing is not new, it's just new in using the words 'human' and 'rights'. Even in the dark days of apartheid people had rights, but unfortunately the non-white people didn't have access to lawyers. Coloured and black lawyers were arrested before they could represent coloured and black people in a court of law. Now the focus has been changed, but the system hasn't changed.

There is a greater shift to humanity; there is a greater shift to victim support; there is a greater understanding of why people commit crimes with a basis of social evils and socio-economic problems. In order to deal with these socio-economic problems the police created the facility of social crime prevention officers. That means you address the social needs of the clients that you serve – 'serve', not 'police'. You address the root causes by employing the service of NGOs and civil society.   **– Inspector Khan**

The transition was difficult. It still is. Any white police officer, if he doesn't say it's difficult for him, he's lying to you. It's about how you adapt to it and with what type of attitude you go about working.

When it came to '94 and when the transition started, it wasn't as bad as it is now. Then it was still happy-go-lucky; you were still basically in charge. Now you're not in charge any more. In the beginning your achievements were still noted, even though there was a change in government. If you were good, you were good. Now it's not like that any more.

We're feeling it now. In '94 we just worked. We carried on doing what we had to do.   **– Inspector (F) Kemp**

Sebokeng is quite a fun place. When I started in the police a lot of people asked me if I was afraid to work in the township. In the beginning I was, but now I don't think I'd ever want to work in a white area. The people in the townships are so friendly. We've had a couple of times where we did patrols and there were funerals or weddings going on, and just because you waved to them or you turned on the siren, they invited you in to come and eat with them. You won't get things like that in the white areas. People in the white areas are snobbish. The township is a nice place to work; it's full of a lot of nice experiences.   **– Constable van der Merwe (2003–2009)**

After the election in 1994, I went to work in Vereeniging and Asanda. Then we were deployed in KwaZulu-Natal and the Western Cape because in the Western Cape there were still problems with drug dealers, PAGAD and gangsters. We worked hard there and we managed to stabilise the place. We were working black and white, mixed, as a team, equals. Some people still had the attitude of the old days. When we worked, we worked together, but after hours we were separate. Whites slept at their own place and we slept at our own place.

Even now, our own black brothers still have that attitude of discriminating against some other people. So if you are working and you don't have somebody who knows you well, then you'll struggle. I don't know when they will get this right – even now it is not right. Now they deprive these young white ladies and gentlemen. They are getting frustrated because of affirmative action. They are suffering for something which they didn't do – it's wrong.   **– Inspector Mampuru (1994–2009)**

In the Western Cape, after the 1994 elections, a lot of coloured males were promoted. A lot of people – especially white people – said, 'I'll never get promoted.' I had a white colleague who said he would never get promoted but then he and his brother both got promoted. They looked at performance – they were good workers, and they promoted them on that. So currently in the Western Cape I think people are being promoted on performance, not race.

I've been around; I've seen the bigger picture. There are good people all over, and if you look at the white men, they are still getting promoted. You have to look at the better ones obviously, and obviously the ones who don't get promoted are not going to see it like that – they are going to see it as 'It's me not being promoted.'

There are some people who get promoted when it should never happen, but overall I don't think that's the case. I recently applied for a promotion and I couldn't have done a better job than the two people who got the position. They were both white.

– Superintendent (F) January (1994–2009)

I'd only recommend a career in policing if you are a fan of Henry Ford's famous quote: You can get a Ford in any colour, as long as it's *black*!

On a serious note, if you haven't got a problem with getting to know other races, you'll get along fine. A white man's future in the SAPS is working in the townships, because of the equity policies. I think Chinese people will also have a brilliant future in the police since none of them are currently enrolled in the police and equity will be in their favour!

— **Constable van der Merwe**

6

ON THE CASE

In the week after I had done the serious and violent crimes detective course I worked on standby. Being on standby means that after you knock off at four, you still have to attend all complaints received at the station. Even if it's midnight, you wake up and you go to the scene.

At about eleven at night I received a call that a restaurant owner had been killed in Craighall. When I arrived at the restaurant, there was nobody there – just him, dead. No witness, nothing. I was puzzled. I didn't know what to do. I told myself I had to make a plan.

There were footprints of an All Star takkie in the blood, trampled all over the floor. The knife was there too. The restaurant owner's cellphone pouch was empty and the safe next to him was open and empty. He had about sixteen or seventeen stab wounds in his chest.

I found a room that looked like an office. There was a list of staff members with their cellphone numbers. I started calling them one by one. When I called the supervisor he said they were still all in the staff transport on their way home. I asked them if they knew there had been a killing. He said no. They made a U-turn and came back to the scene. There was blood all over the floor. It was terrible. All the staff members were crying there at the scene, just crying.

I asked the supervisor how many people had been working that night. He said everyone in the Kombi had been working, except for one person who they didn't see when they knocked off. I asked who usually opened the door when they knocked off for the night. He said the owner opened for them when they left, then he locked the door so that he could stay behind counting money and doing the paperwork. He said the owner was very strict about locking the door when they had left because he didn't want to be robbed.

Strangely enough, when I had arrived the door was unlocked, but the key was in the door, which means someone from the inside had opened the door. So I asked the supervisor about the staff member who had not knocked off with them. I could tell from the key in the door that it was not somebody who had come in from outside – it was someone inside the restaurant. I asked the supervisor if this other person usually used his own transport. He said no, he usually travelled with them. I asked what he had been wearing and he told me that he'd been wearing white trousers and All Star takkies. I asked if he knew where the guy stayed and he said he could show me.

Before I could trace the suspect there was still a lot I had to do at the crime scene. So I waited for the photographer and the fingerprints guys. They took all the measurements of the takkies and everything. Then the body was taken to the mortuary. From there I called one of my colleagues and together with the supervisor we went to where the suspect stayed in a flat in Hillbrow.

It was now about four o'clock in the morning. We knocked on the door. This guy opened. He was wearing shorts without a shirt or shoes. As soon as he opened the door, he pretended to stretch and yawn as if he had just woken up, but I could see that he had not been asleep. The supervisor told us that this was the guy he had been talking about. But we didn't have anything to link him to the crime.

In flats in Hillbrow you can find ten or twelve people sleeping in one room. There were about eight other people there, fast asleep. He was the only one who was awake. We asked him what time he had come home; he said, 'I asked my manager to release me early because I was having problems, so I arrived here at the house at about eight last night.' I asked the supervisor separately and he said, 'No, he's lying, he was there until late.'

Then I searched the room. The clothes he was wearing when he knocked off, the trousers and the shirt, were wet. He had put them on the chair next to his bed. This made me think that he had probably struggled with the deceased and his clothes were full of blood, so that when he arrived home he had to remove the blood. That's what I was thinking but it was not enough, so I searched under his bed and found some jeans. It looked like he had worn them once he had changed out of his work trousers. In the pocket was a cellphone and a lot of five-rand coins in a bank bag. I asked him whose trousers they were. I could see that he wanted to run, so we apprehended him immediately. He put up a fight, so I had to use a saucepan to hit him on the head. I knocked him out. I was afraid he was going to die, but he woke up. Then I called the photographer again. He came to the house and took pictures of the suspect, the clothing, the money, the room itself, everything. I took the wet clothes and put them in an evidence bag, sealed it and sent it for DNA testing.

This guy had previously worked at the restaurant but had stolen some money so the owner had fired him. But because the suspect's father also worked at the restaurant, and because the restaurant owner had a good heart, he would ask the father how the son was doing. The father would say his son was not working; he was suffering. So the restaurant owner decided to re-employ him. This incident happened about three weeks after he was re-employed.

I pushed the fingerprint expert to compare the fingerprints found on the knife, cellphone pouch and till machine, to see if they found the suspect's fingerprints. At his second appearance in court the suspect was applying for bail, but I was ready with the results. The results showed that the fingerprints we found on the knife used to kill the deceased belonged to him. I was happy. I was just waiting for the DNA tests. They take a really long time. If you don't push, you will wait about ten months. So I went straight to Pretoria to push for the results. They did it for me and after about two weeks I had the DNA results. They showed that the clothes that I found in the suspect's flat had blood from the deceased on them.

The case was transferred to the High Court, where he was sentenced to two life sentences for murder and thirty years for armed robbery. That was the first case where I felt like I had really done a good job.

— **Constable Sibuyi (2002)**

This guy in Gugulethu was hijacking people and committing house robberies. It was around 2000, 2001. He would execute them in their houses. He would hijack three or four vehicles a night. The last incident he was involved in before we arrested him, he hijacked a pastor to use the car for a house robbery. Then they went to Delft, they killed four people there, came back, dumped that car and hijacked another car. They searched and robbed the driver, took him to the bank. Then they beat him up and put him in the boot. They were driving to Gugulethu but the wheel came off; they left the car. They shot at another taxi and robbed the people. They continued and robbed a guy who was parking his car in his house. That was all in one night. For them it was like a hobby.

I was on the case from the beginning. I was a reservist and he was one of my priority suspects. We were on standby day and night on that case. On that particular day I was off, then they sent a van to come and fetch me. We got to this guy's house in Barcelona in Gugulethu, and surrounded the house, a shack. We called the other people out. We called the army in; they surrounded the house – about eight army guys. We ordered him to come out; he didn't come out. Teargas was fired into the house. We waited for him to come out because those canisters are very strong. But he didn't come out. Eventually I called the CCU. They came with two Nyalas. They started pushing the shack with the Nyala. Then we heard about three shots being fired. He'd shot himself.

He had said that if he was arrested, he was either going to die with the police, or he'd kill himself. We'd never catch him alive. And eventually he committed suicide during the arrest.

There was already a crowd of people there – the community had spread the news that the guy was cornered. Immediately a march was organised to celebrate.

We used to call him Vox. He was a quiet guy. He wasn't a big guy; he was short and slender. He didn't look aggressive. He would smile when he talked to people.

The three of us got the Catch of the Year for that: we were all reservists.

There was another policeman, who is crippled now. He was coming down towards Lansdowne when some kids on the street stoned his vehicle.

He pulled the vehicle off with the intention to go and investigate. He and his friend were armed and were going back to find the kids. As they turned around a Kombi came. The Kombi was driven by the same guy, Vox, and some others. They stopped and asked the policemen what the problem was, and said they wanted to assist them in driving around looking for the kids. So the policemen got in the vehicle. The one policeman went in front.

In the Kombi, underneath the seat, the owner of the Kombi was lying. He had been hijacked. Vox and his friends shot both the policemen and took their firearms. The one died; the other is now paralysed. They also killed the owner of the microbus. They shot them inside the vehicle, then threw them out.

In one incident Vox went to a house to buy Mandrax. The lady didn't want to give him any. He told the child that was there to take a pillow and hide his face and he shot the lady in the head. Most times he shot his victims in the head.

In Delft he killed a male and a female and their two kids. One member of the family survived because she had gone to visit someone and couldn't get transport to get home. The reason he killed them was that he had a hiding place in Delft where he would take the cars and strip them. This lady had called the police to tell them about it, but when the police got there Vox managed to escape. So he came back to kill the lady who had called the police. He wiped out almost the whole family.

I knew that he knew me at the time. He was also a taxi driver so he used to know us. He knew exactly who was looking for him. But one thing I have learnt in the police is you can't concentrate on the threat. Otherwise you lose focus. You have to stay focused, optimistic. If you are driven by fear you will lose that element of surprise. It's something you live with every day. This job is about putting your life at the forefront. When you are walking around you are a target – it just becomes a matter of time.

So you can't worry about death. You just stay focused and optimistic and exercise all necessary precautions. I'm not saying you should not worry about the threat; I'm saying you must stay focused. If it's your day to go, then it's your day to go. But stay alert; do all that is possible to stay alive.

You can't keep worrying, what if I enter this house and the guy is behind the door? That's a daily possibility. So stay focused, stay positive, follow procedure and make use of your eyes.

Vox was eighteen and he'd killed eighteen people.

— **Inspector Lukhele (2001)**

In Emmarentia, there are a lot of Indians. They are like blacks: if one Indian has a house there then the whole family comes.

This house was owned by a husband and wife. The other people staying there were in-laws. These people had an argument and the wife decided to divorce the husband. The husband was not happy about this and he decided to kill the rest of the family: his wife, mother-in-law, sister-in-law, brother-in-law and his own sister. But he chose not to kill them himself. He hired a hit squad so that it would look like a robbery. Those guys entered the house, tied everyone up and then shot them in the back of the head, one by one, execution style. He wasn't there himself but he alleged that he was there. He had a scratch on the back of his head and he said he had run away.

When I questioned the husband, he contradicted himself a lot. I asked him which car he drove and asked if it had a tracker. He said it didn't. So I phoned the tracker company to see if it had a tracker and I found out it did. I followed the necessary procedures and applied for a Section 205 and asked for the tracker records. The records showed that on that day his car had stopped outside his house and idled, then it drove off for about five or six hundred metres. Then he turned the ignition off but the doors were not opened, which means he sat in the car. After about twenty minutes or so his car started again, all three doors were opened and he drove off from Emmarentia to Soweto. At Soweto he stopped for a minute then made a U-turn and returned to the yard. That's how I found out that this man was lying.

When I asked him who had been driving his car that day he said nobody had driven it; he had had the keys all day. Then I asked him what his car had been doing in Soweto. He kept quiet. That's how I caught him. Then he told me everything. He had dropped these men at his house, then went to park his vehicle. Then they went into the house and did the killing.

That scene was terrible, terrible. There were human brains on the floor. They had used hollow-point bullets. Wherever these bullets exit the body there will be a big hole, so they had taken the whole brain out of the heads. That was the most terrible scene I have ever attended. There were bodies lying all over.

I've never attended a debriefing after attending to a crime scene. It's possible, but it's a long process.   – **Constable Sibuyi (2007)**

My favourite memory is from the time when I was working for the sexual offences unit. I enjoyed it a lot. I got convictions for nearly ninety per cent of my cases. I started there in 1996.

My favourite case was the Baviaanspoort prison case. There were two wardens working as nurses at the prison hospital. There was this guy who normally cleaned – he was a convict. He cleaned during the week, not on the weekend. But he knew that on the weekend there were fewer wardens working and that these ladies were alone. He sneaked out of the cells on the weekend and came to the hospital section of the prison. He raped one of the women and sexually assaulted the other. Afterwards he slit their throats and locked them in one of the laundry rooms, leaving them there to die. He threw the key away and went back to his cell.

He thought the women would die there. Fortunately enough, before he left them to die he had fetched their handbags to search for money and so forth. There was a cellphone, but he didn't take it. So after he left, one of the ladies was able to crawl and get the cellphone to phone control to come and help them. When the people from the prison came to look for them they didn't know exactly which room the women were in so they tried all the doors. Then they found them – naked, full of blood, lying on the floor. It was horrible. I was the officer on standby, so I saw everything. It was very difficult for me, especially with the husbands there trying to give their wives support.

At the end of the day I was happy that that guy got a very good sentence. Both of the women survived. One of them has been medically boarded and the other one decided she no longer wanted to be a warden. She is now working as a nurse at a clinic. She left the prison. It was very traumatic. They were both married; the one who was raped, her husband was a social worker at the same prison.

– **Superintendent Molebatsi (2005)**

If a specialised unit like diamonds and gold needed a female for a certain undercover operation, I would sometimes do it.

There was one with serial raping at Centurion Lake. At night a lot of young people sit around the lake. People were being held up. The men were beaten and the women were raped. They were robbed of all their things. It went on and on.

Me and this guy went undercover. We took fishing rods and a blanket and a cooler box. We lay next to that lake for many, many nights. I just thought, please don't let anybody that knows me come past here and think I'm a fisherman at the lake lying on a blanket! We had a bottle of whisky there too, so what would people think seeing me lying next to that thing! We did that so many times and we still couldn't get them.

Then one night we were working shifts and we bought food. I said to the guy, 'Let's go and eat at the lake.' We went to the lake. Two guys were sitting on the stairs that go up to the bridge. We searched them for no specific reason. When leaving, on the little bridge, I saw a little Okapi knife. I said to my colleague, 'Let's take them in.' When we took them to the car the one threw something down. It was a watch, and on the back was engraved the name of one of the ladies who had been raped.

The victims came in and we did an ID parade. They were nailed big time. So we caught them in the end, not by lying there with our bottle of whisky but just by doing a normal search.

– **Inspector (F) van Niekerk (1995)**

There was a guy in a pub in a small town; he was playing pool. I said, 'This fucking guy has absolutely caused shit somewhere.' Everyone said, 'What are you talking about?' I said, 'Come on, look at the fucking way he looks!' He had tattoos; he had no hair.

I went and played pool with him, had a couple of drinks, found out he was foreign. He was being sought by Interpol and we found him and fucking arrested him and sent him back to his home country. I just looked at him and knew this fucking ou has caused shit somewhere.

It was actually quite funny because I had to make friends with him. Then the day I arrested him I said, 'Look, I'm a policeman,' and he said, 'No, you're not!' I said, 'I'm telling you; I'm a policeman!' and he said, 'No, you're not, we sat in my house drinking together.' I said, 'I know, but I'm a cop.'

'No, you're not!'

'Oh well, fuck you then!'

Still today he doesn't want to believe I was a policeman. He used to carry a revolver on him permanently, so I had to first take the weapon off him. The plan was I would walk onto the pavement with him as we were leaving his house. The guys from the reaction unit would already be in the bushes. I'd say, 'Hey Hans, let me look at that gun of yours again.' As I grabbed the gun I would say, 'Listen, I'm actually a cop,' and they would jump out. — **Inspector Stevens (1998)**

The other time I was undercover we had a lot of schoolchildren being robbed of their bicycles and we couldn't catch the guy. I had to put on a school uniform. When school came out the police would take me and drop me off there with my bicycle, with my gun in it. I would ride around and hope that somebody would try to steal my bicycle. The policemen would tease me so much about this!

The parents looked at me while I was being dropped off by these men in civilian clothes: me with my school clothes and my bicycle. I know they looked at me and thought, we know that you haven't been to school today – we see you!

Once it was so hot – it was November – and I pulled off the road and I sat there on the grass. One of the children's moms said, 'You can't just sit here. They will come and steal your bicycle!' I was thinking, I *wish* somebody would come and steal my bicycle! But no one ever tried.

— **Inspector (F) van Niekerk (2000)**

Before you do a drug deal, the police handler searches you to check that there are no drugs, no money, nothing on you. Then they give you the money to buy the drugs. So when you buy the drugs, you give them the drugs afterwards and they search you again. You're not allowed to take drugs into another drug deal.

I did a deal in Middelburg and they arrested me and put me in an office with these guys. They were busy questioning the one guy in another room. The room we were in had those little *hokkie vensters*. We were on the first floor. I had a pair of pliers and I bent it open. The other guys, the suspects, said, 'What are you doing?' I said, 'I'm going to jump out here; I'm going.' They said, 'No, please don't go – they're going to shoot you!'

The one guy told me he still had some Mandrax in his pocket. I said, 'Give it to me, I'll go to the toilet and I'll flush it out.' So I knocked on the door and I said, 'Open up please, I want to go to the toilet.' Then when I was out I gave the police the Mandrax and said, 'Okay, here's another charge.' When I went back in the police pushed me into the room and I fell on the ground. This suspect's eyes went wide! I said, 'I'm going to fuck up these policemen! They're dogs, man!' It was a lot of fun in those days.

– **Captain de Beer (1998)**

I was with another constable. We were driving around when we received a complaint of a bank robbery in Craighall. We called for back-up and set off. When we arrived at the bank there were two tellers there. We asked them what was going on. They said, 'Nothing is going on; it must be a false alarm.' We asked where the bank manager was and they said he was out at a meeting. So we left the bank thinking that nothing was happening. We got in our patrol vehicle, but as we drove around the corner my colleague said, 'No, man, that bank is always very busy but today there were only two tellers and no customers; there's something fishy there.' So we went back.

The front of the bank was glass and through the glass we saw that this was a real robbery. There were people with guns and everything, so we called for back-up again. We couldn't enter the bank, because it was dangerous. So we just stood by the entrance, pointing our firearms so that nobody could leave. We only had this 9mm thing. One of the guys inside was carrying a bag with what I presumed was money, and an R5 rifle.

He cocked his R5 and exited through the revolving door. As soon as he was outside he started shooting at us, but we were ready for him. We shot him and he died. The others were still inside, so it became a hostage situation. Those inside saw that we were ready for them. We called the special task force and they came and threw smoke canisters inside and then killed all the suspects.

What had happened was that those robbers were clever. There were about nine of them. Immediately when they entered the bank they took the security guard and the rest of the staff members into the manager's office. There they ordered them to lie on the floor. Then two of the robbers took the shirts from two of the tellers and when we entered they pretended as if they were tellers and nothing was going on. They were very brave actually.   – **Constable Sibuyi (2007)**

I liked being a negotiator because every situation was different. A lot of times people would ask me, 'What do you say to these people?' You never ever say the same words twice.

The quickest one was only a few seconds and the longest one was two weeks. It was always something different, always filled with adrenalin. I was lucky; I had a one hundred per cent success rate, but some of the guys who were trained with me weren't so lucky. They would come back home with the guy's brains all over them after five hours of negotiating.

We had lots of suicide threats – some evenings we had two or three of them. There was a guy in Swartkop who was about nineteen or twenty years old. He was sitting in the veld with a gun. We got a report that he'd told somebody he was going to kill himself. When we stopped there, I climbed out and I said to him, '*Dit reën en dit is flippin' koud. Gee my die gun en laat ons ry.*' I don't think he expected that. He just gave me the gun. Maybe he wanted someone to plead with him not to do it, so that totally got him off guard. It was really cold; I really didn't want to negotiate that day.

One time we had a guy in Pretoria who threatened to jump off a thing with a rope around his neck. Every time he saw a blue uniform coming he would swear like hell and chase them away and threaten to jump. I had my uniform on, and when I went in the same happened. So I went out and I waited for a while, then went back in and swore and shouted at him. He just broke down and cried. After two hours, in tears, he begged me not to leave.

You never do it the same way. It's always something different.

Another time, this guy wanted to commit suicide. He fired a shot but it only hit the tip of his nose. I promised that I would take him home and we wouldn't arrest him or take him anywhere else. When I eventually got him to get into the car with me, all four doors flew open and the task force was there, pointing a million guns at our faces. I swore and shouted at them to get away. If you break that man's trust in you, the next minute, the next day, he could do it again.

The guy wrote me a letter afterwards thanking me for saving his life and saying he was back on track. But it could have gone wrong there if they had taken him out of the car.

You don't make false promises, except if you want him to be arrested. There's also a difference for me between suicide and hostage situations. This guy didn't threaten anybody else. Most of the times in situations like that the task team comes out, because it can also impose a threat on other people's lives. These people sometimes just lose their grip on reality and shoot somebody from a distance.   – **Inspector (F) van Niekerk (1996)**

7

COMPLEXITIES AND MISHAPS

I became an agent in crime intelligence in 2005. I have to be on the ground myself, working with criminals so that I can work out their modus operandi, learn how they operate.

When you are working with a criminal, deep in your heart you know you are a police officer and this person is a criminal. You are working with him now, trying to plan something, maybe a robbery or something. This guy will tell you, 'If a cop comes here wearing civilian clothes I will sniff him out!' Meanwhile he's saying that to you, a cop. He says he uses muti to help him sniff out cops. But he can't tell I'm a cop, so the muti doesn't work.

When you are working with a criminal you know when a person is talking shit to you. But you ought to play the game. If he wants a bribe you should give it to him; you are buying a relationship. If he's a criminal and you are an agent and you need to buy something like drugs from him, you feel, 'I can't buy this thing – I'm making this guy rich,' but you know you are trapping him. Sometimes you think, *eish*, am I still a police officer? You just want to say, 'I arrest you,' but because you're working for crime intelligence, you can't. That's your job. — **Captain Ndlovu**

I left the open system and went into a unit where you worked in an under-cover environment. Only you know what you do there, nobody else does. You have a car that doesn't look like a police car, but it is one. Everybody thinks you've left the cops. You don't go to the canteen any more – you're just out of the system. Those who see you ask, 'Oh, when did you leave?' and you just say, 'A while back.'

Working for an undercover unit and having a fake working persona fucks with your mind a bit. I know a lot of people who it's damaged quite seriously. They don't know the difference between reality and the bullshit life you live. I'm not a tough guy, but I managed to tell the difference between reality and fiction and I knew that a lot of the stuff that I did was a lie; it wasn't me. You can't live that life. It's just your job; it's not your life. It's got to come to an end sometime.

Some of the things which were not me were some of the belief systems I would have to have. I would have to be an extreme racist in order to become friends with someone in a right-wing group. I'd have to have no morals on drugs when it came to a drug syndicate. Obviously if you're going to try to get in with a guy you've got to say, 'Dagga should be legal,' and 'Fuck the government,' and stuff which you've got to control. Some of those macho undercover guys out there don't have to, but I was different.

It's difficult because you live a lie. Everything's a lie around you. You're not Mr So-and-So. That's not your car; that's not your money. You don't really live in Hartebeespoortdam in a fucking chalet there – it's just a house you rent for a time. So you've got to distinguish between what's real and what's not and if you can't do that, as they used to say, it mind-fucks you a bit. It just fucking destroys you. You live that lie, you become that person and eventually when the car is gone and the flash money is gone and the safe house is over because the investigation has ended, it's like a cold bucket of water being thrown over you in the middle of winter. It's like *sjoe*, so I actually live in *that* house? I *don't* actually own that car?

It's like a drug: you want to go and do another one so you can have that same experience again, so you can have that bullshit life again until it ends. You can do it for two years or five years, but it has to come to an end. It can't go on forever.

Imagine you're a fifty-year-old guy and you've got to leave. You've bought nothing and built nothing up in your private capacity because you've been living the bullshit dream the whole time. Now you've got to go and buy a car and a house that will be yours. You're actually going to buy your own petrol and you're actually going to pay rent and pay your own water and lights; you're actually going to buy your own food. It's not going to be a sponsored little undercover journey. You've got to be very careful.   **– Inspector Stevens (1996–2006)**

My primary task is to protect the prisoner. He is the one who has killed or raped, but I cannot judge him. I have to be neutral at all times. His safety comes first. There are people out there who want to kill him, so I have to put my life on the line to save him. So I switch off. All of us switch off. Maybe somehow or other it surfaces in our rage when we get cross with each other over some stupid incident in the office and maybe what you heard in court sits somewhere in your subconscious and it just comes up again. I think somehow or other it comes out, but you don't know that that's the cause of your action.

As a police official working in court, you must have a good relationship with the prisoners. They can retaliate big time, or fights can break out between police and the prisoners. So you must connect with them. I'm not saying they should overpower me. I'm the policeman at the end of the day and it's not my fault they're there. They're there 'cause they caused a lot of shit. But there is some way that we handle the prisoners. Anyone who works at Pollsmoor or any other police station, any warden will tell you that they have a connection with the prisoners. You can't think, you killed my mother. You can't; it's impossible. Otherwise you won't do your work. And you will go mad because you will constantly think about what this man has done. You can't.   **– Constable Louw**

There was a big riot somewhere in the Free State. I was there sussing out the ringleaders so that we would identify who they were and then work on them. There would always be one guy sweeping up the crowd, so if you eliminate him you've eliminated most of the problem.

All I remember is a brick coming and it hit my friend right in the forehead. He just collapsed. A brick hitting a head is like a balloon popping. The guy is just gone – he's out; that's him. Hopefully he will wake up in hospital. That's a shocker. And they said, 'Oh, they didn't have guns?' Fuck, try and dodge bricks for two or three hours. You can't shoot the guy, and you can't throw the brick back at him, because of the photographers. Imagine you were to throw a brick at me and I picked it up and threw it back at you. 'Oh, this cop threw a brick at the suspect!' The fact that the suspect threw it at you first will become irrelevant. The fact that you threw it back will become a big headline and it will go on for six months. So that's what used to upset me. They'd say, 'Ah, it's just a bunch of students.' Okay, then *you* go and keep them under control: two hundred students with a bunch of stones and bricks! It's not nice.

– **Inspector Stevens (1994)**

Coming from the army, it was difficult to make the shift from maximum force to minimum force. When you're in the army you go somewhere with fifty or sixty guys. In the police you're only two guys in the vehicle. Then you go to the shebeen with thirty, forty, fifty people there. You can't be aggro. That's the big thing with the South African Police: we've got the British thing – we mustn't be a police *force*, we must be a police *service*. But in Britain you can send one guy with pepper spray out on a complaint. In South Africa you're two guys on a vehicle, you go to a shebeen or tavern or house, maybe there are only three people in the beginning, then the next moment there are thirty, forty, fifty people. You're only two guys. Then you work at a station like Plettenberg Bay. There are only six people on a shift – two in the charge office, two of you outside and the other two on the other side of town. There's nobody who's going to help you. It's only you, the friend next to you and a bottle of teargas – that's it. Then they want to come from Britain and say you can send one guy and go and speak to the people. You can't do that, especially on a weekend, with liquor. But you handled it in the end; you did it. That's just the cowboys-and-crooks side of the police – you go out and come back without your shirt; that's part of it.

– **Inspector Marais**

I've been at a busy station and I've been at a quiet one. At the quiet station you hear the public complaining about something very stupid. At the busy one you work twelve hours and you don't get a chance to eat because you're so busy.

– **Superintendent (F) January**

In the early nineties, I started asking myself: what can I do to be recognised in the SAP? When they talk about crime, what is it that I'm doing? I could go to work for twelve hours and when I booked off no crime had happened. But the next day when I read the news, it said that three people had died in Mamelodi.

Then I started feeling guilty. It simply meant I had not done my job. I was at work, nothing happened, the next day they said someone had died. It started to haunt me. I consoled myself by saying it was impossible; I couldn't be everywhere all the time. In the 1990s there was a scarcity of transport and things. When someone came to the charge office and said, 'There's someone being killed there,' you had to tell them there was no transport. It was true that there was no transport! But it pained you to tell them. Sometimes you felt it was better if you didn't go and talk to the person because they would need transport and it wouldn't be right to tell them there wasn't any.   – **Inspector Kekane (1990s)**

I always wonder if I am doing the right thing in my work. When you arrest a person, you're not sure if it's the right person. We're not the magistrate or prosecutor; we can't judge. We just hear the story, 'This one stole my phone,' and we have to arrest the person.

I once opened a false rape case without knowing it. The lady came and opened a case, saying she had been raped at the taxi rank. I took the statement. Then she was taken to the doctor. The doctor said indeed she had had sex. But she was lying about being raped because she needed an excuse for not being home.

She had been at her boyfriend's house overnight, and in the morning she had to go back to her mother's house. She had to explain to her mother why she hadn't been at home that night. So when her mother asked her where she had been, she lied and said she was taken by force and raped.

When the story came out, the man was released and the woman was arrested for perjury. It's crazy. When I found out she had lied and she had been arrested, I felt she deserved it because she had wanted that man to be arrested for nothing.   – **Inspector (F) Dlamini**

I had cases against me for theft of dagga, corruption and obstruction of justice. What happened was we caught someone on the road with two *stops* of dagga. We asked, 'Where did you get this?'

'No, sir, that guy found it in the road.'

We hit him. 'Where did you get it?'

Eventually he told us, 'I bought it there, at that place, one rand a *stop*.'

We went to the house he'd identified, entered and found a guy sitting with some parcels, busy making *stops*. We seized a bag of *stops* and two or three parcels and arrested him for dealing in dagga. A week and a half later he was outside.

We went back to his house. We got there and found another stack of dagga in the house. But the guy came at my colleague holding a panga as if to kill him. My other colleague shot him through his stomach, but he was all right. He was in the house and he closed the door. Now the dagga is inside, the man with the panga who attacked my *tjommie* is inside and he's been shot – what now?

We called the reaction unit and they threw gas canisters inside. We waited outside the door for him to come out. He didn't come. Then the door opened and he threw the canister out. Now *we* ran away! Eventually he came running out and we caught him.

We arrested him for attempted murder and dealing in dagga. A couple of days later, he was out on the street. We waited two weeks and went back to his house. We found three hundred and fifty *stops* there. I thought, it's not going to help for me to lock him up, because he's got connections. So I took that stuff to the police station. The following day I went back and I found five hundred *stops* and I took them and handed them in. I said to myself, I'm going to make him financially weak.

Then he came to the police station and said, 'That policeman was at my house yesterday and the day before and he took my dagga and he handed it in to the SAP13. I want my dagga.' The policeman who locked it up, me and him weren't so lekker. So they asked him, 'How much dagga was there?' He said, 'The first day he took ten parcels and three hundred *stops* and yesterday he took another ten parcels and *stops*.' But there had been no parcels the second time; the *skollie* wanted to get me back for taking his dagga!

That detective made a case of theft of twenty parcels of dagga, a case of corruption because the dagga was booked into the SAP13 without an arrest and one of obstruction of justice because I didn't arrest the man.

The cases went to the Attorney-General and he wrote a letter saying I had to answer to him or else he would charge me. He wanted to know why I didn't lock the man up. I wrote him a long story about how I had locked him up and he had been released. Then the letter came back: 'Find out what happened to the first two cases.' At the end of the day it emerged that the one docket had disappeared and the other one they had written off without doing an investigation.

My captain was told he had to take remedial action against me. That remedial action was him coming to me and saying, 'You mustn't do that again.' And I didn't – I locked everyone up!   **– Inspector Kotze**

A lot of times when you stand in the court, the accused will turn around and tell them something like you've stolen their three hundred rand. One time when somebody accused me of throwing them to the ground, the magistrate asked him to come out of the box and stand next to me. He was much taller than me and the magistrate said, 'Do you *really* want me to believe that she threw you to the ground?'   **– Inspector (F) van Niekerk**

There was this boy – one of those small boys who steals cellphones and hi-fis from the houses and then sells them so that they can buy drugs. He was in the cells on Saturday. Me and my partner were on standby. That day we took him out the cells so that he could show us where he had sold the property that he had stolen.

He made us forget he was a suspect. We even forgot to handcuff him. He asked for a cigarette and I gave it to him. Then he stuck his hands through from the back of the car to take the cigarette. I said, 'No! You should be handcuffed!' I stopped the car and handcuffed him and held the cigarette while he smoked it.

At lunchtime we went back to the police station. We left him in the consultation office. I don't know what went wrong. We asked a guy to watch him but that young boy escaped. Then all hell broke loose. I started thinking I'd lost my job; I was the one who had signed for him!

I told my partner. He said, 'No, don't worry, we will get him.' We had not eaten. We had a little money. He had two hundred rand; I had three hundred rand. We put it together and we bought a pack of beer and ice. We organised a cooler bag and put it in the police car. It was just a problem of getting that guy back before Monday office hours.

That guy was smoking drugs, so the only way to get him was to go to the ones who were smoking drugs. We went to them and we said, 'Do you know this guy?'

'Yes, we know him.'

'Have you seen him?'

'Yes, he was here not long ago. He said he was going to get some money for drugs.'

We asked if they could help us. They said yes. We asked how. They said, 'We told him we were going to get money to buy drugs and then he can come back and smoke with us.'

'So do you have the money?'

They said no. Then we had to take our money and give it to those boys to buy drugs. They didn't have a cellphone either – they sell them to buy drugs. So I went to my house and got a cellphone, bought a starter pack and airtime, loaded it in, gave it to them, then gave them a few hundred rand to buy drugs. Then we asked them to call us when he was with them.

We were on his trail. Those boys would call and say, 'We are here,' but as we rounded the corner he would stand up and go. We ran after him. He went to his home, went through the gate, then jumped up onto the toilet and over the wall. One bullet rang out. I missed. It was like a movie that day – we were jumping over fences, guns in hand. People came out their homes; they didn't know what was happening.

Then the boy disappeared. We were tired. We'd been drinking some beers and were angry. We got back in the car and parked somewhere else. We just drank and smoked. 'This boy, we are going to kill him!' we said. We could not sleep. Then at six o'clock in the morning, the ones we gave the money and the cellphone phoned to say that the guy had left and was going to Mamelodi West. He was using a taxi so we had to park close to where the taxis drive so that they could give us the registration of the taxi and we could wait for the car. He SMSed us the registration and description (a Mazda Midge) at ten o'clock. We were also driving a Mazda Midge, unmarked. We were driving slowly; then we saw it in the distance.

We wanted to own the scene. My partner parked the car in the middle of the road so that the taxi couldn't go. I got out. The suspect was sleeping. For sure he had smoked a lot of drugs. He was sleeping on the front seat. He didn't even realise what was happening. I just opened that door very quickly, picked him up and hit him against the car.

We opened the boot of our Mazda Midge and threw him inside, because the cooler bag was on the backseat. We did a U-turn and drove to where there was a very big, shady tree. Then we drank our beers. Our problem was solved. We drank those beers until they were finished. Then we drove to the police station but the boot wouldn't open. We had to damage it to get him out.

We had a second option if we couldn't find him. We said we'd give five hundred rand to one of the ones we sent for the drugs so that he could smoke until he got drunk, then we would take him into the cell. They didn't have IDs. Even if he says he's not the person, who would've believed him? But we arrested the right one, so our job was done.

– **Inspector Kekane (2005)**

We got information that there was a large quantity of counterfeit currency being stored in Mdantsane township, and that the suspect was also transporting AKs. I tried to get hold of a magistrate to authorise a search warrant, but couldn't get one. The situation was time-critical, so I had to make the call that we were going to hit the house without a warrant, knowing that if anything was to come from it there was going to be a shit storm. But those are the calls you have to make.

I contacted the local reaction unit to assist us with the operation. We got to the house and announced our presence. We heard people inside, but they weren't responding. Straight away the hair on the back of your neck goes into high alert: now the situation becomes tactical.

We tried to breach the doors but they were bloody steel-framed and we couldn't breach them. We ended up having to break windows, throwing in stun grenades and going into the house dynamically.

I still believe we did the right thing, because we had to consider the safety of the guys. But the biggest thing for me was that here in this house was this woman and her two little kids cowering in one corner. A stun grenade is not a nice thing, especially in a confined space. These kids were terrified. I still remember the tears streaming down their faces.

She confirmed that the guy had been there and that he did have counterfeit currency and AKs, but he'd left a few hours before we'd hit the place. She had been afraid to come out because she didn't want to be seen as an *impimpi*.

That was the type of operation we did. It puts a human face on people who are victimised by the criminals. It was not a nice thing to see. When I look at my son now – he's two and a half years old – and I consider him being put through that experience … It's not something you want to do, but you've got to make those calls and you've got to live with the consequences.

– Sergeant Jordaan (1996)

We got information that they were selling drugs at this house. We surrounded the house. Everything was fine; nobody could escape. We left our posts and went inside. One policeman was at the front door. When he walked into the house he found a lady lifting her dress up. She had nothing underneath. At the same time the brother of the lady was throwing the drugs out the window. They were in the same room; the lady was at the door and the man was behind the door. The policeman was just looking at the lady while the brother threw the drugs out.

He said he had been taken by surprise. He saw a beautiful lady. He was unmarried and thought this was a once-in-a-lifetime chance – being proposed to by a woman. She never said anything. She just lifted up her dress and walked to him. He stepped a little bit backwards but when we came in the lady put her dress down.

At the end of the day we didn't find any drugs inside the house; we found them outside. Because they were outside the house they said we planted them, because we had searched the house and didn't find anything. We had to say okay. We took the drugs and put them in the SAP13 and destroyed them. — **Captain Ndlovu (1993)**

I was still with the uniform branch, working sectors. At that time the army was still assisting us a lot with crime prevention operations.

On one of my night shifts, I was stopped by a man who was completely wasted. He was full of blood and one could see that he was severely beaten. He told us that there was a party up the street where he had been beaten up. He wanted to go and show us, my crew member and myself, where the party was, but I refused him entry to the vehicle since he was blood-soaked. He then pointed towards the house where the party was.

I was over-eager and drove in the direction in which he had pointed. It was a huge party so I drove past the party into another street and contacted crime prevention for back-up.

The crime prevention unit – consisting of a lot of bakkies, a Canter and an army truck full of soldiers – arrived. I explained the story of the assault and we went to the house.

Upon our arrival, the soldiers jumped out and cocked their R4 rifles, pointing them at the people at the party and ordering them to lie face down on the ground. Anyone who refused was beaten up with sjamboks by both SAPS members and the soldiers, but mostly the soldiers.

When everyone was on the ground, the complainant came to me and told me that we were at the wrong party. He then pointed at another house in another street. I then asked around and found out that we had just very rudely fucked up what had been a peaceful twenty-first birthday party.

I was so embarrassed that I just got back into my vehicle and drove off. Crime prevention and the soldiers also got into their vehicles and they went to the other party and arrested everyone for being drunk and disorderly.

It happened about three or four years back and I still feel like a *poephol*, thinking back on it. — **Constable van der Merwe (2006)**

8

LETHAL FORCE

In those days if you wanted to arrest somebody and they ran away you would shoot at them. I was a very accurate shot. I was chasing this guy and I wasn't gaining on him; he was really moving. I was tired and I said, 'Well look, let me shoot him.' I missed him by a mile, but that shot was like a turbo being switched on! That guy was off in a cloud of dust. I never saw him again.

Of course, getting back to the station you've got to report one shot being fired because you've got to account for each round. The warrant officer who was the station commander gave me such a tongue-lashing as I haven't received since, and threatened me with all kinds of things if I ever dared to do what I'd done again. And it was a good lesson in life because it showed me that you can't just shoot at somebody because the guy's running away. Had I been unfortunate enough to hit him, then what? Then I would have been up for murder. As it was, nothing happened. But the crass stupidity that I displayed there was something that I look back on and I shudder to think what could have happened. Ja, you grow up.

– **Director Grobler (1964)**

I was in Potchefstroom. There are coloureds on the one side of Potchefstroom. They drink too much wine. They came and tried to burn our police compound. They threw petrol bombs. When it hits it explodes. There's no time to undress; you are always in your uniform. There is no time to wash. So we shot at them with real bullets. Then the commanders of the riots took us back to Pretoria.

When you committed a crime and they saw it was going to make international news, they would replace you, just like that. From 1983, '84 to '85 too many people died, both by the police and by the community who killed family of the police. **– Inspector Moji (early 1980s)**

I've never had to shoot live ammunition. I've never fired at anyone. In the riot squad there are snipers and there are those with teargas canisters. I was in the gas group. Teargas was all right because you just shoot, shoot, shoot and they disperse. There was no crime in that. The unfortunate thing was when someone had asthma and they fell on the ground. But that was the situation: there was no mercy at the time because if the community found you they would kill you. **– Inspector Rameama (mid-1980s)**

I've fired that old 37mm stopper, the one where you pull the handle out at the back. It takes a rubber bullet or a gas canister. For special duties, we did a raid at a hostel one night for illegal weapons. It was one of those big hostels with long corridors and about twenty rooms per floor. We confiscated about a thousand firearms that night.

I don't know how they knew we were coming; there were a couple of thousand of them. One guy put out the power, so suddenly it was totally dark. We used flares inside the building to make light. The only thing that was close to me was that rubber gun.

We picked up a couple of dead bodies there afterwards. I had fired but it wasn't only me. That was an emergency situation; nobody asked questions because those guys were not supposed to put out the lights.

I've also fired live rounds in retaliation. We were shot at a couple of times in Alexandra, but we usually used Casspirs there – we never used normal vehicles. We had to shoot at least once a shift. But they were difficult situations at that time. A guy would phone and say, 'There's a dead guy; we've put him on the pavement outside such-and-such a number.' You'd never know who phoned. You'd never get the guy who stabbed him – that's how they worked there. Sometimes they would say, 'He's done such-and-such wrong, we're the street court, we've killed him, just come and take him away.'

I don't know what happened with all the people that we shot at, or how many were hit – maybe we missed. Sometimes there were people who were injured and we would get the ambulance, but more often it was like a riot situation or a war situation. Then when you left, it was the two parties against each other again. I never understood that mentality. Sometimes I thought they just wanted to fight.　**– Inspector Burger (1990–1991)**

We were chasing a criminal. I was driving the police bakkie. My colleagues were chasing on foot. They never found him. When we met up I said, 'Where's this guy?' and they said, 'We couldn't find him.' I said, 'Why? I just saw him go in there!' They told me, 'We looked there; we didn't find him.' I said, 'Just go and look there,' but they said no. I said, 'Okay, no problem.'

I faced the car in that direction so that the lights would shine in the space behind the house I was talking about. I took out my pistol and I went to look for him. I looked and looked but couldn't find him. As I was about to leave I heard a click sound behind me. When I turned I saw somebody lying on the ground pointing his firearm at me. As I turned I shot him. His pistol fell out of his hand. My colleagues heard the shot and came running. I said, 'I shot him.'

He must have thrown the firearm on the ground while he was running. Then when he saw me passing, he reached for it. As he slid the gun towards himself the hammer was open and the soil became lodged in between the hammer and the firing pin so when he squeezed the trigger there was no power to hit the firing pin. That's what made the sound that I heard. When I turned, I realised he'd wanted to kill me. I killed him instead. I turned and shot. I didn't speak a word. There was no time to speak. He didn't speak to me so why should I speak to him? I should have been a dead man.

It made me feel bad, bad, bad, bad. In the record in my heart, I remember I killed a person. If there is a record up there in heaven, I will have that record. No matter that I was on duty. I killed him. There was no debriefing, no counselling, nothing. My superiors came to the scene and looked and people made up stories that I'd planted the firearm, said I was supposed to arrest him. It's something that causes me stress. Even now it's still in my mind.　**– Captain Ndlovu (1992)**

There was this time where we had to go and arrest this person who was involved in a murder. He had killed a member of the opposition party with a shotgun at a very close distance. The victim had a big hole in his chest; it was a serious and violent crime activity. We identified the people involved. We went to this specific house and we managed to get into the house. As we were going into the house, this person came out of one of the rooms with a firearm and he shot at us. But it was a handmade firearm and it just went 'click'. Obviously, when we saw that, we returned fire and the person was fatally injured. Afterwards we got this firearm. The bullet had been struck but it didn't go off. We were lucky.

It's also traumatic to shoot someone because there's always the investigation with regard to what happened and the statements that have to be submitted. For a person to die in your presence: it's not nice, it's sad.

– Senior Superintendent Boning (1993)

One night a Cressida drove past us. We saw the guys inside were very young and scared. Suddenly the car stopped and the driver jumped out and ran. I chased.

In those years it was the old Article 49 – you could shoot someone for stealing a carrot or a chicken from a farm. Most of us weren't that crude to shoot someone for a chicken, but it was common practice to shoot people for stealing cars.

I ran after him and he jumped over a wall. I jumped over the wall but I realised I was getting tired, so I fired a couple of warning shots. He kept running and jumped up onto another wall. When he was at the top I shot him and I saw him fall over the other side, but when I got there nobody was there.

Soon control called and said there was a woman in that same area who'd phoned to say her son had been shot. It was just two streets from where I was. I went to the mother and she said her son had been taken to the day hospital. We rushed to the hospital and there lay the ou on a stretcher with plugs and things in him, struggling to breathe. I said to the doctor, 'Do what you can to save him, I know this outjie.'

They took him into the theatre and we went to wait outside. The mother was there. She didn't know that I'd shot him. She came straight to me and said, 'Listen, my son has been stealing cars for a long time and I said to him, "One day the police are going to shoot you." So, sir, please tell your colleague who shot him that he mustn't feel bad because I've warned him.' A few minutes later he was dead.

He was seventeen years old. I felt really bad; he was still a *laaitie*.

Most times I shot people I didn't feel bad at the time. They were the *swart gevaar*. Nothing happened to me. In those days there wasn't an ICD, only an internal investigation. They opened a murder case, but then they just closed it. My captain who had to report this incident came to me and said, 'You can't say you shot eight shots; they will say it was murder. Just say you shot two warning shots and then you shot him, and it will be all right.' So that's what the report said. Everyone had spare rounds so they wouldn't notice the other rounds missing. That was what we did.

The bad thing was that a few years later they said you can't shoot someone for stealing a car. But that's what we did. It wasn't right. You couldn't punish the policeman if the guy died; it was a section in Article 49. So we shot people and there was nothing they could do. That's what we were told to do. When I look back I feel bad, but that's what we did. He stole the car for joyrides; he made a mistake, a big mistake. But you can't shoot someone for a car – the insurance pays out.   **– Inspector Kotze (1994)**

In Van Ryneveld we noticed a bakkie loaded with housebreaking stuff. We chased them and they came down at Van Ryneveld Avenue and turned left into Hans Strijdom. They rolled the bakkie, jumped out, jumped over a fence and ran into a veld. I was still wearing my dress in those days, but I decided they were not getting away and I jumped over that fence and shot.

At the time I only had a 7.65mm gun – we were issued with smaller guns, the men had bigger. While I was shooting I remembered in college they taught us that this thing is only accurate up to thirty metres. I could see the suspects far away and I imagined my bullets dropping down before getting to them. I only had seven shots, so when my magazine was empty I was cross.

Eventually some of the flying-squad members arrived. Some of them had R1 rifles and most of them had the 9mm. A few magazines were emptied that day. The dogs went and caught the guys in a waterhole. They came back and the paramedics said, 'What's this small-calibre shot? Where does this come from?' I said, 'What?' They said, 'Come and look here at this tiny little thing in his shoulder.'

After that I started wearing pants instead of a dress so I could have a proper belt with a 9mm.   **– Inspector (F) van Niekerk (1994)**

We were patrolling in Manenberg. One of the Clever Kids came along. We stopped to search him. Because he was drunk, he was violent. A struggle broke out and we used hand teargas. Then he ran off. At Nyanga Junction there are seven flats. We patrolled further and we entered the flats. As we entered, the shooting started. We were in the middle. Our crime prevention unit came. It was a wild shoot-out. Gangsters were shooting; we were shooting. It was so dark, you could see the people but you couldn't identify the faces – just shooting, shooting! They were shooting from the flats, from the houses, from behind walls. We had to shoot back to get them off. Unluckily – or luckily – one person was shot dead. We were charged with twenty-three attempted-murder charges and one murder charge. Three of my colleagues were arrested. We had the ID parade. The case went on for almost three years. Then the pathologist came to say that this guy was shot with a .38 and not a police round. It was nerve-wracking.

– Inspector Lakay (1994)

When I was the head of planning and research we did a project on the *kitskonstabels*. I sent one of my guys to Oudtshoorn. He came back and he said to me, 'Sir, we'd better talk.' He said he went there and gave them a questionnaire with the question: 'It's twelve o'clock at night. You're on foot patrol. You're walking down the street. Suddenly someone comes running past you at full speed. You shout for him to stop, but he ignores you. What are you going to do?'

About ninety per cent of the respondents said they would shoot him. Some would shoot a warning shot, but some would shoot at him directly. That made me think very seriously about what I'd done. You have no idea why the guy's running, but you're going to shoot him because he's running, because he's not stopping. You assume that he's done something illegal. But what if he's on his way home and it's his curfew and he's got to run? He's not going to stop and explain and say, 'Look, I'm late.'

So one of the things we came back with from that was, if you're in Oudtshoorn, don't run! — **Director Grobler (1995)**

We tested a car in Khayelitsha, a blue Mazda 323. It wasn't positive, but the car fled so we chased it. We pulled up next to them and they smashed into us. Then they stopped, jumped out, ran and jumped over a wall. I thought this car was stolen. They were about forty metres away so we shot, hit a guy and he fell down. Then we stressed, because control said this car hadn't been reported stolen. We went to the address in Melkbosstrand where it was registered. It was in the night, twelve o'clock, but *sjoe*, luckily it *was* stolen! He lived. — **Inspector Kotze (mid-1990s)**

I took a transfer to George just for a short while. When I got there some of the policemen would ask me questions like, 'Have you ever pulled out your gun?' I realised that some of them had never had to pull out their gun in fourteen years in the police! — **Inspector (F) van Niekerk (1995)**

When I started in the police you could still shoot in any high-profile situation. Your biggest thing in Plettenberg Bay was housebreaking. If you got to a housebreaking scene and you shouted at the guy to stop and he didn't, then you shot. It changed with Article 49. In a housebreaking the value of the goods is not worth the value of the life, but when I started that rule wasn't there and we were involved in lots of shooting.

There's a difference between whether you *had* to shoot – did the *book* say you had to shoot, or did *you* want to shoot? On paper I shot about five times, but in my police work I must have shot about fifteen times. You used your weapon when you needed to use it, but that didn't necessarily go down on paper. But you get to a point where you think, 'Okay, it's time to quiet down now, no more cowboys and crooks.'

I fatally wounded people twice in Plettenberg Bay. The one was at a house; I shot him with a pistol. The second time was after a housebreaking.

We waited on the national road between the town and township. If you had a housebreaking in town you went to the national road and dropped four or five guys every twenty metres. That night the three guys who were in the housebreaking came over my side. I shot the one guy with a shotgun. They don't fly back like on TV – only if you shoot them within a metre. I shot him across ten or fifteen metres. The pellets start spreading so they covered his whole back. I think three or four went to his vitals.

I didn't feel anything. I think it had to do with my age. Perhaps not *nothing*, but nothing worth talking about. In both of those cases I was still single and lived in the barracks. I think it would be a different story now that I'm married with children. It wouldn't be different in terms of shooting the guy – not to sound heartless – but today if you've got to shoot somebody you will think about your family because you are going to get into shit, even if you do it by the book. In those times it was different because of Article 49. At that time the duty officer came out and did what had to be done, the guy went to the mortuary, they did a post-mortem and that was it. Today if you shoot someone, that's it – a murder case.

Lots of police don't use a firearm any more, especially in detectives or organised crime. It's not worth the hassle any more. For my last five years, if you had a firearm in your possession, even if it was a *geregverdigde skietvoorval*, you're going to be in shit. So when that law changed lots of the guys said, 'Listen, it's not worth it.'   **– Inspector Marais (mid-1990s)**

One night we were in an unmarked vehicle. My white colleague and I were in civilian clothes, and we had a black colleague with uniform on. He sat at the back. We were driving in E Block, Khayelitsha. There were lots of *skelms* in E Block. We saw this old Toyota Corolla with two black guys in the front. The car was idling, so we stopped behind it and tested it. Control asked, 'What car do you have there?' and I said, 'A green Toyota Corolla.' They said, 'The car is positively stolen in Plumstead earlier in the evening.' So I told my colleague to let the car idle, and me and the black policeman got out, pointed our guns and said, 'We're police!' They could see my colleague was a policeman; he was in uniform. The driver looked at me then looked at his friend, and then he just started driving.

We began shooting at the car as it drove away, me and the black policeman; it was just part of our job. The car stopped. We saw the driver jump out and run but the passenger was sitting. We jumped into our Sierra and drove up to the car, and there lay the passenger on the driver's seat, blood everywhere; his head lay on the side. He was saying, 'Help me, help me!'

I stressed. I didn't want to shoot him dead, I wanted him to stop – and he wasn't the driver; he was the damn passenger. I climbed in that car – there was just blood everywhere – and I rushed to the hospital. I said, 'Doctor, you must save this man's life, now!' I stressed. I said to my friend, 'Listen, I shot a lot, give me a few rounds.'

Shame, this man is paralysed from the neck down – he was shot in the head and the back, but he lived. I don't know if I shot him or if the black policeman shot him, but the damage to that car! We shot the windows, the dashboard, the clock and the back – it was bad.

That shoot-out was the last one. I said I couldn't work in Khayelitsha any more. He was the seventh person I had shot in two years. He nearly died. I felt really bad. He wasn't even the driver of the car – he was the passenger. They opened a case, but nothing happened. We had identified ourselves, we had asked them to stop and they fled.

That was a bad year. After that shooting I went home and said to my wife, 'I'm finished, I'm finished.' I phoned my captain and he asked me to see a psychiatrist. We talked, everything came out, and he said, 'You must leave.' Two weeks later I was transferred to Bellville. That was the fastest transfer I ever had.   **– Inspector Kotze (1996)**

I was on standby. My wife and I went to visit a friend. As we pulled up at his house I looked across the road and saw one of his other friends' cars parked there. There was a guy in the car so it definitely wasn't Sarah, the owner. In those days we didn't have cop cars with aircon so you ended up driving with the window down. Then the police radio squawked. This guy looked at us – it was almost as if time froze. He looked, realised I was a cop, and literally while the car was in motion he jumped out and hauled ass!

Of course all your training kicks in. I pulled up the handbrake and I jumped out, drew my firearm and went down on my knee. Using some very colourful language, I challenged the guy to stop and I pulled the trigger. This was before the change of Section 49; this is what you've been trained to do. But at the last second as I pulled the trigger I realised at the back of my mind that my wife was sitting in the car watching, and I pulled the shot just off to the left. That bullet must have missed him by centimetres. The guy ran off into the bushes. My wife said to me that night she heard the gunshot and wondered why the guy didn't drop. She knows I'm a fairly good shot.   **– Sergeant Jordaan (1997)**

When I was still a young dog handler a friend of mine and myself were working. We'd just finished an operation in Atteridgeville and were coming through Pretoria. As we came down Zambezi Road we got a call about a couple of guys that were trying to steal a car about two blocks up. We decided we'd have a look.

As we stopped we saw the guys running. They jumped over a wall and I went around to see if I could block them on the other side. I turned around and as I turned I walked into them. This guy was five metres from me and he started shooting. I was standing on a corner underneath a lamp post, which is not the best cover! I can remember looking down and seeing the bullets hit the grass in front of my toes. I ran across the street looking for cover.

That evening I shot one of them. With the help of a whole lot of other police officers and the police chopper, we arrested all three of them and got back three guns that they had had on them.

That was the first time I'd ever been in a situation like that.

Afterwards I felt scared. At first it's more anger. I thought, he had the audacity to shoot at me! Where does he get off?

It was quite a traumatic experience. I couldn't actually remember running across the street and looking for cover. When one of the guys who responded to our calls came down the street, he said to me, 'Jenny, when I got there you were on the other side behind the trees.' I said to him, 'No ways, I was on that corner under the lamp post.' I think it's a natural reaction. It's not something you think about. It's just something you do – self-preservation, probably.

I don't know when I returned fire. I probably started while I was standing there and then while I was running I was probably shooting as well. I remember shooting and I remember the other policeman coming with his car and blocking the fire between them and myself with his car. It was quite an amazing feeling.

I just wounded the guy I shot; he didn't die unfortunately. They were actually linked to about twenty-five armed robberies and the death of a police officer.

If I were in the same situation again, I would do the same thing, but the Christian part of it is a bit difficult. I'm not God and I hope I never have to play God again. But if it's a decision to save my life or someone else's life, I'll do it without thinking about it.   – **Inspector (F) Kemp (1998)**

I was working in Bellville and there was a group of guys who were breaking into businesses every second night. They were working all over. We didn't know if they were brown or white or black, but every night or every second night they were breaking into businesses and stealing computers and things.

One night we were working in a white bakkie. I was the passenger and my colleague drove. At 4 a.m. he said he was too tired and asked me to drive. I said, 'Ja, let's go,' because I wasn't tired and I wanted to get these guys. He said, 'Drive nice and slowly because I want to sleep.'

After a while I saw a bakkie fully loaded with stuff. I woke him up and said, 'Here are the guys!' We approached them and when they saw us they sped off. There were three in front and two at the back and as they drove they threw computers and keyboards and everything off the back. We got up next to them and knocked them to the other side of the road. It was a lekker chase! Then we shot the back tyres out; the bakkie rolled. They all climbed out – everyone was all right – and they ran off into the dark bushes where we couldn't see them.

I don't know if it was the excitement or what, but we stood there and we just shot into the bushes. When everything was over, we called for back-up and we walked into the bushes. We found the one guy, dead, and a little further we found another guy. The others were gone.

The ICD was very difficult. They would not understand, saying, 'You can't just shoot at them!' We said, 'No man, it was attempted murder!' We wrote attempted murder on the docket, always: if a case didn't look good then you threw in attempted murder. It's often difficult; there's a grey area – 'Can I shoot or can't I shoot?' We shot.   **– Inspector Kotze (2000)**

I have shot at people but fortunately I have never injured somebody. It was private defence, I didn't want to but I was protecting my life and other people around me. I am a policeman, I was issued with a firearm, so I must use where it is suitable. I felt this is part and parcel of my life. I didn't shoot at people; they started shooting at me first. I didn't do anything wrong.

Usually you just sleep with that. Nobody can say the job doesn't affect you. It really affects you. You become very unhappy. Every day you're unhappy. That's why you find many police get divorced. I don't know how this can be overcome. There's no happiness in the police, then you take that thing home. That's why you find the policeman shot his family and wife, and you ask yourself why.   **– Inspector Ramela**

The first time I used lethal force was in Gugulethu. We were three in the van, all sitting in front. This guy crossed the road in front of us. My colleague said, 'This guy looks suspicious. He has something at his side and it looks like a gun.' Immediately as the guy saw the police van he took out the gun. I told the driver to ram him with the vehicle because we were too late to climb out. We drove straight at him but that guy opened fire. I was in the middle. The guy next to me opened the door and jumped out, then the driver opened the door and threw himself out and the van moved on by itself. I was still inside but I managed to lie down while the guy was shooting. Fortunately he had a revolver and he shot all his rounds out. Then we chased him and I shot him and killed him while he was running. Later we found he had spare rounds in his pocket.

It was not illegal to kill him; he still posed a threat when I shot at him. The fact remains that he shot at us. And now he's running with a gun, so what is his intention? – to shoot again. I am effecting an arrest. I saw him shooting – it was attempted murder. There's no better way of me arresting this guy than by shooting him – killing him – whether from the back or anywhere. If he shoots at us and turns his back, does he expect that I'm going to shoot past him? That guy was moving; there was no intention of surrendering. So I took the R5 and I shot him in the back.

The other time, we were patrolling in a Kombi. We saw three guys and stopped to search them on the road. As we opened the doors, they took out a gun and started firing at the vehicle. I ran to the back of the vehicle. The houses in Gugs are joined in a row, so they had to run next to the houses, on the road. I went to the back of the Kombi. I opened fire and I shot one in the back. I killed him. He fell with the revolver. The other two escaped. I emptied my pistol there. So incidents do happen.

The most recent killing was during the xenophobia thing. I was using rubber bullets. This guy came at me with a knife. I shot him with a rubber bullet. He continued to come, so I shot him again. I was standing against a wall. When he was two metres away, I just dropped the shotgun and pulled out my pistol and I shot him twice in the chest. I killed him.

– **Inspector Lukhele (2001; 2001; 2008)**

One Saturday night me and a black policeman were driving in Thembalethu. It was a very quiet patrol. A *laaitie* came running, and said, 'Sir, two guys just robbed me of my pay! They had knives!' I thought, okay, it's the end of a fortnight, he's probably just been paid. It's probably four hundred or eight hundred rand. We must help him. 'Climb in the bakkie,' I said. He said, 'Sir, drive between the shacks.' We drove and we saw the two guys. The one had a lekker long knife and the other had an Okapi knife; it was closed. We stopped at the guys. The black policeman climbed out and the guy ran.

There were no lights. It was a gravel road. He ran through the wire fence of a shack. He fell, stood up, ran to another fence and jumped over it. We went from one house to another chasing him. At the third plot I said, 'Stand still, police!' The man turned and he stood still. I said, 'Put that thing down!'

You could see he was drunk. He then came running at me with the long knife, running and running. I said, 'I'm going to shoot you!' I didn't want to shoot. I fell on my back and he came and stood over me. I stressed.

The safety was off on my gun and I am always one up, so I knew I must just shoot. I shot him in his hand. He remained where he was and I said, 'But I just shot you!' He saw the blood flowing. The next moment I shot him dead. That was my third murder. — **Inspector Kotze (2005)**

I've got eight murders — I've killed eight people. I don't know how many attempted murders I have — maybe more than forty or fifty where I've used my firearm. Sometimes it was in the course of affecting arrest, and dockets were opened. It's something I don't worry about in Cape Town. If I shoot someone, I always feel good. It's one less problem for the innocent and the defenceless. I don't bother worrying about that. For me, having a gun is a privilege. Those who are killed and robbed every day don't have the same privilege. So I feel that it's my role, when chances avail themselves, to protect them.

Once, I was driving off duty and stopped at a pedestrian crossing to wait for the pedestrians. They robbed somebody's child. Then the child's father went to confront them. But they came, about eight of them with knives. They took him down and one guy got on top of him. When that guy lifted up the knife to stab the guy whose son had been robbed, I pulled out my gun and I shot him in the neck. He died.

Another time two of us were working in the train. We were just going to observe the people who were robbing in the train. The next moment I heard people crying. When I looked I saw this guy had grabbed this police official's gun. I saw the suspect had a knife. The policeman had the suspect's hand in his, and the suspect had the barrel of the policeman's firearm in his. They were busy fighting. Hey, that train had been full! There were people at the doors. But suddenly it became empty — there was a big space. People were jumping out the train; others were praying.

I thought the best way to stop the fight would be to shoot the guy in the head. If I shot the guy in any other part of his body he would realise he was dying and he would do anything in his power. If I shot him anywhere else, he would take that gun and he'd do a lot of damage with it. I took out my gun and I aimed it at his head and I pulled the trigger. As I pulled it the train jerked. The bullet scratched the guy's forehead. I lowered the gun and I shot him in the knee. Then he released the gun. At the next station we informed control that there was an incident in the train and everyone had to be offloaded. — **Inspector Lukhele (2006; 1998)**

After my first shooting incident, when I accidently killed an innocent guy in a shoot-out, a docket was opened against me: an attempted murder docket. I had been executing my official duties, but a docket had to be opened against me. I had to attend court. How are we going to fight against the criminals if we don't have the necessary support from management? If the criminal has a firearm, he will shoot you. He won't shoot a warning shot; he will kill you directly. The management of the police ignore such issues.

Since that first incident I've only fired warning shots because I've learnt that once you've done something in the police you have no one to cover you. I've fired warning shots at people protesting for service delivery. They were marching. They were throwing stones at us and I had to shoot a warning shot. I used live ammunition. Afterwards I just put another bullet in my magazine. You can't report such things; they will take the hell out of you if you report it. We know we are not covered for some of the things that we do, so you need to use your discretion.

— **Constable Shabangu (2009)**

Even though you are not allowed to fire warning shots, it does sometimes help. You feel quite nervous afterwards. Then you start realising your life wasn't in danger so you must cover your tracks, pick up the cartridges. Always carry some spare ammunition and reload your firearm so that if they come and check, you have the correct number of rounds. When you get home, the first thing you do is clean your firearm. Then you just wait nervously for the cases of attempted murder to be opened against you.

— **Constable van der Merwe**

Crime is out of control. If they manage to change Section 49, we will be back where we were before. The reason we are where we are is that the criminals have no respect for us. They have far too much leeway; they have far too many rights in this country. Our hands are literally tied behind our backs. I'm not saying we should go out and shoot and kill everyone running around, but they need to give us back our respect. When they give us back our respect, the crime rate will come down. — **Inspector (F) Kemp**

9

IN THE LINE OF FIRE

It was night. There was a robbery in progress at one of the factories in Khaya Sands. The suspects came in and handcuffed the security guards. They entered with bakkies and loaded some computers. Then we received the call.

It was a complex with different factories inside; there was only one gate which they could use. When we arrived we heard shots from AK-47s. There were about ten police cars there. We started taking cover, then the suspects came out. They came straight at the policemen, driving a big bakkie. It was just like a movie – I thought I was dreaming. They came at us just like *ba-ba-ba-ba-ba!*, shooting from the car, approaching the gate. They rammed our cars. Then they jumped out, left everything in the bakkie and ran away.

Everyone was down; nobody even went after them. We'd tried to fire but we didn't know what was happening. There was a hail of bullets. I pinched myself after everything was over. I think we just stood there until other policemen arrived. We were down with our hands on our heads. I thought I was dead. When I looked up, I found cartridges all around me. We found plus-minus two hundred AK-47 cartridges. No policeman was injured. It was a shock. The counsellors came and booked us off duty after that. It was a very big crime scene. **– Inspector Ramela (2004)**

I was off duty and on my way to the train when somebody called me. There was only one police official in the charge office. He said there was a rape in progress and I must go and investigate. I was alone. I couldn't think twice; I had to think about the other person.

I got there, got the suspect and was walking with him back to the station. He was a little bit violent so I had to use some force. I didn't know he had a friend with him. His friend was very close behind me.

Along the route the friend took my gun out and the suspect grabbed me so that I couldn't run. I looked at him and I saw him cocking the gun. I even saw the bullet going up. The suspect said, 'Shoot him! Shoot him!' I don't know what happened; I don't know how I turned that guy, but I grabbed that guy in front of me and I turned him around. The next thing I heard the shot and the suspect was falling in front of me. He didn't die; he was shot in the leg. Then they hit me with a plank. So I suffered some injuries and had to lie in hospital. That's when I realised that if it's your day to go, then it's your day to go. There was no cover there – it was an open field. I had a ninety-nine per cent chance of dying. I realised that it was not my day to go.   **– Inspector Lukhele (1998)**

One day in Sebokeng, Zone 7, we were working night shift, travelling in a Casspir. People had dug a trench in the road and covered it. When the Casspir got to the trench, the front wheels fell inside. It couldn't move forwards or backwards. Those people knew they had caught us. They started to fire AKs at us. The bullets couldn't penetrate the Casspir. They turned the Apollo lights – the street lights – off so that we couldn't see them. We stayed there trying to call for help until our radio battery died.

There were fourteen of us. We waited until it became quiet. Then we opened the door slightly. Two of our colleagues leopard-crawled to the nearest house. They knocked, but the people inside were scared and didn't want to open the door. They forced their way into the house and found some small boys and an old lady. She was scared so they said, 'Don't be afraid, we are the police – we just need help.' The old lady allowed our members to use her phone. We phoned Unit 1, who then phoned the Alexandra unit. They sent four cars to give us manpower and pull us from that trench. That's when our lives were saved.

That time was terrible. You think to yourself, if those people had come closer and thrown petrol bombs and they had caught fire beneath the

Casspir, that thing could have exploded. But because God was with us, we survived that incident.

It's not nice. If you take what happened and you think about it, you realise you were halfway dead. Without training we would not have survived. Many people survived because of our training. We stayed in our group; in there we were safe. No bullet could penetrate.

Every day when you left your home to go to work you prayed, 'Oh God, help me God. Let me come back home when I've finished my hours.' Sometimes if you believe that God will help you, then he will help you. But if you don't believe in that, sometimes you will see an example. Even now, before I go to work, I have to pray. I have to thank God for protecting my life until now.   – **Inspector Mampuru** (1992)

In certain incidents when there's fierce fighting, you see your death. You just hope God doesn't lower his hands that time, because maybe it's two days to pay day! There's a thread of wire that keeps you alive. In your mind there's just that thread; it keeps you going forward. But deep in your heart, you know you can go at any moment. Entering a house with thirty, forty gangsters – you don't know what arms they have. Life and death is around every corner. Do people always appreciate what you do? That's a question I ask.   – **Inspector Lakay**

If ever a policeman is shot, the first thing from management, the first thing they say, is, '*Waar is die vuurwapen*? Where is the firearm? Remove it from them. Search for the firearm and get it.' That is the first thing they ask about. They don't say, 'How is he?' or 'How is she?' Any policeman will tell you: they don't ask about the condition of that policeman; they ask about the firearm first.   – **Inspector Ramela**

I was called in to negotiate with a woman with a .38 Special who was threatening to commit suicide. A guy who had been chosen to go on the negotiator course but hadn't yet done the course thought he would handle the situation until I got there. When I came I was supposed to take over the scene from him. When we were both in the room he thought it would be a good idea to grab the gun from her. But it was cocked already. I was sitting next to her on the bed and he was on the other side. When he tried to grab it I got up and she got up and she tried to pull the gun away and the shot went off. It went between my arm and body. They made a joke about it – that if I had had bigger boobs I definitely would have been shot! I remember thinking for a split second, I wonder if this is going to hurt now? **– Inspector (F) van Niekerk (1996)**

I was at my house watching TV. I had my daughter with me. She was very young – four or five years old. My colleague came to pick me up. When I left, she started crying. She had never cried before, but that day she cried.

In that period we had a project where at twelve o'clock every night we knew the place was quiet and we wouldn't have many complaints. We had a list of the most wanted suspects, so we would form a convoy with other police cars and go and look for suspects.

There was a group of suspects. They called themselves the Tupac. The leader's name was Blood. They were a gang of little boys, about five of them. That night we heard where we could find them. It was our car and another car. When we got the information about the gang's whereabouts, we contacted everyone and met up there.

It was an undeveloped place, a squatter camp. These guys were in the shack. They had locked it with a chain and then twisted the chain so that the lock was on the outside and it looked like there was no one in there.

There were about fifteen of us and about eight cars. We saw the lock dangling outside and we all relaxed. Some took out their cigarettes and started smoking and talking about how we would hit them when we found them.

Me and my partner were close to the shack. I heard a movement inside. The shack had a wooden window, so I jumped up and kicked it. When I kicked it a second time, it fell in. At the same time I saw a red shirt and a spark of red light. The guy had shot me.

When you have a gun in your hand and you see a spark, your hand automatically pulls the trigger. I shot at him at the same time. As I was falling down, my left leg couldn't support me. It felt as though it was falling into a very deep pit. Should I not have fallen down he would have killed me, because he shot twice.

Now I was lying outside and the other officers started shooting towards the shack. They did not see me. All I could see was the bullets flying above, and the dust when they were shooting down. But the one said, 'Inspector Kekane?' I said, 'Yes!' He said, 'Don't shoot, it's Inspector Kekane!' That guy was brave – he struggled and struggled and grabbed my hand, pulled me over the fences and got me to the van, then left for hospital.

I took about five days in the intensive care. He had shot me right below the second rib and the bullet had exited at the spine. The reason that my left leg could not support me was that the bullet had hit the nerves along the spine and affected the leg. My kidney and intestine were severely damaged, but they managed to repair them.

When I came back to life, I tried to move my hands and check if everything was okay, but when I tried to lift my lower body nothing happened. When I asked the nurses and the doctors, they said I would be fine. The doctor told me I was lucky. I could have been paralysed, but I would be fine. He said it would take time. I was frightened I would be paralysed because at the station we had two guys who were paralysed. I started thinking about them.

At that time my family went wild. When I woke up my wife told me that after my daughter cried that day she had become quiet when the police came and brought the news.

From what I understand, one of the suspects escaped. I don't know how. The one I shot died. We were face to face with each other. There was no need to aim – I could see the spark and I shot at the spark.

I felt some kind of pride going through that. That group was known in Mamelodi: they were committing a lot of heinous crimes. They would get into a house, grab the daughter, take her away and rape her. When they found you selling your cigarettes or vegetables, they'd just take your money and go. After this incident I heard that even the commanders went to my house and talked to my wife and came to the hospital and talked to me.

I felt proud that everyone appreciated what I'd done. The fact that I killed someone did not bother me that much. I only concentrated on the fact that what I did was not wrong. Everybody appreciated it. I felt like someone brave, like a hero. — **Inspector Kekane (1998)**

We got a complaint. A hard-working constable and an inspector who was useless at his job – he's now a captain – were shot outside a nightclub. When we got there the constable was lying on the ground, the inspector was shot through his hand and the suspect was also lying there.

Apparently they were sort of ambushed. The inspector had been sleeping and holding on to the hand rest. They stopped the van. A guy came up to them and said he had been robbed by two guys. But when the constable asked which direction it had happened in, the guy pulled out a firearm and shot him two or three times in the chest. He had his bulletproof on underneath his jacket, so by the third shot he just played dead.

When the guy picked up his firearm the constable started to fight with him and a shot went off. It shot through the finger of the inspector. They wrestled outside the vehicle for a while and eventually the constable pleaded with the inspector to shoot the suspect. The suspect was shot three times in the head.

When we arrived the inspector was actually standing on the throat of the suspect in an attempt to choke him. Then when the paramedics came, he stopped. When the paramedics wanted to treat the inspector, he told them to treat the suspect first. That was very traumatising, seeing the constable lying on the ground. At the time we didn't know he was wearing his bulletproof. He must have passed out afterwards due to the impact to his chest. He looked like he was dead.

— **Constable van der Merwe (2005)**

I had a friend shot in Orange Farm, shot with an AK-47 in the leg. He still has the scars today. He was shot in 1995. He's never been seen by a police psychologist. He's never even been phoned by a police psychologist, not even to say, 'Hey, prick, are you fine?' Nothing. Just, 'Fuck you.' He went on sick leave and went back to work.

That upsets me – they could have just phoned to say, 'We can do fuck all for you and we don't actually give a fuck,' and I would've felt better. But they didn't even phone him. I look at him today and I shake my head. He's still a cop. He has to have an operation every year. He has to have shoes built up every year. He can't walk properly. It's not right.

There are some things I don't want to remember.   **– Inspector Stevens**

10

FEAR AND HORROR

In this job you can't think of death and still expect to perform. If you think of those things, you can hardly do anything. That doesn't mean you don't get scared. You get scared but you must deal with it. You get a call that there's an armed robbery in a shop. You arrive and you don't know who has a gun. You expect to see a criminal but not all criminals will have their guns in their hands. You are sent to an unknown place. You get there and you are tense and your eyes are wide open because anything is possible. You see police with their firearms in their hands, trembling, shivering, because they don't know who's who, what is what.

One day we were looking for a guy for a cash-in-transit robbery. This guy had an AK in his bag and a 9mm in his pants when we caught him. When we interviewed him, he pointed at one police official and said, 'You! If I had wanted to kill you, I would have killed you because you walked past me.' Oh, I shivered a little bit! He said, 'I saw you run past me; you were on the phone, but because I was lost I stayed inside the hostel. You went past me and I knew you were phoning the police.'

You hear these stories and you really start to shiver.

– Inspector Lukhele

Today, I am still working with rape cases. I daily see how the victims come and sit in my office and cry because they were raped by someone. I do not trust people near my children. I have this fear of rape. I still have it. It's something I cannot get over.

When rape cases are reported, I give support to the women. A lot of the time I take their statements. You must pull all the facts out of the women. Sometimes they talk easily, other times they don't want to talk. Sometimes I take the statements, sometimes I just come in and put them at ease, show them our facility where they can spend the night, give them soap and toothpaste – the support things. Then later on we still work with the women and give them support afterwards. Every month we have at least one rape. It is happening, even among the children. There are a lot of sexual things happening, things with each other and things with adult people who are doing things with them.

I still have a fear of being raped. I work with people every day and I see what people can do. But I think my trust in people has improved.

– **Inspector (F) Basson**

We went to a house where they had stabbed a seventy-year-old woman, an old lady. They had stabbed her in the body. She had about twenty-seven stab wounds. When we arrived, she was still alive. When she breathed, all these holes were puffing blood. It was horrible. Very sad. It makes you feel afraid and scared. That day I won't forget.   – **Inspector (F) Dlamini (2000)**

In FCS you see things which you don't think exist. Things which you read about in the newspaper and you think, no, this is not happening, it's just a story. A father raping a toddler, his biological child. You wonder what's wrong with that person. My first case at FCS in 1996 was a case of a four-year-old child who was raped by her neighbour. When the child was explaining to me what the woman did to her, I couldn't believe it. They have their own language to tell you things. She would tell you, 'She took a nail and poked me with a nail.' She is trying to explain what happened, the pain inside that she felt. It was bad, really bad.   – **Superintendent Molebatsi**

The murder cases didn't affect me, but the rape – I've got two daughters at home. I don't like rape cases.

When I was finished with detectives there was a motor vehicle with four students. Three died. The one wheel burst; they hit each other at the crossing. On the scene we had two dead and one died in hospital. The next day I had to do the identification at the hospital and I was sitting with the parents and the grandfather crying. I said to myself, 'Now I'm finished, no more murder cases, no more dead people.' I got to that point.

– Inspector Marais

With us being on the police station for six months before we went to college, by the time we got to college we knew a lot. After I was sworn in at Bosman Street, when I arrived at the police station as a new student they said, 'I don't have time for this; do you want to see blood?' We got into the car and we attended my first accident scene. I think it must have been the most gruesome one that I saw in my twelve years in the police – five minutes after I was sworn in!

Actually it was quite good – it really let me know that this is the real thing now. You don't just join the police and one day you might see something. You're there and anything can happen any time. They made a joke and asked me if I would take the dead guy's jewellery for myself. I thought, Okay, this is expected of me. I'll do it. Then just before I did it they said, 'No, no, don't do it. Don't touch him!'

It was bad; it's still very much in my mind. I can still see exactly what the scene looked like and how it happened, but it didn't make me not want to go on. I think it just made me want to do it more and more and more: the adrenalin was quite a thing for me; I was quite hooked on adrenalin.

– Inspector (F) van Niekerk (1990)

I had to attend an accident on the N4 from Witbank to Pretoria. People from the location cross the N4. This person was hit in the fast lane. He entered through the windscreen and landed next to the driver. But it was only half his body with his cap still on his head. When the car stopped, the driver found this half-body sitting next to him with his cap on. He couldn't believe it. He got out of the car and ran. When he tried to explain to us, he just told us, 'Go and look at that car. I can't believe what I saw!'

On the road we found this foot here, that foot there. But when we went into the car we found this person sitting there. He was still holding a plastic bag with meat in it that he had gone to buy. It was like a joke. I was very traumatised. I had to stay home for a week.

– **Captain Mthembu (1997)**

One day at seven o'clock in the morning we attended a car crash. There were two females in the front of the car sitting with their heads leaning against each other. They both lay dead. Nothing gruesome, just that little bit of blood coming out of their noses.

Then I started picking up all their things that had landed in the veld. I found the one ID book and it said T.J. Stein. Then I found the other ID book and it said C.S. Stein, and I thought, this is weird. Then I picked up one deodorant – it was a certain make – and I got the other deodorant and it was exactly the same make. Then it hit me that they were twins.

I went back and I saw how they had died sitting with their heads leaning against each other. That was terrible for me. The more dangerous situations weren't bad for me because then I had an adrenalin rush. In a situation like this there was no adrenalin. It was just that human factor that got to me. It was bad. – **Inspector (F) van Niekerk**

In 1984, in July, they took me from Pretoria to the Western Cape. We were guarding ward counsellors' homes. They ran away and left their homes, so we owned their homes as security. A man is a man. When you see a beautiful woman, you have to talk. The neighbours had children and we talked with them. We would get ration packs of pap, boiled eggs, two slices of bread and a hamburger patty for the day. Then you gave that food to your neighbour and she would become your girlfriend.

We maintained those families that were suffering there. They became my in-laws; I was the boyfriend. We left our wives. That was the procedure, because we didn't know how long we would be there. Some are still there today. We were the good and the bad, but not the ugly!

The community knew that one woman was a girlfriend of a policeman in the riot squad from the Transvaal. A brother of mine kissed her, so they burnt her alive. They used a tyre and petrol and burnt her alive. Then they sang and stoned her.

I saw it first hand. They took her out of the houses to a soccer field. There were more than ten thousand people. She was burning. We shot and they ran away, but she was still burning. She died helplessly. We couldn't even cry. When we carried her, we had to put her in a body bag, but when you touched her, her body broke. That smell is still in my mind. Like burnt cow leather mixed with hair, but slightly different. Your stomach is full of rubbish, intestines and things. Those things cook. When shit is cooked, how does it smell? That is the smell of a person who has been burnt. We took a shovel and collected the soil around where she lay. There was fat in the soil.   **– Inspector Moji (1984–1985)**

I worked with lots of dead bodies in Khayelitsha. The morgue driver wouldn't come out on the weekend and often the ambulances were too scared to come out, so we had a little room where we kept the bodies.

On weekends there were lots of murders and suicides, and some people were burnt in their shacks. So you had to go and put the body in a black bag. It was burnt – an arm falls off, a foot falls off; it's not nice. And that smell – it sits in your clothes. You zip the thing up and throw it in the bakkie. Then you get to Khayelitsha station and you throw it in that room. On Monday morning the morgue van comes.

– Inspector Kotze (1994–1996)

The first time I saw a dead body, I was afraid. Imagine, alone in a restaurant, in the basement, and you're just there with the dead body, blood all over!

Another thing that made me feel a little bit afraid was that the mortuary still fell under the police service back then, so for every serious case the IO had to be there for the post-mortem. So I had to attend that post-mortem and I saw how the doctor cut open the brain, the chest, everything. Human flesh is like chicken. For about a month or so after that I couldn't eat meat. Every time I wanted to eat meat, that image of him being cut up by the doctor came back to me and I wanted to throw up. It was bad. After a while I got used to it. Today I don't feel anything.

After that there was one incident where we suspected that the man was murdered, but our investigation found that he wasn't: he was just sick and staying alone in the house and he died. He was dead for about a week or so. His daughter in Cape Town used to call him every day to find out if he was okay, but for a week he hadn't answered his phone. She suspected that something bad had happened.

When I went there, I could smell the stench coming from the house. The door was locked. I broke down the door and I saw him lying in the passage. The passage was full of maggots. The smell was terrible. I put this thing in my nose to prevent me from inhaling bacteria but I could still smell it. It was bad. After that I couldn't eat rice. Every time I wanted to eat rice, I thought about maggots.

Most of these incidents happen at night. You're alone there in the house with a dead body until you arrange for other people to come and assist you. You are the first man at the scene most of the time. Even if you are not the first person there, crime prevention will just hand the scene over to you and they're gone. They leave you alone there. So it's very scary. But I'm no longer afraid; I'm used to it. I've done it for a long time.

I don't feel anything when I see a dead body now. If somebody has been killed and has not been identified, I have to go to the government mortuary and take fingerprints from the dead body and take them to Pretoria to see if they can identify them. So I'm used to it. If you see those guys who work at the mortuary – I've realised that those people are pretending like they are not affected, that they don't feel anything, but I can tell you they are affected.

What they do there – it's strange. I went there one day to take fingerprints from a dead body. This guy had a Coke bottle. He put the Coke in the drawer, between the legs of the dead body, and when it was cold he took it out and drank it. That is not normal. Those people are affected bit by bit. And they are always laughing! What are they laughing about? So even me, I feel like this thing is nothing, but maybe it is slowly affecting me bit by bit. I don't know.   – **Constable Sibuyi**

I used to do mortuary work, especially when I was in Laingsburg. If I was the investigating officer on a certain accident, then I was responsible for all the post-mortems. Say, for example, someone was stabbed with a knife.

You would put your pen through where the knife went. Then the doctor would just come and fill in the form. The doctor was meant to establish what the cause of death was, but didn't, so you would put a pen in the wound and open it and establish what the cause of death was.

That's the way the doctors worked there. They didn't open the body; they didn't close it. Only if the head had to be opened, then they did that themselves. I was expected to do that job, and the doctor would just make sure I had done it.

We didn't have mortuary trailers, so if someone died you would put him in the back of the van and transport him. Now it's two o'clock in the morning and the district surgeon refused to come out, so we would drive the van to his house. He would come out and look through the window, and say, 'Yes, they're all dead.' I said to my wife the other day, 'I wonder if I've ever put a living person in the mortuary?'

– Inspector Burger (1988–1994)

I don't like looking at dead people. All unnatural deaths upset me. I can remember the first unnatural death that I had to attend. A guy in Sunnyside had been standing on the balcony of a flat. He leaned over the balcony, his foot slipped and he fell down and hit his head on a brick wall.

It was a really gory sight. That was upsetting to see. And then you would marvel at the absolute callousness of the guys that work at the mortuary. They come along; the body is just like a piece of meat to them. They pick it up, put it on a pan and cart it off. I don't know if it affects them – maybe it does. That's why some of them start drinking, I think. Many guys have a drinking problem. Why? Because of these things that they see and hear and experience. Working with dead people for a long time must cause you to hang on to something, some handle, some lever somewhere, to be able to deal with these things.

One particularly gory thing that I remember – a black guy committed suicide by hanging himself from a black bottle bush. I got there and the corpse was hanging: now what do you do? You've got nothing. You can't undo the knot; this guy's been hanging there for quite some time. You cut the rope and get the mortuary van to come out and collect the corpse.

They say to me on the radio, 'Hang on, you must get the ambulance.' So the ambulance arrives and I say, 'What are you doing here? This guy is dead.' He says, 'I'm not transporting dead people in the ambulance.' So he pushes off. So I get on the radio and call for the mortuary van. They say, 'Oh, now it's your problem. You must see to it that he gets here.' I say, 'I'm not putting him in the police van; it's not a mortuary van.'

Then the doctor arrives and says to me, 'Who are you to say this guy's dead?' I say, 'Well, the guy's been hanging from a tree for a couple of days, he doesn't smell too good, I can already see some maggots in him and I've asked him who he is and he refuses to answer me – I assume he's dead.' Everybody keeps quiet because there's going to be a confrontation between the constable and the medical practitioner.

Then the mortuary van arrived, they picked him up and they took him away. The process is that you identify the guy at the scene and you've got to go to the mortuary and identify the guy there to make sure it's the same person. So I was there and of course the doctor was there too. I said to him, 'Is he dead?' 'Yes,' he said. 'Well, he's in the same condition he was in when I found him!' I said, and I pushed off. Clever doctors.

– **Director Grobler**

Working with dead bodies never bothered me. It's only at a later stage where you feel, I don't want to do it any more. I think I've done my part. If that's what you need to do to say you've done your part, then I've done mine.

We had at least one serious accident a week in Laingsburg on the N1. I've seen a truck that ran over a bus and cut it in half. It cut everything in half. That's the worst experience I take with me, scenes like that. It seems like those things happen without a reason. An 'accident' – that's what the word means, 'accident' – it's not supposed to be. Other things happen where you can say, 'This was the reason,' but an accident seems so meaningless.

– **Inspector Burger**

11

OFFICER DOWN

There was a guy in my platoon at police college. He slept two bunks from me. We passed out on a Friday night and on that Saturday he was posted to one of the riot units. That Saturday night he went out on his first patrol and was killed. Literally on his first day on the job, he was killed.

It was a feeling of absolute disbelief: 'No, man, you're shitting me. Things like this don't happen.' But they do. It was literally that disbelief – 'But he was here just the other day.' That was a brutal wake-up call. This wasn't a game any more. This was real. People die and they don't come back. It's not like a computer game where you press the reset button. When you die, you die. It certainly tempered my viewpoint on the job. It didn't change my enthusiasm, but it made me realise it was time to grow up.

– Sergeant Jordaan (1991)

We worked the whole day together. He was supposed to pick up students who had finished their training in Graaff-Reinet. He dropped me off at about eleven at night. Five minutes after he dropped me off, they phoned me to say he had been killed – shot dead in Lavender Hill. I was in shock. I almost ran back to Manenberg police station. I couldn't believe it. We'd just been together.

They shot at the van as he drove past the flats. They shot an artery in his leg. He drove into a wall and bled to death. He was still young – three years permanent, just married, wife was pregnant. They just shot 'cause he was the police. Gang violence. **– Inspector Lakay (2004)**

I had a friend who was on course with me. Her fiancé was killed while she was on course. He was a cop with the reaction unit in PE. Driving back down to East London with her, constantly trying to console her the whole way – it guts you when things like that happen. You try to be there for the people, but everyone deals with loss and grief in that scenario on their own terms, in their own way. It's not nice.

One of the guys in the platoon and I tried to round up everybody who had been at college with us. There were thirty-six of us in the platoon. Virtually half of them had died in the line of duty. Every now and then I look at the photos from police college and I wonder which of us are still around. **– Sergeant Jordaan**

I was in the open unit. In the morning meeting with lots of haste and excitement, everybody jumped up and said there's a house that's got weapons in it and we are going to go and bust it. In those days we never used the riot unit, we just did the houses ourselves.

So there was a white policeman and a black policeman and they went and knocked on the door of the house and the black guy stood in front of the door. The next moment they just shot through the door. They shot the black policeman dead. Then they shot my white police colleague too – shot him in the arm. That was quite a shock to me. That guy was shot dead; that was the end of his life. That was the first time a colleague of mine was killed. It was sad.

What goes through your mind is that you want to kill the guy that did it to him. He's got to pay as well. We tried to catch him but couldn't. Fortunately he died in a car accident five years later.

There was no debriefing at that stage. That was the old 'cowboys don't cry' era. You didn't show any emotion, nothing. You just looked at the body and walked away; that was it. You didn't ask questions, nothing. Some things were not discussed because you might become emotional about it. That didn't change in my days. **– Inspector Stevens (1991)**

In my fifth month in the SAPS, I was driving the patrol vehicle with one of my inspectors. It was at night; we were driving and driving and the inspector fell asleep. We received a complaint of an armed robbery in progress somewhere in Craighall Park. I woke the inspector up, told him and we went there.

Because I didn't have much experience at the time, I didn't even think of calling for back-up. We just arrived, the two of us, with our blue lights on. I wasn't thinking properly. In the suburbs they usually have automatic gates. When we arrived, the driveway gate was open. So, stupidly, I didn't park outside, I drove inside. As soon as our patrol vehicle was inside, the gate closed behind us. I wondered what was going on. I thought maybe the complainant saw the blue lights and opened it for us.

I got out of the patrol vehicle, but the inspector stayed inside. He didn't care; he was just sitting there. I went around the house. I didn't see anybody. The lights were off inside the house. I heard a gunshot inside the house. I didn't know what was going on. I had my hand radio with me so I immediately called for back-up. I couldn't see anyone. Then I slowly went back to my vehicle. The front door of the house was open but still I couldn't see anyone. The inspector was still sitting in the vehicle. I called, 'Inspector, get out of the car, come this side!' When he tried to open the door, shots were fired at him. It wasn't a 9mm; it was a big gun, a high-calibre weapon. I started shooting from where they were shooting in the house. I couldn't see anybody, so was just shooting to scare them. By luck I shot a suspect in the chest. He ran out of the house with an R5 rifle and fell down on the veranda next to our vehicle. Luckily by then all the back-up vehicles had arrived.

I hadn't realised that my crew was shot. I thought they had shot and missed, but they had shot him in the forehead when he tried to open the door. He just slumped down in the seat and died. We managed to arrest another four suspects in the house, but my inspector was gone. That was my first such incident. I hadn't even been in the police for a year.

It's a terrible feeling. Just imagine, it's this person that you work with every day; you do everything together. You drive around with him, you go to the restaurant to buy food with him, you share everything with him. Whenever you go to work, you pick each other up and go to work together, and you drop each other off after work. I felt terrible. Terrible.

The police service asked me to go for debriefing, but when you are brought up in our culture you are taught that a man mustn't cry; a man must be brave. So I refused. But as time went by, I could feel that this thing was not leaving my head. I had nightmares, thinking about it, remembering the pictures of my parents and my brother from when I was young. I couldn't cope; I couldn't eat – my appetite was gone.

Later I realised I had to do something about it; I had to go for a debriefing. I went about five times. After that I was much better.

The thing that made me feel so bad was guilt. I had come out of the vehicle and left my inspector behind. Maybe if I had gone with him to the back of the house this would not have happened. Secondly, when I came back to the front I shouted at my inspector to get out of the vehicle, and when he tried to open the door, that's when he was shot. It made me feel bad. I felt guilty, like I was responsible for his death.

That was the first incident where I used my firearm and where I was shot at. It felt terrible because my partner was killed. I killed a suspect but I was not worried about that. I didn't even think about my killing the suspect; I felt nothing about that. The suspect was shooting at us, which meant he didn't care about our lives – he wanted to kill us. They never bothered to run away. Why not? They were ready to kill somebody. I still hate that guy, the guy that I killed. If he was still alive and I met him today I would still hate him. I'm not proud of it, but I had no choice. I hate him because he shot my crew.

The suspects we arrested were sentenced to life in prison, but my inspector's life is gone. I will never see him again. He's gone forever. But I've accepted it now. I've learnt that this is what police work is all about. Sometimes you lose your colleague's life; sometimes you kill a suspect. That's how it works in the police service.

Ever since then I have hated a suspect with a gun. I hate them with all my heart. If I kill a suspect with a gun I won't feel anything. I hate them with all my heart.   – **Constable Sibuyi (2001)**

Two of my friends died in accidents on the same day. You were on the road about seventy to eighty per cent of your working time, so the probability of dying in a motor accident was high. So I was surprised when I had a heart attack; I always thought I'd die in a motor accident. But I've been through a few and I survived them.

To cope with the losses, we drank a lot. Even when they died in car accidents. We went to the other side of Witrivier, near the Kruger National Park, for a funeral and it was just one big drinking session. That's how it works in the police. If your friend dies then you drink. The first one is on the ground; for him. How wrong can you be to do things like that? But that is the way we did it. That's what we believed he wanted. I mean, one of my deceased colleagues didn't even drink, but we drank to him. And the next morning you walk into the office and he's not there, his place is empty, his things are taken out and you just carry on. He's just another number that's wiped out.

I said to the reverend one day after my heart attack, 'I've been given a second chance.' He said, 'No, no, no, you're wrong, boy, you've been given a lot of chances, but this one you have to take.' – **Captain de Beer**

A drunk policeman came to the police station one night. He wanted to tell the guys about what had happened the week before in the charge office. He just wanted to tell the story. A policeman was at the counter busy writing something. This drunk policeman took out this guy's gun and put it against the guy's head. He didn't know that the gun was one up. He pulled the trigger. The guy was shot dead by that drunk policeman who had tried to tell a story. It was an accident.

That was very bad. You come in there and you have to work in that charge office the next shift. You just have to go on. You can't just say, 'I'm not going to the charge office any more.' You just had to go on. But I think it took all the policemen quite a while to get over that. The brother of the guy who was shot was also a policeman at the police station. We still had to work with him and that made it very difficult, knowing the pain that he must have been feeling. But even him, he just went on. He didn't stop being a policeman or ask for a transfer. He stayed.

– **Inspector (F) van Niekerk**

In 2008, I lost a colleague who was close to me. He was off duty but he was tracing somebody on foot. He was walking with his girlfriend. The guy he was tracing shot them both. He killed them both.

Another colleague was killed in the line of duty. He went to buy something; the other police were waiting in the vehicle. When he came out and was approaching the van, these guys shot him and took his firearm.

One thing I tell myself is that it's a price you might have to pay at any stage as a police official. With a bulletproof or without a bulletproof, it's a price. It's always there. Sometimes you are lucky enough that it doesn't happen in the course of your duties. Unfortunately there's no hundred per cent safe tactic in the police. If someone really wants to kill you, he will kill you.   — **Inspector Lukhele**

Two of my colleagues have been killed on duty. I remember the day the first was killed. I was coming back from maternity leave. He picked me up at home. That was the last real conversation we had.

We were at college together and then we worked together at a busy station as field-training officers. At the time I didn't have a student, so I worked in the office. He had a student, so he worked on the shift. A call came through as a burglary. He responded, got out of the vehicle and went into the house. As he went in he was confronted by a guy. It was a house robbery, not a burglary. He was shot and killed. It was his anniversary that same day.

He had come to work, but then gone back home because he'd forgotten his supper. His wife was there and she asked him to take his bulletproof. He said, 'No, it's okay, I'll get it later.' So in a way it was meant to be. That's how I look at it. The fact that that night he didn't wear his vest – he always wore it but that night he didn't.

The second guy was a reservist. I could always rely on him to help me out. We worked well together, but he was working on another shift that night. He gave someone a lift home, a lady who was stranded. I don't know why they shot at him – maybe they were doing something and they thought he was on his way to catch them. But all he was doing was giving this woman a lift home. He actually pushed the woman out of the way to protect her and they shot him.

It was very upsetting. I am the kind of person who doesn't get too emotional about things. It could be good or bad. But I still think about them every day. I think about them both.

— **Superintendent (F) January (2000)**

If I hear about a police murder today on the news, I immediately recall scenes where police people were brutally killed. As I'm talking now, I recall this young police officer who was killed in this small place in Davel.

He was a white guy; his van crew was an African guy. They were on duty, patrolling. There were some problems in the township. Davel is a very small place, so late at night there's not much happening. They wanted to go to a café to buy some cooldrink and so forth but the one in Davel was closed. So they went to the township. The only place that was open at that time was the shebeen.

The mob there was already under the influence of liquor. Immediately, they saw the enemy and they went to them. The policemen saw that there was a problem. The African guy had a pump gun with him. He wanted to fire a warning shot, but he forgot that it was a pump gun. So he fired a shot and it injured his colleague in the leg. Then he ran away, because you have to look after your own life. The injured guy couldn't walk, so he crawled away.

He crawled from one place to another until he got to a house where he could hide for a while. But this mob was following his blood and eventually they traced him to the house. They went in, brought him out, set him on fire and shot him in the head.

I can still see him lying there in the street with his uniform burnt. Those things don't go away. — **Senior Superintendent Boning (1992)**

We had four guys in our unit die within a period of four years. But it passes; now it's just another day. Luckily we haven't lost a guy in quite a while.

One of the worst was a guy who was part of our unit for a very long time. He transferred to Carltonville Dog Unit and about four months later they shot and killed him.

He had stopped at a garage and the guys were going to rob the garage. They walked up to him and shot him. They pushed him aside and drove his police car away with his dog in the back. They shot him nine times. They then drove into a mielie field where a getaway car was waiting for them. They took his gun and left him there with his dog.

I was one of the coffin-bearers at his funeral. They arranged for the police chopper to do a fly-by as his coffin was being lowered. It was the most amazing, heartsore thing that I've ever seen. That was very, very bad. There are things that you never forget.

There are a lot of good people that die and not enough people who kill them are arrested. That's the heartbreaking thing. Their death is for nothing then.   **– Inspector (F) Kemp (2005)**

There had been a heist. The chopper had just passed. We chased the criminals, but they shot at us before we could shoot. It was just a bang and then my colleague died on the spot.

It's a bad memory. To this day, I haven't forgotten it. I can't. We were in the van. He was driving; I was on the radio. These police vans, they mean nothing. Chasing a BMW with a Toyota 1800 … We are two – one talks, one drives. Who's going to shoot? There should be a middleman to shoot, because I can't use the radio and shoot and the driver can't lose control of the vehicle. Our safety comes first. I was a failure; I couldn't shoot first. I was calling back-up to close the roads. There was no back-up. We were looking for cars for assistance. I was busy talking to radio control. I just heard *boop-boop!*   **– Inspector Rameama**

I had a colleague; we never worked without each other. I was in Pretoria doing training for a peacekeeping mission in Sudan. When I came out of class, I had almost thirty missed calls. When I started calling back, the first one asked where I had run off to. I said I was in Pretoria. Then I was told my colleague had been shot twelve times in the stomach, and his arms and legs were broken. It was at Nyanga Junction, cash-in-transit. He went there at the wrong time. They robbed him of his firearm while he was in his uniform, in front of the charge office at a substation there.

Because we were that close, I had a guilt trip for a long time. What would have happened if I were there? His wife was still pregnant. So it took me quite a while to make peace with myself. But he survived.

— **Inspector Lakay (2005)**

I had a colleague who we called 'Russian'. He once got a hiding: he had thick lips and his lip split and looked like a Russian sausage with a slit. That's why we called him Russian. He was shot dead in a trap. That was bad for me.   — **Captain de Beer**

I lost colleagues during my time in Joburg at the flying squad. You stand parade there – there are twenty people for example – and then you go off duty and they say, 'A minute of silence for Lance Sergeant So-and-So', and someone is not there. It was quite bad. None of them were close to me; they were just working on my shift. I remember one guy who died was standing two places down from me that morning. You just say, 'Thank God it wasn't me.' But I've always had faith in the Lord, so I knew that if something happened it was meant to be; it was my time. But you mustn't go and look for it.   — **Inspector Burger (1989)**

Going to the funerals, that's the worst. That's the bad part of the job. You have to see the families, see what's left behind: the mothers, the wives, the widows, the kids …   — **Superintendent (F) January**

My colleague bought a house in Soshanguve. He invited us to his house-warming party. We had a nice time, a braai. Then a friend of his arrived. He was not a police official. He came in asking us if we had bullets of the same calibre as his firearm. We asked him what type of firearm he used because we used the 9mm Z88 at the time. He showed us the gun – a .38 Special. He showed us the bullet and it was very different to ours, so we told him there was no way we could help with the bullet.

We were sitting in a circle. Everyone wanted to see the gun, so we passed it around until it got to the last person, the owner of the house.

He asked for the bullet. He then told everyone he had seen people play Russian roulette on TV. When the bullet got to him he put it in the gun and spun it, held it to his head and pulled the trigger. People told him not to do it and he said, 'Look, I'm a cop, don't tell me about guns.'

He continued. I think he did that three times. The fourth time, he shot himself in the head. The bullet came out the other side and he died on the spot. — **Captain Mthembu (1993)**

I attended some suicides where police officers had committed suicide. One of them was a schoolfriend of mine. We went to the police together. Later he was stationed at Koevoet in Ovamboland.

I was the detective on standby and I went to the incident. I knew his mother and father as well, so to be part of that is not nice.

I knew him for a number of years before he committed suicide. He said he experienced things, like when he was driving at night he felt that people were looking at him from behind. He was starting to hallucinate. But he wouldn't show signs. Depression, especially in the police, is much like HIV: you can talk to me but you can't see if I'm positive or negative. I talk to people who've got depression or post-traumatic stress disorder and you will not always see it; people will keep it to themselves. Then you will say, 'But I talked to this person yesterday and he looked fine. Why did he commit suicide?' You can't see what's happening in his thoughts or in his mind.

I think that one of the reasons is that you're abnormally exposed to gruesome scenes, crime scenes. You develop post-traumatic stress disorder as time goes by, but you are not aware of that. Unfortunately with this type of psychiatric disorder you are vulnerable to get depression as well, and depression can cause suicide. The other thing is that police officers have financial challenges. If you look at the constable or sergeant, or maybe even the inspector with a family, he is usually struggling financially.

— **Senior Superintendent Boning (1989)**

I was on a course. This policeman received a call from home. After the call, he went into the bathroom and shot himself.

Another time, a policeman mentioned that he was having a problem. We took it as a joke. We said, 'Don't make your problem our problem.' That man shot himself dead in front of us. He was serious, but we thought he was joking.   — Inspector Ramela

A friend of mine shot himself. He was at SANAB first, then he was transferred to the detectives. Everything had turned upside down for him. His marriage was going down the drain; his wife and kid had moved out that Saturday because of his drinking.

A week before he killed himself, my wife and I were sitting in a restaurant and we saw him talking to himself. I tried to speak to him, but he didn't want to speak to me. My wife said to me, 'He's going to commit suicide.' All the signs were there.

It was a Thursday morning at two o'clock when he shot himself. That Wednesday night he had been out drinking with senior officers. They realised there was a problem but they didn't say anything.

— Captain de Beer (1998)

A policeman friend of mine, his wife had just left him and he was left alone in the house. He said he was going somewhere and wanted to have a braai for us, so we went to his house. He told us that at twelve o'clock he was going to leave us. He said he wouldn't lock us in the house. We were thinking he would come back.

Five minutes to twelve he went to the bathroom. He shot himself dead at exactly twelve o'clock. The party was destroyed. How can you party when something like that happens?   — Inspector Ramela

What is important is what makes a person commit suicide. What kind of person commits suicide? People will say, 'It's a weak person that commits suicide.' It's not the weak person; it's the strongest of people who has the guts and determination to turn his hand on his own life. No weak person will commit suicide.

So don't look at the weak guys that cry easily or who talk about their problems easily. The ones who commit suicide are the people that will surprise you; the people who are uncompromising, level-headed, strong-minded – they are your candidates for suicide.   **– Inspector Khan**

This white female captain, she was crying every day. She had been ordered to work night shifts without a vehicle, without any support. She was having marriage problems. There was no support. Now she is dead. She shot herself. She was still young, brilliant.

    I was traumatised. But we know this is the same road everybody's going to go. This is the life of a policeman.   **– Inspector Ramela**

12

THE PSYCHOLOGICAL TOLL

We were brought up to believe that cowboys don't cry. It was a no go for you to cry. You just had to carry on. That's why so many police assaulted their wives and children and committed family murders. Policemen shooting at their wives, wives shooting policemen because they get drunk at home ... It happened and it's still happening, that trauma.

— **Captain de Beer**

I was hospitalised for stress: family problems and work-related pressure. I had a big gang fight, threats on my life, problems at home, my house was attacked – lots of things happened and I just needed to have a break. So I went to hospital for three weeks to unwind. SAPS booked me off. I came back, started again with social crime, recharged my batteries. At that time our unit was shot at frequently, every day, in the gang fights, so it was stressful. I was attending crime scenes with five-year-old kids, innocent kids, and seeing them lying in their blood. It leads to breakdowns. Sometimes you started crying at the scene when you saw them.

I had a murder in Surrey Estate where a small girl was shot, apparently by PAGAD. In the morning her father came out to start the bakkie. As he started the bakkie, she came running out and a car pulled up. Guys jumped out with R4s and started shooting at the father. She ran back to the house. As he ran in, he pulled her and threw her through the kitchen door. He was lying there dead and she was lying just in front, shot through the head, blood all over. It was scenes like that where ... I don't know ...

There was only one solution at that time. We worked long hours – sixteen, seventeen, eighteen hours. We'd buy brandy and just speak about what happened. After a shift we would sit, have two, three bottles of brandy, just to relax and debrief each other. We couldn't just go home. It was hectic. That was our support structure. There was EAS, but not like they are now. If you speak about the issues you can get others to speak. You speak about how you feel and how we can bring change, how we can make the negative into the positive. Some see it differently, but when we chatted I tried to steer it in a direction so that at the end of the day we would go home satisfied. We can't all get rid of stress in the same way. Some of them would go out and receive professional help for that immediate pain, so as not to go and take that back to their families. That's what we did.   **– Inspector Lakay (2000)**

I've found ways of dealing with my stress. Most of the time I go to places outside of the townships. But some people deal with their stress in a different way, through alcohol. I believe you wake up the next day and your problems are still there. In any given situation, people's responses will always be different. Your family has certain expectations at home; your employer has certain expectations. The community, the people that we serve, they have certain expectations of us. Sometimes people find it very difficult to balance.

That's why, at some stage, you need support from external sources. Other people get into habits of collaborating with criminals or creating the impression, 'I'm not the bad cop, I can do you favours or drink with you.' There are some people in the police who will sell dockets because they think it's a better way of getting cash. Sometimes these things are inexcusable. Other times people are really being driven by having reached a level of hopelessness.   **– Inspector Lukhele**

My first posting was a rural station in Laingsburg. At that stage, when I got to Laingsburg, there wasn't a single black person staying there – only whites and coloureds. There were about thirteen of us at the station. There had been eleven when my colleague and I joined after we came out of college, so with us there were thirteen. There were two members on a shift, one in the charge office and one in the van. It wasn't manageable; we struggled. It was always difficult – especially the accident scenes on the N1.

At the time that was normal. 'Cowboys don't cry,' they said. But later some of the incidents and the scenes came back. It made a definite impact on me, especially where kids were involved. When you've got kids of your own and you see bad things happen, you realise it could happen to you or your kids as well, because it happens so quickly.

I think we all feel a bit of stress after a couple of years. I can't remember ever having had a debriefing in those years, not in my first ten years of the SAPS – it just didn't exist.

In Laingsburg I had a colleague who shot himself. We had played rugby together and worked together. He had been very stressed. He turned to liquor first and then to suicide. Then there were only twelve of us left.

– **Inspector Burger (1988–1994)**

In sixteen years I didn't have a debriefing. There was a superintendent in charge of the Criminal Records Centre in Witbank. He was complaining of stress because of all the scenes he had to attend and he was never debriefed. He wanted to leave the police. When anti-corruption closed down and I wanted to join them, the first thing they asked me was whether I would manage attending scenes without any trauma counselling. I had to go and think about it for a month and I came back and told them I couldn't.

The one time I was on standby and I got a call. It was not far from where I was staying. The people got home at three o'clock and saw this person lying at the gate and they called the police. When I got there I found that this person had been shot in the top of his head.

Those were the kinds of things which were normal, very normal. At those scenes you ask yourself, what kind of person can do that, shooting someone in the head then leaving them to die there? Even if you're very angry, how can you do it? A person doesn't deserve to die like that. I couldn't understand it. I grappled with it every day. You ask yourself what is happening. What can make someone so angry that the only solution is to let that person lose his life?

It still affects me today, very, very much. When you think of it, you become emotional. I believe no matter how strong you are there are incidents that touch you.   – **Captain Mthembu**

I was held hostage for one and a half hours in a drug deal. There was a big drug smuggler, Naidoo. I was doing a drug deal with him in Witbank. I bought from him three times. Then the fourth time I went to show him that I had fifty thousand rand for a big deal. He and a Frenchman just drew guns. They held me hostage, me and a reservist. He hit me with a cocked .45 on my forehead. He was on crack, totally unstable. They took my wallet, my cellphone, everything. My insurance had to pay for it, not the police. The police even wanted me to pay for my appointment certificate. They got the fifty thousand rand too. But we caught them. The Frenchman we caught the same day; the Indian guy we got three months later in Durban. The one got thirty-seven years and the other got thirty-two.

The first words from the police after the incident were, '*Skors hom*. Take him out of the system because he stole the money.' That's the first thing that they thought. Not, is he well, has he been shot?

I had a tape on me for the operation. The drug dealers didn't get the tape. I was also camera-bugged and had the camera hidden in my rave bag, but they didn't get it. Once the police got the transcripts of the tape, they just kept quiet. They didn't say sorry.

From then on, there was a contract on my head. The drug dealers were part of a syndicate and they had photos of my wife and my eldest son. They got them from my wallet. He took them out while they had me hostage and said, 'I'm going to fuck them up!'

With the money on my head, my wife couldn't sleep at night; she went through hell. From 14 October 1998 to 1 February 2006, my wife and my children went through hell with me. There was no support. There is no support system.

I went to church with my gun on me; when I swam I put my gun under a towel; when I went to a restaurant I took my gun; when I went to a party I took my gun; when I went to the movies I took my gun. Wherever

I went, I took my gun. I've got about seven or eight types of holsters. You'd never see the gun on me. I never went without a gun. But since 2006, I don't take a gun any more. If I die now, I know where I'm going, but at that stage I would have gone to hell. I was a really awful person. I swore at people. Even a complainant: he didn't need to talk too much to me before I would swear at him and chase him out of my office. I only had my buddies and if you didn't drink you were not my buddy. I was a difficult person after the hostage event. I didn't know how to handle the trauma I had been through. There was nothing to help me.

When I drank at night, in the morning the problem was still there, so I had to start drinking again. On 1 February 2006 at three o'clock in the afternoon I had a heart attack. That day the first call came in at one in the morning: a guy was smoking dagga on the railroad and he was struck by a train. Later that morning, at about ten o'clock, I went out to attend a suicide, an old lady. Then I got back to the office and I was busy; I was really busy. I felt something in my chest. I wanted to buy a soda water to get it out, but I didn't get to that. At about ten past two I realised something was wrong with me – water was running down my face. I went to the hospital to draw blood and when I was leaving, right in front of the hospital, I fell over. I was lying there in casualty and the doctor said, 'You're in the middle of a major heart attack.' I was gone. I'd seen hell; I had gone there and back.

That night my whole world collapsed. That's when I realised my wife and kids were going to leave me. I was going to lose everything. Then I was sent by the doctor to a psychiatrist; I was admitted at Vista. I've been admitted five times now and I'm still being treated.

After the heart attack I quit smoking; I quit drinking. Before, I smoked forty-plus a day and when I drank, I drank until it was all finished. If there was one bottle, I would finish one bottle. If there were two bottles, I would finish two. If there were two bottles and a bottle of wine, I would finish them. I finished everything there was. I had a drinking problem – I didn't know how to handle my stress. You go out to crime scenes, or you've just come from an accident where there were people splattered all over the highway, then you get into bed – nothing is wrong. You wear a mask:

'No, it's fine; everything's fine,' you say. But it's not fine. I was off sick for a year and nine months, then they sent me back to work for a year and three months. Then everything collapsed again. Sending me back put me right back to where I had been before.

I will come right; I will heal. I healed quite well, but then they sent me back. The EAS people in the police saw me once a month at 8 a.m. when I had a lot of sunshine tablets in my body and I'd say, 'No, it's going well – no problem at all.' Until my wife said she couldn't take it any more and she called them. They said, 'We don't know how to handle it; we haven't handled a serious problem like this before but we will come back to you on Wednesday.' Since then, we've never heard from them. I'm not cross with those people; it's the system.

I used sleeping tablets for a year and five months after I was diagnosed with post-traumatic stress disorder, because I never slept at night. My mind never stopped; it just went on and on and on. I was put off on PTS and major depression from March 2006 to November 2007. In that time I healed quite a lot. After about a year and a half, I quit the sleeping tablets. Then in November 2007 they said I had to go back to work or they'd stop my salary, so I went back. Most of the guys go back and then book off again. I thought, okay, I'll go back; I'll try my best. Now I'm back on sleeping tablets again. After that year everything just came back – I was just put back to where I had been in the beginning. If I don't take a sleeping tablet at night, my mind just goes on and on.

In the morning you can't recall what was on your mind. When I worked, it was about work – that story, that scene, that docket. Previously it hadn't bothered me because I would have a few lekker drinks, and I just slept. The next morning you *skrik wakker* and you say, 'What did I do last night? I can't remember.' You drink like an eraser; you can't remember what you did. I didn't realise it was part of post-traumatic stress disorder.

Today I don't know where the pictures of my family are. That guy sitting in jail for thirty-seven years, maybe he gets a reduced sentence or whatever – say after twenty-five years he comes out, do you think he's going to like me? Even though he's older like me, a gun doesn't get older, so what is he going to do when he comes out? I don't have that guarantee that I'll be all right. The only thing I do now is trust in God, that he will protect me, because I took him as my saviour. If that guy tries to get to me he's not going to get to me because God's angels will take him out. Except he's not going to try to hurt me; he's going to try to hurt someone close to me. But the SAPS forgot about that.

Today I see a psychiatrist once a month and I'm on medication. But the psychologist, that's a lot of bullshit. I went to Vista several times and I think the treatment there is good. I've said to many people in my life, 'Go there, that's a hospital that helps you.' They give you lectures and you do therapy, and it really helped me. If I feel I'm going down, I phone the doctor and he admits me.

I know quite a few guys who've suffered from stress and depression. I met a lot of them at Vista – most of them are policemen. I met a director-general in a section of government. That's when I realised that everyone can get this sickness. I always said to people, 'Pull yourself together and go on,' until it happened to me.

My family went through hell because of my drinking and smoking. My wife sat up at night and watched outside. She smoked about fifteen cigarettes a night. She was afraid of the fact that they had a photo of her and our child. She had dreams of a vehicle stopping and taking our child and driving off. Until today she hasn't had any support from the police. I take my hat off to her because she went through all this and she's standing strong for me. Sometimes it just gets too much for her. A woman cries. I have also learnt to cry. I no longer believe cowboys don't cry. I've learnt to have emotions as well. I can also sit in a movie now and cry. I didn't used to do that.

I had some raw deals in the police. It's not that they owe me anything, but it's the way they treat you when you're in a crisis and when you're going through trauma: they're not there for you. The police was my life; it was my life. The first five priorities were the police. They were the police, the police, the police, the police, the police. And then it was my kids, and then it was friends and liquor and parties, then it was the dog and the pot plants, and then my wife. God didn't even figure in my life; I didn't have any priorities except the police. I gave my everything for the police, because the police was my passion.　　　　　　　　　– **Captain de Beer (1998–2009)**

They took a whole intake from field training and they made us the crime prevention unit. It was just a bunch of constables with a superintendent and one inspector. We wanted to go and arrest a suspect for bicycle theft. He ran away, so we chased for a long way until the Golden Highway bridge, then we saw one of the reservists catching him and we thought, okay, he's caught, we can stop running now. Then that small, tiny little guy *moered* the shit out of the reservist and started running again. More policemen came. There were about six policemen and that guy *moered* all of them.

When we eventually got there we managed to handcuff him but we had wrestled him out of his shoes. We were still young and naive and we said, 'Ja, you can put on your shoes,' and we all let go of him. As he was putting on his shoe, I saw him turning towards the Golden Highway and looking to the right, and when I looked I saw the truck coming. I shouted but it was too late and the guy jumped. I saw the truck hit his head. He spun around and fell to the ground. As he lay on the ground he looked directly at me and I could see the blood coming out of his mouth and his nose and that look of disgust in his eyes, and he died.

When the paramedics came, they saw the handcuffs and that I was the only white guy there, and they looked at me with disgust too. There were people there who said they saw us throwing the guy in front of the truck. The parents came there and they asked me, 'Why did you kill my son?' The inspector just disappeared and left us there. We were just a bunch of constables left to attend the scene.

It was a couple of years after that when I started getting flashbacks about him. It was chaos. I got drunk and caused trouble at home and I got in the car and just drove around aimlessly. In the end I went to a captain's house. He wasn't there. Suicide was on my mind. I left his house, but he came and found me. He recommended a psychologist. In my first session with the psychologist she booked me into the psychiatric ward. I stayed there for a week.

A year or so later something similar happened and I couldn't get rid of all the flashbacks. At Gold Reef City, they have photos that are golden-brown; they're old photographs. The whole flashback takes place in that sort of colour tone. It plays, rewinds, plays, rewinds. It's all that you think about, all that you see, until you just break down. I ended up in that hospital again. I was eventually diagnosed as being bipolar and got the right medication and now I'm fine. But going to that hospital taught me some coping mechanisms. It's something that the police don't teach you; they just throw you in the deep end. Like that inspector – he just left us to handle the situation by ourselves. There was no debriefing or anything like that even though everybody knew what had happened. That's why a lot of policemen get depressed and commit suicide – they don't teach you any coping mechanisms whatsoever.

I used to dream about my work before I went on the medication. I used to struggle to wake up in the morning because when I got home the night before I would go to sleep and dream about my whole workday all over again. The dream would start when I wake up, prepare for work and take a bath, then I'd go to work, do the job, come back and climb into bed. At the point in the dream when I climb into bed, that's when I would wake up and have to go to work again. So basically before I went on the medication and had counselling, I relived my whole workday the moment I got home and went to bed.

The second time I was in the hospital, the SAPS chaplain came and spoke to me and he asked me what had happened. I was halfway through the story when he interrupted me and spoke for an hour and a half. He then said, 'Okay, if you ever feel the need to talk to me again feel free to come and talk.' I thought to myself, but wasn't that what this meeting was meant to be? You asked me to talk and then you interrupted me.

Before I went to hospital the second time, I spoke to a social worker and she said, '*Eish*, you're like a balloon. If you blow the balloon up too big, it's going to burst. I can't help you.' So I asked her who could help and she said she didn't know.

I met my fiancé at the psychiatric ward. Her father, a policeman, was a patient with me and he introduced us to each other. We are still living together, very happily. That's one good thing that came out of the whole story.   **– Constable van der Merwe (2004–2007)**

One day I attended a burglary in progress. I was the detective on standby. When I arrived on the scene there were only a few uniformed people standing outside. The owner and I went in and found the suspect inside the roof. I climbed up to him to take him out because he didn't want to come out. He turned around and stabbed himself with a knife, in his heart, twice.

We took him out and he died there in our presence. It's a strange kind of crime scene because the person stabbed himself. You don't get that often. Immediately the suspicion is there: 'Didn't *you* kill him?' At that stage we had a culture that every morning at six o'clock the standby detective must report the more serious crimes of the previous day to what was at that time the regional office. So the next morning when I phoned the brigadier he said to me, 'You are a murderer!' He made a joke out of it, but it affected me. Not that much then, but later. At one stage I became sick. You start to have guilty feelings. What if that person was there looking for something to eat or drink? You don't know. But then the other side of the story is that you were doing your work; he was prepared because he had a knife with him. So maybe he could have killed you or the owner, or any other person. But it stays with you. That's the moral of the story – it stays with you.

– **Senior Superintendent Boning (1987)**

Soon after the passing-out parade, just after I arrived in Sebokeng, there was an incident that I got involved in, a shoot-out incident. There was a complaint in the hostels. Control called for police assistance.

When we arrived at the address, we parked the car outside. As we were about to go into the house, the lights were switched off. I knocked; nobody responded. I knocked again; nobody responded. I kicked the door open and went inside. It was me and this other inspector. I don't know how it happened – I don't know how the bullets missed me – but as soon as I kicked open the door and went inside, there was a shoot-out. The thing is, we couldn't see those people, but they could see us. We threw ourselves down, took out our firearms and shot and shot and shot and shot. The unfortunate part was that one innocent guy was shot. Ballistics proved that the bullet had come out of my firearm.

From the station to where I stay is about five kilometres' walk. I walked from work to where I stay. The following day at work they provided me with a private psychologist because I was not functioning all right; I could not execute my duties all right. I was late. Problems were starting to arise. I was having nightmares. I was traumatised. I was shocked. So I went to see a psychologist at the station level. The psychologists in the police don't know how to do their job.

I attended that psychologist. She gave me sleeping tablets and asked me how I felt. I told her how I felt, but every time I saw her I came out worse. Every time I went there she asked me how I felt. It didn't do it for me. My drinking got out of control. I couldn't control some of my feelings; I started isolating myself from people. I couldn't socialise with people any more. It's still happening. But the old inspectors told me they had experienced such things before. I asked them how they coped and they told me, '*Bra*, you just have to drink.' The drinking went from bad to worse. I couldn't manage my finances; I couldn't do anything properly. Even today it continues, but it's all right.

I felt I had shot an innocent person. I don't even know if he's still alive or not. He is innocent; he has a family that he must look after. It was hard for me. The management in the police are useless. If you are in a shoot-out, they won't ask you if you are all right. The very same day that the incident happened, the superintendent wanted an incident report. How can they take it from a traumatised person? So the managers made my trauma worse. The only thing my commander wanted from me was a statement. He didn't ask how I felt – he didn't give a damn.

Just imagine me as a junior member, a student constable, already being negative towards the management; already having that negativity, that feeling that the police are just exploiting us.

I still have a drinking problem because I am stressed. I drink every day, even when I'm working. I go to the shebeen when I'm on duty. We are used to drinking with the people there – they don't do anything. I drink about three beers when I'm working. My colleagues also drink on duty. All of us drink. Everyone in the police is drinking.

– **Constable Shabangu** (2007)

I don't drink. When something happens to you, find some people to talk to about it and you will relieve yourself of the stress. But if something terrible happens and you don't talk about it, it will trouble you. That thing will always be on your mind if you don't cough it out. Sometimes if I am having problems I will try to organise a psychologist or social worker to talk with me and reduce my stress. **– Inspector Mampuru**

It was early 1994 or '93. I'd literally been worked to death. We were carrying heavy docket loads and I was investigating a big corruption and fraud case at the local traffic department. It was the regular problem with the issuing of professional driver's permits. My commander at the time wanted statistics. It was all about statistics: 'If we have more cases, then we'll get more staff.' Generally, the policy would be that if you were investigating a docket, it could have multiple counts in it. This warrant officer gave me an instruction: 'You *will* open a docket for *every single* count!' Now when you're talking about ten thousand counts of fraud …

For a period of several weeks, literally all I was doing was opening dockets. I wasn't sleeping. I was getting by on an hour's sleep a day. Then all of a sudden, a docket inspection gets sprung on us. I totally cracked under the pressure. I remember the evening that it happened going to my mom's house. She took one look at me and I collapsed in her arms, crying. I ended up in the foetal position in the corner of my mom's room. I had a nervous breakdown.

The fallout was that some other cops perceived you as being weak if you had stress, but I learnt to deal with that. Ironically, it has made me a stronger person. Now I know when enough is enough. I think that's part of the problem. Most people in South Africa join the police young; they're still growing up. We thrust them into this hostile, unforgiving, unfriendly environment and we expect them to cope without any support systems. A breakdown is not fun; I don't recommend it to anybody. It was a tough time.

I've seen it happen to colleagues of mine, colleagues who virtually became alcoholics. I went through a stage early in my police career where I drank very heavily. It was nothing for me to drink a bottle of whisky a day. Luckily, after having a breakdown you tend to take a close look at your life and I'm now only a casual drinker. It's not an easy thing to talk about, having a breakdown, but people need to realise that when a cop does have a breakdown, they just need support. Unfortunately, the structures in the police are not tolerant of people that have those problems. You get worked to breaking point by your commanding officers and then when you crack, you're seen as weak.

– **Sergeant Jordaan (early 1990s)**

I've got a serious problem with them appointing people who don't have a police background in operational posts and in top management. I've got a problem with that because you need to have a police background to understand the culture, to understand what these people are facing. If you have never been shot at, you will not understand the trauma that that person has experienced when he's shot at.

That is the problem we're having today: people don't care. I don't care if my colleague is shot. EAS doesn't even debrief the person. What is that? Why do police officers shoot each other? We are supposed to be close colleagues who assist each other, help each other, are there for each other. I must back up my buddy – that's the concept, but now I'm shooting my buddy. What is that?

So there's a problem with care and understanding. Understanding police trauma is a big problem. There's stress in the police that you don't find in all other jobs. You can't compare it to someone working at Shoprite.

Because they take these people from the university and place them there at EAS, they don't have a cooking clue about policing, and now they want to debrief me. When I spoke to this one lady I think *she* needed to be debriefed. She didn't understand, because she's never worked in the police environment.

There's a culture that you don't speak to these professional people because cowboys don't cry. Go drink a few more whiskies.

– **Senior Superintendent Boning**

I had a colleague, a uniformed officer. He was having relationship problems. I got a phone call from the charge office from one of the other cops.

I still remember him sitting in the stairwell of the police station in uniform, with his gun in his hands, cocked.

Nobody was standing around. A lot of the time, people abdicated their responsibility: 'It's high risk, so we're not going to go there.' The guy had a loaded gun; he could snap at any minute and shoot you. It must have been about two to three hours that I talked to him – 'It's not so bad; things will be fine' – just getting to a point where he would relinquish his gun to me. I took his gun and kept it with me and gave it back to him two or three weeks later.

There was no official record of it, because it would have killed his career. He was a good guy, he was having a really shitty relationship problem and he literally felt that he had no future. Those were the kind of scenarios where sometimes the guy just needed to talk, but the culture didn't allow that. Guys have to be macho. Cowboys don't cry. Maybe having been in a situation where I'd had a breakdown made me a bit more empathetic towards people who were in that scenario.

That was a hair-raising night. That's the kind of scenario that you don't want to screw up. You can screw up an investigation; you can screw up a lot of things, but you don't want to screw up talking a guy out of trying to kill himself. **– Sergeant Jordaan (1996)**

In 1996 I was a detective in Plettenberg Bay. This uniformed guy lived with me at the time. He and another guy had come back from the disco. I heard them having a fight in the hall. One guy went back to his room, came back and I heard him cocking the pistol. I thought, fuck, you're drunk! I opened my door and said, 'Give me your pistol,' and he said, 'I don't want to be here any more!' and he shot himself. That was it.

I went downhill for the next two months. I had a nice captain at the time. He told me one Friday afternoon, 'Either I'm going to file a complaint about your shit work and your missing work, or you book yourself in, get yourself well.' So for a year I was on antidepressants and saw a psychologist once a month.

I'm better off now being out of the police, even with the security work I do abroad. The police will always be part of my life, but I've been better off these past few years. Now I can switch off. When you work detectives or organised crime or a task team, if you finish at six o'clock or seven o'clock, you don't switch off. At seven o'clock, you're already thinking, where must I start again, what did I not do today that I must do tomorrow morning? There's never a switching off. I got my grey hair from detectives, ask my wife! Now, working on the security side, the mortars fall, but then it's finished. After two months you go home and there's nothing else – you're home.   **– Inspector Marais (1996)**

Sometimes you come back from work being cross. Maybe you've had a conflict with the other police members, or with members of the public. When you get home, you just go to church and when you go to sleep, you relax.

The stress is caused by an overload of work. Maybe the other members are off, or the work is too much: there's no manpower; there are no resources. You want to do this job, but you can't because of the lack of these things. You become stressed.

I've never been to EAS. My remedy is just church. I sleep very well after going to church. The other day, there was a taxi that was involved in a car accident and it burned with the passengers inside: fifteen of them; you couldn't identify anything. They were black, black, black. I didn't go to church that day. I didn't sleep very well. All those things were on my mind. Even when I fell asleep, I was dreaming of those things. The next day I went to church and everything was fine.

– Inspector (F) Dlamini (2001)

I've been offered leave for stress and I went to the doctor myself, personally. He said to me, 'The only people who get stress or depression from work are the ones who are actually doing something, or who are worried about things that must be done. The people who just go through a career for thirty years without doing or caring about anything, they're actually not the right ones for the job.' I don't know if it's true, but it was interesting for me.

It's not only the work which is stressful, but especially the accident scenes where kids are involved. I had one which wasn't nice: a mother and father and twin daughters. I had just come on duty on the Friday night. I was driving past the mall in George to Hoekville. The car in front of me's tail light had just disappeared over the hill and I just heard *boof!*

It was a guy from the opposite lane who had gone head-on into them. The mother and father and one of the twins were killed. The twins were already bathed and dressed in pink pyjamas, about four or five years old.

That night I told myself, 'That's enough, now.' The other idiot only had a broken arm; *totally* drunk. His blood-alcohol level was close to dead.

That was quite a thing. I just felt, I've had enough of this, especially when children are involved. That was just the final straw. I didn't want to deal with it any more. I wanted to stop while I could still make a clear decision. Because some people go over the limit and then they're not the same any more. I wanted to stay normal. I've made a decision – not to get away from it, but just to stay normal. Because that is not normal – to see things like that once a week, or once every two weeks. It's not normal. Sometimes you wake up and you still see that.

You get to deal with the people afterwards, with the relatives. It goes on forever for them. Sometimes they phone you and ask how you are, say they are coming by and can they come and see you. You feel their pain as well, especially the grandparents of those people who were killed. They passed by here the other day and said, 'We're going to buy you lunch.' It will stay there with them forever.

Luckily, at this time I'm not that old; I'm not forty yet, so I've still got time to do something else. I won't be able to show what I've done in terms of finances, but at least I'd be more normal; I'd be more relaxed at home; I wouldn't go to work on a Friday night. **– Inspector Burger (2007)**

13

FAMILY LIFE

I think the one group of people who really suffer the most is the women: the wives, the people who stay at home. Because you were out on investigation, you didn't come home on time, you didn't phone, didn't have a cellphone. What's a cellphone? Never heard of it then; we read about that in science fiction. You couldn't phone home – you never thought of it.

One particular incident when we were on a hot pursuit, I ended up in Pietersburg. We had to spend the night and I didn't have anything with me. I phoned my wife at about seven o'clock and she said, 'Where are you?' I said, 'Well, I don't know; I'm in Pietersburg at the moment.' 'But I've already made dinner,' she said. You don't think of that. She said to me later on, 'If I had had the money I would have divorced you.' She would have married me, but she wouldn't have married the job. That is the biggest problem of any police officer, I would imagine. The job interferes with your family life. Social life is okay, because policemen are all the same – you give them half a chance and they'll knock back a couple of beers and have a braai. But the people who really suffer are the wives and children.

Policemen aren't all that well paid; you've got to really plan. You've really got to look after your money. Would I do the same thing again? Yes. Would I make the same mistakes? I probably would. But I would certainly be more sensitive to my wife. It's a good organisation to work for if you believe in the purpose behind a police service. But the most important thing is your support system at home. You've got to keep that right, make sure that your wife knows where you are. You don't have to tell her everything you are doing – you will bore the hell out of her – but at least keep her informed so that she knows what to expect.

A colleague's wife spoke to my wife at a year-end function and asked her, 'Will this ever end?' My wife said, 'Yes it will. It will end at some stage.' She divorced him. They remarried at a later stage.

It's one organisation that really puts tremendous stress on interpersonal relationships. Is he going to come home sober or not? Is he going to come home at all? Is he dead or is he alive? Those stresses, they can't deal with that. That's why I say it's probably *the* most stressful job. And I think policemen's wives aren't ready for this.   **– Director Grobler**

The memories come back. I wake up at 2 a.m. and I can't sleep any more. I dream about the past – nightmares. I have flashbacks. This work is beautiful work, but it causes stress to my family. It gives my wife hypertension, because sometimes I don't sleep at home and when I'm not at home my wife doesn't sleep.   **– Inspector Moji**

My son is with my aunt in Limpopo. He's at crèche. I don't have a house this side in Joburg, and even if I did there's nobody to take care of him here. It's not like I work from seven to four. Sometimes, when I get information on a case, I'll have to rush somewhere and I'll get home late, so there's nobody to fetch him from crèche. I can't take care of him. So he needs someone who can look after him full-time. That's why I'm putting him that side. But I go there often.   **– Constable Sibuyi**

I enjoyed the speed; that was nice. I enjoyed the adrenalin, the danger. Once you get to a scene, you don't know what to expect inside, but you know it's a dangerous situation. I soon realised that by staying outside you don't over-come your fear, so I began going in first. I confronted my fears. That also gave me an adrenalin rush and made me want to do it more and more. You get a lot of policewomen who work outside in vehicles, and once they get to a dangerous situation they will stay in the vehicle or outside. I preferred not to do that. Face your fears and go in and take it from there. I enjoyed it. I didn't think I had it in me, but once I started doing it, it was quite nice.

At that stage I didn't know it was an adrenalin addiction, so I just did it. It was my job and it was what I did. I knew my mom and dad were worried sick, so I kept from telling them what had happened when I came back in the morning from a night shift where they'd shot at me, or whatever. I didn't tell them that, because I knew the next time I went out it would put more pressure on them to be afraid for me. So in the morning when I came home and they asked how my evening had been, I would say, 'Boring,' while in reality it had been anything but boring! You can't let them stay awake the whole night. I stayed with my mom and dad until I was twenty-eight years old – a lot of that time I was serving in the police force, so I couldn't do that to them.   – **Inspector (F) van Niekerk**

This kind of job is very traumatising. It gives you stress. Most of the time you are at work you spend with suspects who give you a hard time. Then after work you expect to go back to a family that will understand that you are going through a tough time at work; a family that will console you and love and support you in whatever you do. If, after you've fought with a suspect and been shot at, you go to your wife and she starts shouting and calling you stupid and saying you can't afford things, it affects you a lot. She is treating you as a suspect would. That's when people resort to abusing drugs, alcohol, domestic violence. To do this kind of job, you need a family that understands and supports you. If you don't have such a family then you can't make it here in the police.

For instance, while we were looking for a suspect in Yeoville one day, this constable went to the highest floor of the building, to the roof. Then we heard a shot go off. We thought he'd been shot, but after investigating we found he had committed suicide. Before he'd left for work that morning he had had an argument with his wife and he'd told her that he wasn't going to come home, that he was going to kill himself. He shot himself and fell from the roof down to the ground. It was terrible. He was a very quiet guy, always laughing. You wouldn't have suspected he was having problems. He didn't tell you about his private life. I was shocked; I couldn't believe it. Even on the way there, he was joking and laughing.

– **Constable Sibuyi**

Sometimes you are posted to work in the client service centre. Many black people end up working there, because white people don't like to work in the client service centre unless they are forced to work there. Some other people want to be served by their own race, not by black members. You get pressure from them; you are very tired. When you arrive at home, you have to take care of your children but you are tired, you are stressed, you don't have time for them, you don't bring happiness to the family.

Sometimes you get paid and then the money just runs out; it just gets finished while it's in the bank. Then you can't send your children to a proper school, you can't feed your family properly. That's why they say many policemen have financial stress; that's why we have too many suicides in the police. And we ask ourselves why? Sometimes your wife doesn't understand your duties – she starts shouting at you. That's when policemen take firearms and shoot the whole family.

I was having a marriage problem due to stress. I approached the station commissioner. He said, 'You must divorce your wife.' That was the only thing he could say. I couldn't believe it.   **– Inspector Ramela**

I brought the aggression home; shouting and swearing. But thank God, I never assaulted my family. If I had struck my wife, I would have killed her. Same with my children – I never touched them. I never gave them a hiding if I had a beer or two. Thank the Lord for that. If I see how many policemen shoot their families, how many policemen's wives just crack and shoot at them, and how many suicides there are in police families … But I shouted at them, and verbally abused them, very much. You don't backchat me. If I can't hit you, I'll just shout. I was nasty to them.

These days I testify in churches about the life I lived. It's not something I'm proud of, but I must tell you where I was, where I am now and where I'm going to. Most policemen go through these things; some go through more serious things. But thank the Lord my wife never had to call the police to come and take me away. There were many times when I just went out, got into the car and went to drink. Stuff them, I thought, and I only came back a day later. That's why I say my wife really loves me, otherwise she would have been gone a long time ago. She went through all that and she's still here.

– **Captain de Beer**

My first marriage was an unmitigated disaster! Being a young cop, you don't listen, and I hooked up with a young girl who was working in the police as an admin officer. Biggest mistake of my life. But we all make stupid mistakes. The relationship didn't last. Being a detective, I'd be called away in the middle of the night. I worked late, and she'd say I was having affairs because I was working late. Insane jealousy. I don't think she could adapt to that kind of lifestyle. Even though she was in the police, there's a difference between being an admin officer and being a detective in a specialised unit.

My current wife has been very accommodating with me – she's always understood my career. I've tried to involve her in it as much as possible. The first time she came down to East London for a holiday when we were dating, I took a week's leave. The Thursday night I got a call – there was a syndicate operation and I had to set up a sting. It's not like I could have left my girlfriend – she'd come all the way down to visit me – so I said, 'Okay, you'll have to schlep along with me and see what's going on.' So there she was with me doing surveillance on the top of a building in central East London, literally seeing me in action.

Often I would pick her up from work on the way to a scene and she'd have to sit in the car while I processed it. So she was very supportive of my police career. But I used to see how stressed she was when I went out on an operation and she didn't know if I was coming back or not. I saw the impact that it had on her.   – **Sergeant Jordaan**

We become so professional in our duties that we start to become abusive in our homes towards our kids. Not by beating them, but by violating their rights. When your kid comes and says, 'Daddy, I want to go there,' and you say, 'No! Do you know what happened there?' You become overprotective. It's a way of violating their rights.   – **Inspector Lakay**

The job influences family life tremendously. The knife cuts both ways – it's either positive or negative. At work you have a standard, a way that you treat your clients. Then when you go into your private home, you forget that you still have your police shoes on. You think you're dealing with your clients. So your child is treated like a suspect or someone who is reporting a crime, even though it's an ordinary household conversation. You cannot switch off, can't forget you're no longer at the police station. You're a civilian at home, and you shouldn't address your family members as 'Sir'; you should call them by name. If you spend long hours at work, you forget about those small little things.

Because you are in a disciplined environment at work, you are sometimes very unforgiving if your own household – your friends, your family, your children – do not follow the strict line of discipline. Yes, your wife might say you're too strict, your aunties and uncles and grandparents and parents might say, 'Please, this is not a prison, allow your children some freedom.' It's very difficult – sometimes you need the input of family members to calm you down. Sometimes you just need to take a break, do nothing, calm down on your own, and get it into your head that your shift of twelve hours or eight hours is over, you're a civilian and you need to behave as such.

As a disciplinarian you will always, knowingly or unknowingly, conduct your life on the basis of strict discipline. You become very uncompromising about the minor errors made by your own family and you treat them with the same assertiveness that you use in dealing with your primary client. You see how thin the line is between being a policeman and a father? The line between respect and fear is so thin that you can't even see a shadow between them. You have to teach yourself the art of switching off. Don't bring your home problems to work and don't take your work problems home; leave them in the office. 					– **Inspector Khan**

Sometimes you get home and you're frustrated and you haven't switched off. It's difficult to leave the work at work. There are things that come home with you. Then the wife goes on at you, 'Don't come with your work things here!' When you go to work at night, the kid says, 'Stay here!'

You get frustrated, because you are always working with the negative. The positive only comes from your side, things that you initiate. We do that to win the people, but mainly we are working with negative things. It's human. It takes effort to get rid of that. You don't just walk out of work and everything stays there and walk into your house and everything is different.

I think anyone older than thirty, with a wife and kids, needs a little bit of stability. You know your breakfast is at nine o'clock in the morning and you will be home at night and you can check your kids' homework. That's the negative side of the shifts – you can't be there.   **– Inspector Burger**

I switch off when I get home. I switch off completely. I stand in court and I hear these cases where somebody gets raped; somebody gets stabbed seventy-five times and has a log thrown on her face; a three-year-old child is raped by a seventy-six-year-old man. You cut off; you can't get involved.

– Constable Louw

I think you change through the years; you become emotionally blunt. You start to evaluate things that are happening within your family against what you've experienced. Say for instance something is regarded as a crisis in the family. I will say, 'But no one is dead.' You've come in from a place where ten people were shot at and six people died in one night. A hit man was driving around just shooting people accurately with a Tokarev. He killed six of them, five immediately on the scene and the sixth died in hospital.

So you come from this scene where people were lying there dead in the street. Their family members come to the scene and you see what they experience when they see their loved ones lying dead in the street. And you come home and there's a problem with regard to X, and you say, 'Well this isn't a problem!' You begin to feel emotionally blunt.

– Senior Superintendent Boning

I've never hit a suspect; I don't believe in it. I don't believe in torture or anything like that. I've always believed in dealing with people civilly – it's how I was brought up.

I'd arrested this guy who was quite a significant role player. He said to me in the interview, 'Sergeant Jordaan, I just want to say something. You have treated me decently and because of that I won't have you killed.' Straight out. That was the environment I worked in. It was an environment in which I received death threats. Everything I owned was in my wife's name just in case I got taken out, so she could at least get by. Everything we owned was in her name. She didn't even change her surname when we got married, just to try to protect her from that type of thing. So I accepted the reality and she accepted the risks.

The biggest shock for me, ironically, was after I'd left the police and I had to testify in a particular case. It came out in the trial that the suspect's Filofax contained my details – the car I drove, the registration details, my cellphone number, the car my wife drove, her registration number, where she worked, where we lived. That hit home. Those were the types of people we were dealing with. She understood the risks. It was never nice, but I felt she was owed the right to at least know the potential risks.

– Sergeant Jordaan

My husband is also a policeman. I met him at the police station. We are the only married couple at the station. There was another man and his wife, but they left. There's one other relationship, but we're the only married couple.

He is a detective now. He was working shifts and crime prevention. I think he is more committed to the work than me. It's not that I don't work as hard as him, but when it's time for me to go home, I must go home. One of us must be with the children, so I take that responsibility. I leave him so that he can go on with the fighting of crime and the investigations. Sometimes the two of us live apart in a way. There is no problem. Because I'm in the police, I understand that he must deal with the work. I can be with the children and he can do the work, but sometimes we don't see very much of each other. Sometimes this isn't good for us.

He has a good relationship with the children. He gives more attention to them than I receive from him, but I think there is a good balance.

Sometimes the children will say, 'Oh, Daddy is going to work again …'
I think their relationship with me is better, because I'm there for them.
But I think we handle it well.   **– Inspector (F) Basson**

In the beginning, your family fears with you. They don't always agree with
the things you have to do, so to an extent it affects your married life. I've
twice been threatened with divorce. She said the police were sending me
on camps and trips. You get accused of being a bad father and having
affairs. This police work – how can it be normal to work sixteen hours,
eighteen hours, yet you don't bring that kind of money home? How do
you explain it? So it's explain, explain, keep on explaining. It has a negative
impact on your marriage, but you've got to make the best of it.

    – Inspector Lakay

My present wife is my second wife. The first wife couldn't take the pressure
of me going all over the country and her being alone. She found a boyfriend.
Ultimately, when I came home, she was at her boyfriend's place. Then
I had to work again – what could I do? I would drink and drink and drink
and smoke drugs and drink and drink. Then I got divorced. The pressure
is in the mind. I found a girlfriend and she said, 'Marry me, marry me!'
and then we had children.   **– Inspector Moji**

The police sometimes ask a lot of you as a human being. You must work
difficult hours during December when other people are with their families;
it's Christmas time, they are at the beach and we must work. Sometimes it
is difficult. You cannot go on holiday in December because that's our peak
time, when we must ensure that the rest of the community is safe.

    – Inspector (F) Basson

In the morning you greet all your children and your wife. They leave; they
go to school. You say, 'I'll see you in the afternoon,' but within the hour
their father could be dead. You just say bye-bye at home; they kill you
on your way to work. They want your firearm. It is a difficult situation.
You feel afraid. That could happen to me at any time.   **– Inspector Moji**

I was married for seven years, from '97 until 2005. My job affected my marriage very much, because I moved around. I went to Kameeldrift, in '97 I married and in '98 I was transferred to Mpumalanga, to Witbank police station. I worked as a detective there, and from there I moved into anti-corruption. So I was moving around for anti-corruption and detective work. I could communicate with my wife, but it becomes too much because you are away from home so often.

When I came back to crime intelligence, I had to move around to different provinces because we were vetting our own members. That's when it had a very serious effect on my marriage. We fought about the moving around. She did not believe that I was going for work – she didn't trust me, even if I brought something that said this is my itinerary and I'll be going with these people to do one, two, three. There was a lot of damage done.

I slipped into having affairs while travelling, but I could contain my relationships. There was never a time when my wife got information about me having a relationship. I think it was more about her thinking than about getting hard evidence that I was busy with something. I usually only met women once on my trips; I didn't really have steady relationships.

– **Captain Mthembu**

They wanted to interview your wife when you were up for promotion as an officer. We always jokingly said it was just to see *what* you had married. But the wives of officers were expected to form part of the Officers' Wives Club and also to do their thing for the community and for the SAP. My wife was very seriously involved with the promotion of a recipe book given out by the ladies of the officers' club.

If your wife was found to be not quite acceptable, you wouldn't be promoted. There was a guy, a lieutenant. We were at a function at the police college one evening. His wife had on a red evening dress, very low-cut and very revealing. She was really dancing and carrying on. I remember the powers-that-be frowning on that, calling him in the next day and telling him that his wife's dress and behaviour were not acceptable. He was not promoted. – **Director Grobler**

My wife knows it's a rough, tough job. Before I married her, her family was telling her, 'You're getting married to a police officer; you're in trouble!' They used to tell her stories about how when a police officer gets stressed he often kills his wife and himself. But now she is used to the job I'm doing.

Sometimes I take her with me so that she can see the job I'm doing. But sometimes when it is stressful, I don't want her to get stressed the way I do. Sometimes I try to debrief myself by telling her the terrible things I saw, but a pastor at Pretoria Central said, 'No, don't do that, because then you are putting your stress onto your wife.' For me it helps, though. She knows and understands what's happening in the police.

– Superintendent Molebatsi

I got married in '93, so my wife went through the whole system with me. I can imagine it was awful for her, I can only imagine it. I absolutely have all the respect in the world for her – to know that your husband gets called out at ten, eleven, twelve, all hours of the night to go and catch somebody, and then he comes back and one of his colleagues has been shot dead.

Working in an undercover unit, being a husband with a fake working persona, was difficult, because I didn't ever speak to my wife about my job. It still affects me today, because I don't speak to her about my present job, even though I can. I drive into a petrol station and I take my safety belt off when I come around the turn – before my car stops, my safety belt is off and the door is open; that's a habit. People look at me now in this private-sector job and they say, 'Where are you going? The car hasn't stopped yet – what's the rush?' But it's a habit. I struggle not to do it.

Now my wife knows more or less what I did, but nothing detailed, nothing bad. I just told her, 'We punched a guy round a bit once; it wasn't right.' Nothing serious. The secrets did interfere with the relationship, but luckily they weren't secrets about other people that could influence my marriage. They were things I kept confidential to protect her. I didn't want her to be scared for me.

– Inspector Stevens

If I wanted to be a good policewoman, I had to be available twenty-four hours a day, like for hostage negotiations. It's different if you just have a normal eight-to-four job. Being a policewoman you have to go and do your job. Your children are looked after at school and then at night you're a great mommy. But just when I wanted to put my children to bed, I had to go and negotiate.

When the eldest was born we had a situation where Nigerians on the internet would kidnap people who came from France or wherever for a business deal; then if we didn't come up with the money or the demands they wanted very quickly, we would find the victim lying next to the highway, shot. This went on for two weeks. I would come home, dress, get something to eat and go back to work. It took two weeks before we could catch those guys. You can't miss out on the negotiation stage. If you take the day off, then you have to find out about every single demand that's been made, everything that has been said in your absence. You can't do that while somebody else looks after your children twenty-four hours a day. You can't be excellent on this side *and* excellent on that side.

– **Inspector (F) van Niekerk**

My fiancé is a pre-school teacher. She works with three-year-olds. I do not have a lot of time to spend with her; that's why I did not connect my TV aerial. We thus cannot watch TV and we are forced to spend time together. This works like a charm. We have a great relationship!

– **Constable van der Merwe**

My first police dog, Nisha, was the apple of my eye. I had had him since he was about a year and a half. He was part of my family. He was my child. He was the most amazing dog. He was great with children. A friend of mine's daughter used to play with him and roll all over him and he would do nothing. I used to do dog sport with him.

He was getting old, so in 2008 I put him down. That was the most heartbreaking thing I've ever done. They cremate the dogs. I have his ashes at home. It was a very traumatic experience for me. He did a lot of good work.

Ninety-nine per cent of all dog handlers have that same bond with their dogs. I have a friend who works in the dog school. He had two very special dogs that he'd had for a long time. A month before I had to put my dog down, he had to put both of his down on the same day. After we've each had a couple of beers we still get a tear in the eye. They're really part of your family. It's like losing your child. — **Inspector (F) Kemp**

14

POLICE AND THE COMMUNITY

In the police service there is no money. The only thing that makes you feel good is when the people you serve come and thank you, and say, 'You've done a good job, well done.' Even though they are not giving you anything, their words – just a mere 'thank you' – it makes you feel good. It feels like you've got money, even though you don't.

— **Constable Sibuyi**

A family living in Bloemfontein made enquiries about their son who was on holiday in Cape Town. The landlord of the flat he was staying in was on holiday in Pretoria so you had no access to the flat, no way to make enquiries, because the person was not known to anyone in Rondebosch.

Sadly enough, a person fitting his description had been killed three days prior to that phone call on the railway line in Newlands. You do your local run-around of mortuaries, hospitals, clinics, holding cells, and no trace of this white man can be found – which leaves you with only one unidentified white male of this age being found dead on the track. Now you sit with a parent whose son may be dead on the phone line 990 kilometres from your area. How do you convey a message like that? You don't know if the incidents are related, but I decided to ask the father to come down to Cape Town.

Prior to that I had arranged with the mortuary to prepare the body. When a body's been run over by a train, most of the time it's not even identifiable, apart from a piece of jewellery. Fortunately this body was ninety per cent intact and identifiable.

I met the father of the deceased at the toll gate in Paarl, the Huguenot Tunnel. We drove down to the Salt River mortuary and the man viewed the body. He didn't hesitate. He turned around and said, 'Mr Khan, that is my son.'

When we got back to my office the man looked me in the face and said, 'Mr Khan, when you phoned me yesterday I knew that my son was dead. I knew you had found him and I knew that when I came to Cape Town I would meet you where you said you would be. You just made that impression on me, even though I'd never met you. I had an irrevocable trust in you.'

That is a testimony that you wouldn't get in any paying job – working in customer relations, the classroom, a workshop, as a priest, whatever. That comes from the heart. And when you get people who relay such feelings of trust in you, it's the highlight of your career.   – **Inspector Khan**

This civilian was killed and we had to go and tell his family what had happened. Oh, it was bad! Screaming! They threw themselves on the ground – a whole lot of noise.

You try to comfort them, but a lot of times they will blame you. It's natural for them to want to take it out on someone; you need to be careful. That's the worst – death and what goes with it. Whether it's a colleague or someone you don't even know, it still affects you, no matter how you look at it.   – **Superintendent (F) January**

Sometimes you know why the community doesn't say thank you and sometimes you *need* them to say thank you. If you see how we work, we are not the same. Some police are very negative. The people can't say thank you when you have a negative attitude but you *need* them to say thank you when you are nice to them, when they are satisfied.

– **Inspector (F) Dlamini**

I believe in what I do. Circumstances are not always the way you want them to be, but you need to get past that and carry on doing what you believe in. Sometimes I think to myself, is it really worth it? But then there'll be one little incident where you help someone, and the gratitude that that person shows you makes you think, wow, and you carry on.

I believe that everything, no matter how small, makes a difference. If I can make a difference in one person's life, then it makes it all worthwhile.

People don't always express gratitude to me. Mostly I get bad-mouthed because we are the 'terrible police force' and so on. For instance, some of the guys from the task force were in Mamelodi. A stolen car went past them. They didn't know it was stolen, but they turned around to check it. The guys sped away from them, got out and shot at them, and then ran. We arrived to help them. We got two of the suspects. While looking for the guns, I pulled a piece of wood out of a shack to see if they hadn't put the gun in there. The lady went and opened a criminal case against me for malicious damage to property. But the suspects were found in her house!

One day we were working a night shift and we stopped at Pretoria Central police station to check the crime statistics. There was a lady; they had stolen her vehicle. She was crying – she didn't have insurance, she was a divorcee with two kids and what-what. So I said to her, 'You know what, madam, don't worry, we're going to go and find your vehicle now.' She said, 'Really?' and I said, 'Yes, really.'

So me and this friend of mine, off we went to Atteridgeville and we found her vehicle and an hour later we brought it back. It was the most amazing thing ever! I didn't actually think we were going to get her vehicle back, but we got it back. It was still whole, one hundred per cent. She said, 'Is there not something I can do for you?' I just said, 'Have your vehicle.' She was so grateful. **– Inspector (F) Kemp**

I wish the people would trust the police and the police would trust the community, and that we would work together. The police must be loyal to the community. The community doesn't trust us because the police are corrupt. **– Inspector (F) Dlamini**

It's becoming embarrassing for me when I am at a private place, for instance at church, and they ask me, 'What do you do?' and I say, 'I'm a police officer.' You can immediately see for yourself – these people, if you don't know them well, they will immediately withdraw a bit and think you are corrupt, or illiterate, or a poor performer. It's sad that that's the association with the police. **– Senior Superintendent Boning**

Some of my old schoolfriends, when they found out I was a policeman they would say, 'Okay cool, now I have somebody who can get me out of trouble when I'm arrested.' They take your number for that, but then they generally try to avoid you. I wasn't friends with the best of people before I joined the police, so it's not a surprise that I've lost most of those friends. Some of them were into drugs and going out to assault people, so that was basically the crowd I was mixed up with. But some of my other friends have been victims of crime and then they come and bad-mouth the police. Obviously not all police are like that. You try to explain it to them and they get upset with you, and in the end you get frustrated about arguing with them. It's just bad always dealing with negative things about the country when nobody's doing anything about it. Basically it's you getting *gatvol* of your friends. So now my colleagues are my friends. **– Constable van der Merwe**

Being a woman, I've had the community questioning my ability. The one lady even said to me, 'You're not even seventeen years old, and you're a blonde – what do you want to come and talk to me about committing suicide for?' I was twenty-four. But a lot of people's opinions changed. They saw me doing my job and they wrote letters saying what a surprise it was for them to see the capability of a woman and the extent of what a woman can do. **– Inspector (F) van Niekerk**

Many times people told me, '*Fokof.*' That's the first guy who phones you when he's got a problem. Then he says, 'Sorry about the previous time, but please help me here,' and then the next week you get the same thing, '*Fokof!*' He uses you when he needs you. Sometimes when he's drunk he tells you, 'I'm paying taxes, so I'm allowed to tell you to help me.'

There are certain things you must just forget. If you're going to be affected by every little thing in this business then you'll never make it;

you'll end up in some institution in your first year. You need to become a little bit hard. But it comes with a price. There are certain things that you forget to share in life. You grow up with 'cowboys don't cry', and you try to be too tough about some things. I've changed my perspective – just be normal. Sometimes we try to be too superhuman. You have to cry from time to time. You have to feel bad.   – **Inspector Burger**

One time I was sitting waiting for a friend near the zoo in Pretoria. At the time, there were bus stops for whites only and blacks only. Because I was tired, I walked down there in my full uniform and I sat down at this bus stop that said 'Whites Only'. I just thought I was a better black because I was a cop. There were these guys who drove past in a bakkie, two in front and three or four at the back, all whites. They saw me sitting there. They stopped, reversed, and asked me, 'Do you think you're better, so you can sit there?' They wanted to beat me up. I had to run away. Imagine, a cop running away from the public! But at the time I couldn't resist; I couldn't say, 'Hey, I'm a cop!' They would have said, 'You're not better because you're a cop; you can't sit there.' So I had to run away.

– **Captain Mthembu (1988)**

At my first station I experienced that there was a kind of separation between black and white, how the service was rendered by police and how people were treated. I was in the suburbs. Only white clients were given professional service. Black people came last. Many black people used to sit in the community service centre without being consulted.

There was a man who was a state witness from the apartheid regime. This person was with others who were arrested for killing innocent people due to apartheid. The orders came from that station that this person had to be protected. I was posted outside his house during the night while my white colleague watched TV inside. The owner didn't want me to go into the house. I couldn't guard outside because it was a threat to me – any time I could be attacked. So I left the post.

– **Inspector Ramela (1995)**

I worked better at Thembalethu than I did in George with the white people. In Thembalethu I got more respect from a black person opening a case. You knock on that guy's door at 2 a.m. and say, 'I'm here for your case. Where's your witness and where's the guy that did it?' That guy will climb out of his bed, get the witness for you, get in your vehicle and find the suspect with you – because he's got someone doing his case. Do that with a white person in George and they'll say, 'I'm not available, make an appointment.' You do that three or four times and he doesn't get back to you. Then that's the guy who writes a letter and says you're not attending to his case. When I left George detectives we had eighty to a hundred cases on the table. At Thembalethu we had forty or fifty cases on the table and you could finish those cases in a month because the people wanted to work with you.

– Inspector Marais

The police job is very tiring. Then you get pressure from management and the public. There's a lack of resources. You find that they put only one or two bakkies on the road to cover an area where you have to give your service to about a hundred thousand people. You find you are attending a complaint, opening a docket, and then there is a complaint somewhere else; something is in progress, a robbery or something. So now you need to leave that complainant, you rush, and the complainant becomes very angry and starts shouting. You finish the job, you arrive late at the next complaint and they shout at you. There's too much stress.

Once I attended a complaint where black people were trying to rob a white man. I was very early there at the scene. On my arrival I asked what time the people came and they said, 'They were here just five minutes ago.' I quickly asked for a description of the suspects so that I could contact my radio control to tell other vehicles. I couldn't believe it. That complainant said, 'Those people looked just like you; they were black just like you.' I said, 'No, describe their clothing,' and he said, 'No, don't you understand what I mean? They were black just like you – I don't need you in my house.' I called my control and said the complainant wanted to be served by white people and I left.

This is what is giving some people stress. Some of the white people complain too much.   – **Inspector Ramela (1998)**

There's this perception that it's a white–black thing in this country. This whole racial thing irks the crap out of me, because it's not like that. On the streets it's really not like that.

We bust a whole bunch of Sicilians in a beautiful operation. We took them down at a taxi rank. So, three white cops took down the suspects at a taxi rank which was thronging with non-white guys. You always get told these are the militant situations. My partner at the time spoke fluent Xhosa. One of the guys in the rank said, 'What's going on?' and he spoke to the guy in Xhosa and said this is what's happening. We had to go down the street for the operation and drive back out again to get to our offices, but halfway down the street the word had spread about what we had done and all the guys in the taxi rank were shouting, 'Viva SAP! Viva SAP!'

That feeling of pride! It didn't matter that I was a white cop and that these were black civilians. They didn't see me as a white cop; they saw us as police officers doing our job. That was a real sense of pride for me. It still brings a lump to my throat. We did good work. Cops do good work and people do appreciate it.   – **Sergeant Jordaan (1997)**

When I joined the force, one member would manage to arrest more than sixty people at a time. He would just push his bike, tell ten people who are drinking in public, 'Sit here I will come back.' They would sit there; nobody would move. He would go and find fifteen more and say, 'Go there,' until he had forty or fifty. Then they would go to the police station. He would lead them; they would follow him. It could be a white policeman or a black policeman.

After 1976 they lost respect for the police in the townships, but in the suburbs they still cooperated. Now there is no respect for police officers. Some people, those who understand the duty of the police, they still appreciate it.   – **Inspector Mampuru (1975)**

In the community, if you are a police officer living in the street, everybody will come to your house when you are off duty and try to report something. They report things like 'Uncle is slapping my aunt' or 'Mama is fighting with Daddy; come and sort this thing out.' They will go to your house before they go to the police station. You are off duty; you are relaxing. You can't have a private life with your family. If you don't help them, you might get into trouble with the politicians. They'll say you are a police officer; a member of the community came to your house and you didn't assist them, why?

— **Captain Ndlovu**

What I enjoy is the support from the community. They are so scared, but they are not stupid. They know a person who is honest.

Usually I leave the city when I want to relax. I can't relax in the townships. There's always something happening that is not right. When I'm in my room a phone call will come saying this or that is happening and I must go there. I must assist if someone phones to say they have been robbed. I must get on the radio. I've got a radio on a full-time basis; I must call for help for the person. So there's always activity. I stay in the police barracks, so if I have to go out and assist at least I can get a few guys from the barracks to help.

The one day I was driving out on my way to Spier. I like to go that side to Stellenbosch; it's nice and quiet. As I was going out, I saw an old man getting robbed on the road, so I had to stop and assist. The old man was already on the ground – two suspects were busy on him. I shot one of them in the arm.

— **Inspector Lukhele (2006)**

I was off duty. It was over the weekend and I went to Witbank to see my family. I was in town. I saw some people trying to rob a man from Pretoria. They were on the street and had knives. They were in front of me, so I drew my pistol and I warned them, 'Stop, I'm the police, leave that person!' They said, '*Voertsek! Fokof!*' Then they pretended to run at me. I said, 'Just leave that guy!' and they said, 'Don't tell us what to do, he's just a white guy.' The three guys were standing in my way and continuing with the victim. Then I shot one and the others ran away. I was aiming for his hip because the leg is easier to miss. He'll be damaged but he won't be dead. I just wanted to stop him from what he was doing.

I was then surrounded by many people in the community who wanted to kill me. They said, 'Why did you shoot that guy?' I said, 'I will kill you too.' I kept repeating, 'If you touch me, I'll kill you! If you touch me, I'll kill you!' until the police came. They opened an attempted-murder docket against me, but nothing happened with the case. I had witnesses.

– **Captain Ndlovu (1996)**

There are still a lot of problems in Sebokeng. There are areas where policemen are still seen as enemies. Partially it's because of things like crime prevention. It's like they're working on the old curfew system. If they find you on the street after a certain time or something, they beat you up and throw you in the cells for being drunk even though you are sober. Especially in the shack areas where if they do see a police vehicle they would rather avoid it, or when you do a weekend operation where you close shebeens and they start throwing rocks at you.

We have been fired at a couple of times as well. Especially on weekends; there are huge parties there. I hadn't ever seen anything like it before joining the police. Then you get a complaint that someone there has been assaulted or raped, and you have to go in through all of those people. You get some people who are drunk and friendly, others who are drunk and angry, people who like the police and people who hate the police with all their hearts. It's a difficult thing. You have to be strict, but sometimes being strict can get you into trouble. You have to know where the light is and sometimes it's difficult to see that light. So I've been in a lot of fights. It can be chaos. Your evening starts off nice and quietly and all of a sudden you've got all hell breaking loose around you.

If you arrest someone in a crowd, it can get out of hand if the community doesn't know the whole story. So you can't just arrest; you have to explain to the whole community, explain everything that you are doing. If you're not in the mood and you just go ahead, it will get difficult. You will end up having a lot of fights.

We had an assault case and wanted to arrest the suspect, but the family was obstructing us. While we were busy fighting with the two brothers the guy actually smashed down the back wall of the shack and ran away. We ended up arresting the brothers and some of the community members who were trying to obstruct us. But it was quite funny because he actually took down the whole shack wall. As I went around the shack I saw this tiny, tiny little man *crashing* through the shack and over the fences until he disappeared. — **Constable van der Merwe (2007)**

I have to find my own transport home from work. How am I going to transport myself with a firearm, a bulletproof, a tonfa, pepper spray – all that equipment? I'm going to get into a taxi.

The community that we live in, they hate us. These people hate the police because we arrest them when they are drunk and they've assaulted their family members. Now, how is that person going to like you? Even my next-door neighbour – if I was called to do so, I would have to go and arrest him. The same taxi driver who is driving the taxi I am using – if there was taxi violence I would have to shoot him with rubber bullets. Then if I got into that taxi again, that person would kill me.

That is the frustration we have in the police – they don't care. As soon as I put on that uniform, I am doing so on behalf of somebody else.

— **Constable Shabangu**

We were doing a raid where people were squatting on some land. They were staying there without the landowner's permission. The people had been warned to vacate the place but they hadn't.

We arrived. The people were harassed – the policemen just kicked their doors down, pulled people out of their shacks and smashed the shacks. In one shack, we found somebody sleeping. It was morning, so we tried to wake the person, but he wouldn't wake up. I think he was drunk. A captain took teargas and shook it, then sprayed it straight into that man's nose. That man jumped, he hit the roof and he came down. He produced a green liquid from the nose and the ambulance was called.

I was very cross with the captain. I told him, 'You know what, I don't want to quote colours, but you are white and you have transport; you have money for a vehicle 'cause you've been here a long time. I don't have a vehicle. When I go home I use a taxi. You are a policeman; whatever you do here, you put other people's lives in danger.'

Whatever one policeman is doing, he's damaging the image of the police. Now when they see us using taxis, we can be killed – we will not be trusted; we will be viewed as enemies. This is what encourages people to do things that we then blame them for. We shouldn't blame them because we have done bad things to them. We didn't have the right or the power to destroy their shacks; we didn't even have documents from the court. It's just because the people didn't know their rights. I cried that time.

– **Inspector Ramela (1998)**

I lost lots of black colleagues who were working at Khayelitsha. They lived in the shacks. Going home the *skollies* would get them and take their guns and shoot them. Lots of them died like that.

– **Inspector Kotze (1994–1996)**

In the past there was not a good relationship between the police and the community. When I started in the police I was working in the Vaal. It was bad – the community was attacking the police officers, especially the black officers who were living in the same vicinity as the people who were rioting. That's when I lost a colleague. That guy was my friend but he was staying with the community.

That day I had an assignment to do. It was during the night when it was quiet, so I usually took my books to read. My colleague said he wanted to do a patrol. I said he should go with someone else, because I wanted to do some work on my assignment. He left. After a few minutes I heard on the radio that he'd been shot. They rushed him to the hospital. But he was shot with an AK-47: you won't survive an AK-47. The bullet passed through him. When he arrived at the hospital, he died.

At the time, it happened for a reason. The people were right about the system being bad – but my purpose is to serve the community, to bring that trust back to the community to help them understand the way the police work.

– **Superintendent Molebatsi**

People are scared. They live in fear. As a police official you cannot worry about death or getting injured because once you live in fear you become trapped; you see yourself as hopeless. Our communities live in fear – like they are trapped in an ice block. They don't see themselves as active participants in the fight against crime, because of fear of what criminals can do. Because of that fear, there is apathy – people sitting back: 'I'll only attend to things that happen to me, otherwise I'll turn a blind eye.' That's the problem we are sitting with. But we need to be hopeful. We need to confront this problem head-on. It's not an easy thing to do but the question is, for how long will we sit and pretend that nothing is happening?

At this stage somebody runs away from a house and says, 'There's something happening there, you go!' Not saying, 'Let's go there together,' because it's better. He runs and says you must go there while he ran out of that same house. That's a problem. But if he runs out and tells me, 'Come!' I'll say, 'Fine, I've got a gun, I will assist, but maybe you can also be there to assist.'

It's a battle, the fight against crime. Although people say it is not an overnight thing, I believe that if we take a stand, things can change. It's just a matter of communities taking a stand. It's not everybody; it's just a couple of people that we need to deal with in those communities. But people these days have become so individualistic: we are so concerned about our own lives. They say, 'If I'm seen talking badly about a criminal then they will come and kill me.' I can understand that, but the question is, how long are we going to go on living in fear? The fact remains that most people are afraid. But how much longer are we going to be afraid? Until when? Until we die? **– Inspector Lukhele**

They broke into my neighbour's house. Everyone in the complex knew I was a policeman, so I was expected to go. I'm like Superman: 'Shaun, they're breaking in there, you go catch them.'

'Why don't *you* go catch them?'

'No, I'm not a cop; you go catch them.'

It was dark; I walked over to my neighbour's house. Behind the complex was open veld and the highway. As the guy came out of the flat he had a bag in his hand. I saw this other thing in his hand, but I couldn't tell if it was a gun or a knife. I asked him to stop and he just ran. I shot, I think three or four shots, at him in the veld. I didn't know what else to do and I didn't know if there were more guys. I'm standing there and I'm thinking, is this guy going to turn around and shoot me?

It's something I still don't understand: 'I can't stop the guy from breaking in – the policeman must do that.' Something makes the cop different. That's wrong. A policeman's a human being. He's also scared to walk towards that car. He also thinks, is that guy going to shoot me? The public can definitely do more. There are individuals in the public who stand up and that's good, but to go and call a cop because you're too scared – what makes him any better?   **– Inspector Stevens (1993)**

It's not only up to the police to prevent crime. The police can supervise everything, but the whole community – all the people of South Africa – it's their responsibility. It is the public's responsibility. They must stop pointing fingers and start reporting crime. We are not everywhere that the crime is being committed, but the community is. Maybe it's your brother, maybe it's your uncle, maybe it's your son, maybe it's your child who's doing crime, but you don't report them. The police won't know the person is involved in criminal activity until you report it.

– Captain Ndlovu

During the apartheid era a wall was built up between the community and the police. Now the police expect the community to break down that wall. But if I, as a policeman, take a hammer and start chopping from this side, won't the wall fall down faster?   **– Inspector Lakay**

15

CRIME AND SOCIETY

Most of the time, these are innocent people who are being killed, like someone who didn't want to give over his wallet. Sometimes when you arrest that person you look at the age of the person vis-à-vis the victim and you find there's a big discrepancy. Sometimes you ask yourself, 'Where is the respect?' Most of the people committing the crimes are youngsters and most of the victims are elders. People who are being robbed are just innocent people – mothers and fathers to some of these perpetrators. You ask yourself the question of moral values in our society.

If you step on someone's toes in Cape Town, 'sorry' is not good enough. It's a violent city. If you are wrong, you just go away and wait for the person to do something to you. In Cape Town people even go to church with guns. We had an incident where a pastor in Gugs was chasing a guy with a gun in the church – the pastor had a gun! We had a case in Nyanga where the priest killed someone right inside the church. They say the guy came to rob inside the church. Three priests came to the station in their church gowns to report that they had killed someone in the church. The priests were assisted by some members of the congregation. I understand it – in Cape Town anything is possible. Where I stay in the barracks in Nyanga, there is a Vodacom container and a spaza shop outside. But I can't afford to leave my room and go there without my gun. Anything is possible in Cape Town. That's the way things go, so I carry my gun everywhere.

We had an incident in Gugs where a teacher was knocked down by some guys. He approached them and asked why they had driven into him. They got out with a gun, killed him and drove away.

There are gangs who operate only in the trains. Then there are other people who specialise in robbing people at the train stations. They will wake up in the morning and rob people on their way to work. And then you have people who rob people in their houses. So there is no sphere where you can say, 'Once I'm out of this, I'm safe.'

I worked on a case where a guy was in a shebeen. He asked for his friend's phone to check a number. He was standing outside. Somebody came and grabbed the phone. Then they stabbed the guy in the neck for the phone, killed him. They killed the guy for his phone!

It's a question of lack of respect for the other person's life and for the rights of individuals. But when they come to court, they will tell you that if you assault them, they will open a case against you. They know their rights, but they don't feel that the same rights that are applicable to them are applicable to others.   **– Inspector Lukhele**

I grew up in a rural area, where people still believe in humanity. I didn't think there were such cruel human beings on this earth, people that could kill as cruelly, as those in Gauteng. There are a lot of people who are very cruel. I've just finalised a case where the suspect got a life sentence. I think I must go for a debriefing for that case. I still think about it sometimes.

It was a house robbery in Craighall Park. There was an old white lady in the house with her friend. The lady was about sixty-five years old and her friend was about twenty-seven. The old lady had nothing, she had nothing. In Craighall Park you can tell by the fences that people have money, but this house had an old fence and the house was not renovated. Three robbers entered the house and tied the women up. They demanded cash. The poor old lady didn't have anything, so they said, 'No, you have the money here in the house; give us the money!' She said, 'No, I don't have anything. Take my card. I'll give you the pin code; you can withdraw whatever is left in my card.' They refused.

Even the TV was old – it was one that didn't have a remote; you had to press the buttons manually. They didn't believe her. When they were busy going through the drawers they found a bullet. They asked her, 'Hey, where is the gun?' She said, 'No, I don't have a gun. The gun that I used to have

I surrendered to the police long ago.' They didn't believe her. They took an electric kettle and boiled some water. Then they took the kettle and poured the whole kettle of hot water over this old lady. They asked her, 'Where is the money?' She said, 'I don't have money. I'm telling you the truth; I don't have a cent!' They boiled the water again, did the same. They did it ten times. I don't know how many litres the kettle held; I think it was about two litres. Hot water. You can see how soft human flesh is – it's soft.

The old lady had a little dog. When the robbers entered the house, the dog started barking. They chased it out of the house but the dog barked continuously until the neighbour realised there was something wrong and called the police.

When I arrived there it was terrible, terrible. She was in pain and the skin was peeling all over, almost everywhere, peeling. The suspects ran away. I called the ambulance and she was taken to Baragwanath Hospital because it has the best burn unit in the province. But she passed away.

How cruel. How can somebody do that to a sixty-five-year-old lady? Even if they hadn't tied her hands behind her back she couldn't have put up a fight. She was helpless. So Joburg has taught me that there are people who are cruel, and I don't know why they are so cruel. Very cruel people who do terrible things. Before, I didn't believe that a person could do that to a sixty-five-year-old granny, but now I know they can. If you enter a house to look for money, how can you do that? Especially with two ladies who cannot put up a fight. What kind of crime is that? Is it a robbery? Is it rape-related? I don't understand it. It was terrible – the worst thing I've ever seen.

– Constable Sibuyi (2008)

In Cape Town the question of humanity, especially in the townships – I don't think it's a word that exists, really. The reason I say this is because of the number of serious incidents that take place. Child rapes, murders – is it possible to understand the meaning of the word 'humanity'? That's one thing I don't understand: the question of moral values. You cannot speak about humanity and then exploit moral values. I believe what I value as an individual, other people value too. When I go out in the street and somebody else is just walking in the street on their way to take a train, how do I start confronting that person? That person isn't worried about my existence, but people confront people, to the extent of killing them. 'Hey, I want your shoes.' If he doesn't want to give you the shoes he has worked for, then you kill him. Where's the humanity there? That's one thing I can't comprehend. How do you justify that when you are sitting at home alone and you ask yourself, but why did I kill that man? He doesn't owe me. He doesn't want to know me.

When I shoot and I kill a person, it's something I don't worry about because at least I know that I've killed someone and I can justify it morally. He was committing a crime. He was causing injustice to somebody, and I have to protect the innocent. But I wonder how the criminals do it. And they go on and on – there are guys with eighteen murders. Those people were sitting in their cars with their girlfriends, then they hijacked them and they moved them around to the banks, then they lined them up and they killed them. What for? They don't even stop there – they go and kill the children. How does this person justify that? Humanity goes with respecting the other person. If you can't respect the other person, then 'humanity' is just a word. — **Inspector Lukhele**

The police can't prevent crime from happening; there are a lot of different issues that need to be addressed. We have a lawless generation being raised. Children go to school and they don't get hidings for doing the wrong things, so when they are big they don't have good morals instilled in them. That's where it starts. You can be a policeman out there but you're not going to change anyone's moral attitude. That needs to be addressed.

Then poverty: when people don't have a lot of money and things, I can understand why they are committing crimes, 'cause they want to eat. That needs to be addressed. Government needs to do a few things, society, households – everybody needs to play a role in this. You can't just expect the police to change the crime in South Africa. — **Inspector (F) van Niekerk**

Alcohol misuse, especially in the Northern Cape, is one of the biggest problems. And also the way people are brought up. The parents do not teach the children. In the Northern Cape, a lot of the mothers leave the children and go to a bigger town to work. They leave the child in Groblershoop with a grandma or aunt. The child doesn't grow up with the supervision of the mother. Most of the time, the fathers are not part of the children's upbringing. This causes a lot of problems. If we can somehow help the people to teach the children more values – this is a job that we have to do to fight crime.

We are going to the schools; we are speaking with the children about alcohol misuse, drug misuse. We are showing them what drugs can do to you; we are doing projects with the children to promote moral rejuvenation. This will be a very good thing if we can just get it in place.

Once I was doing a project with children during the school holidays. We were playing games. I was moving from one small settlement to another. That was very special for me. I could see that our children really have a need to grow in another direction – not just sitting around every day. They want to be better human beings than their mothers or fathers who are working on the farms, who don't have matric.

Some of the children need to be loved. They will stand close to you or look into your eyes. They look up to you and wish to become what you are. I'm not an officer yet, but you can see that these children in Groblershoop are in need of becoming something more than their own father and mother, the way they look up to me. When I'm in the township, they greet me and they want to touch me and they want to speak to me. The children are in need of something more.

What I can do for them is tell them that my mom and dad couldn't send me to university so I have worked hard to get matric. The police gave me the opportunity. I tell them, 'Just work hard. If you get matric, you can join the police and it will not cost your mom or dad a penny.' I tell them that my family was also poor but I got this opportunity and now I can ensure that my children have better opportunities in life than myself.

– Inspector (F) Basson

As a police official, I am part of society; I grew up in society. My job is not only to arrest people and lock people up. I interview people; I talk to them and ask them what the problem is. I talk to them in a brotherly way.

Sometimes you can pick up if a person can be rehabilitated or not. Some people will say to you, 'Just take me away, because I will never change.' That is my job.

I had a situation in Gugs. This *laaitie* was wanted by his gang colleagues. I used to talk to him sometimes. I phoned him one day and told him I wanted to meet him. He told me I must come alone. I said, 'Fine, I'll come alone.'

I stopped at the corner and phoned him to tell him I was there in a police car. Eventually I caught sight of him between the houses. That guy had a gun on him. He came and sat in the van. Then he gave me that revolver – it was fully loaded. He told me he wanted to change, but he knew he'd never change. He knew he'd die someday because he was wanted by some of his colleagues. He told me straight – he could not live without a gun. I said I would take the gun and book it in. I was thinking about the options I had as a police official: what could I do?

One option would be to take the person away to see if he could be rehabilitated, but we don't have such institutional alternatives. I don't think our society has systems in place. I don't think that our country has the support structures.

When they go to jail they give themselves ranks and orders. So when he comes out he is ready for revenge. They come out more aggressive.

He was young, that guy, fifteen years old. He has since passed away in a house robbery.   **– Inspector Lukhele (2002)**

The stats that we see are being manipulated. We deal with them daily and if we find the slightest reason to change something to something less serious, it will happen. It's definitely being manipulated.

If I must take all the cases that people want to report when there's a possibility that they will withdraw it the next morning, there would be ten times more cases. So you settle things with them and you work things out, otherwise you will be told you haven't done your job. I've seen a case where it was nearly a murder and the victim said, 'Just pay the medical expenses and I will forget it.' They knew each other and were drinking together. Liquor is definitely the main contributor to crime. That's why it's so busy over the weekend.   **– Inspector Burger**

The levels of serious crime in the country, such as house robberies, are much higher than what the public knows. I say this because I've attended many crime scenes where the complainant will tell you straight that there's no use in opening the case; they don't want to open the case. The crime stats don't reflect the real crime levels.   **– Constable Sibuyi**

The police manipulate the stats. They change 'rape' to 'indecent assault'; they change 'housebreaking' to 'trespassing'. This has happened since Selebi.

At the end of the month you see, oh sherbet, I've got five 'theft out of motor vehicle'. Make this one 'theft of radio'. Make this one just a 'theft'. The people do that. I've seen it. I don't like it, because you need the real stats on your chart so that you know where to patrol.

You'll hear it from all policemen. It's serious.   **– Inspector Kotze**

16

ETHICS

It doesn't matter whether you condone a law or not. Once a law is written and approved by a government, that law is a law of statute. It doesn't matter if you like it or not – you have to enforce the law. How you execute your duties as a police officer will make the person that you're dealing with understand you, make them appreciate your duty. You're not the creator and designer of the law; you're just the enforcer, irrespective of what it is – like the pass law, or the curfew law in the early eighties, where black people couldn't be on the streets after a certain time. If you have to enforce a law like that, which is blatantly racist, even your worst opposition will accept it if you do it in a dignified manner.

If you have a law like the pass law which prevents people from movement – a person who is required by an inhumane law to have a pass in a certain area and at a certain time – your approach should be to treat that person humanely. That was my calling, unfortunately. — **Inspector Khan**

They sometimes tell you, 'Go and take all the homeless people off the street,' but I'm not going to do something I'm not happy with. I'll never do that. I'll tell anyone that I'm not going to do it. They can do whatever they like to me. — **Inspector Burger**

I've probably done things that others would find unethical, but I've never done anything outside the law. I've locked up homeless people and I'd do it again tomorrow, because the homeless people that we detain, ninety per cent of them are also criminals. They sleep on the street, so what do they do?

They steal. It would be different if they stole an apple to eat, but they don't – they steal your car radio and they steal from old people walking down the street because they're easy targets.

I don't think he learns a lesson from my arresting him. I think he comes out and he's more pissed, but it's one less person on the street to commit a crime. I don't think anyone goes into a police cell or jail and comes out with a 'Wow, I've been saved!' attitude. They probably come out and if he was using dope he'd probably be selling it by the time he comes out. But at least it's one less person on the streets, temporarily. Temporarily, there are so many people off the streets, so I think it's better.

– Inspector (F) Kemp

I think it happens all over South Africa, but I became used to it when I worked in Thembalethu. Every Friday and Saturday night we would make a train of police cars, lots of cars. We would go from tavern to tavern, chase all the people out and just fill up the vans. Some of the people weren't even that drunk. Some people had to go home because there was a small child waiting for them, but we locked them up.

You don't have a choice: the stats say last month you arrested five hundred drunks – you're in the green. This month you must arrest five hundred and one otherwise you're in the red.

It happened in Bellville too. You must arrest at least twenty drunks every weekend. At the taxi rank the people sit and drink. That's where you get your twenty drunks. But they are respectable, churchgoing people who are having a drink while they wait for their taxi or train. We want to give them a J534 but the captain says, 'No, lock them up; drinking in public.' They say, 'But sir, my child is at the house!' But he says, 'I'm not interested in your child!'

I don't like to arrest people for that. Yes, if people are *poepdronk* in the road, they are a danger to themselves and others, so lock them up. That's right. But not someone who's quietly having a drink. Leave him. The policeman drinks worse. Policemen also drive drunk – they take the *work car* and go to a tavern and get drunk! 						– Inspector Kotze

One captain, it seems like he's working on the pass system. If he says, 'Arrest this person,' then you arrest the person. But you can see the guy is not really drunk. Sometimes you get police officials who call the guy out of his house to the street and then when he's in the street they say, 'Okay, you're drunk,' and they arrest him. If I were in that person's shoes, I would sue the police.

Sometimes you've got people from the child protection unit and a girl comes in who's just been raped and they tell her, '*Ag*, you're talking shit,' without even sending her to the doctor. Yes, they have experience, but sometimes afterwards I say, 'Talk with me around the corner,' and then you hear the story and you help her and you find out that the story is actually true. I question what some of the other people do, chasing people away or arresting people for no reason. Especially if there are a lot of people around and they're fighting with them or embarrassing them, then they arrest the person just to prove a point – 'I'll show you.' It's not right. People abuse their power; there's a lot of that going around.

I can understand if you pick up drunkards. Then you get a drop in serious crimes – less accidents, less rapes, less assaults, less robberies – because the drunkards either get robbed or rob; they rape or get raped. You don't want to arrest them, because you try to put yourself in those people's shoes. They're just around the corner from their house. But if you don't arrest them, tomorrow you're going to sit with the docket. Unlawful arrests are really the thing that can get to me sometimes.

– **Constable van der Merwe**

I once had to arrest a guy who stole a small packet of Viennas at Checkers Hyper. His words to me were, 'I'm hungry.' I asked the guys at the hypermarket, 'Can't I pay for him for the *wors*, for the Viennas, and just let him go?' They said, no, they wanted every single theft in their shop to be recorded and they had to have a case number. I really felt that guy wasn't a criminal – he was just an old bloke stealing. He didn't go and take a big bag of Viennas, he took a small pack of Viennas because he was hungry. That was terrible for me. – **Inspector (F) van Niekerk**

Sometimes when you arrest somebody you have to interview them, talk to them. I might find he is hungry. Maybe he asked people for money to buy food and nobody wanted to help him. Maybe he then goes to the shop and steals something. I get there; I talk to the owner of the shop. If the owner feels that the person was hungry, if he says he wants to forgive the person, it's up to him. I can't force him to do that. But if he says he wants to open a case, then I have to because he is the owner of the property, he is the one who was offended. Even if I see that person did that thing because something forced him to do it, I have to open a case.

— **Inspector Mampuru**

When someone is not working and is hungry, they just steal food. You ask why and he says, 'I'm hungry, I've got no place to stay, no parents, no brothers.' Sometimes we have to feel for him. But a crime is a crime. Then you have to talk with the shop owner or the manager, appeal for that man. If you've got money, then you just pay for that food because that is not a serious crime.

It's just like someone walking on the street: you stop him, ask him for his passport. You can see he is a foreigner. Why is he here? He will explain why. Then you just take him. This man is going to stay in the cells for up to two weeks before he is deported. That is detention without trial. It is illegal. Then you will take him to Krugersdorp; they are going to open a file for him. He is going to stay there three months before he is deported. I don't feel good about that. That is a human rights violation. But we have to arrest him. The law says we have to arrest him. We don't ask Americans and British people for their passports. It's like apartheid is still in existence. Now it's black-on-black. It's a black man who is going to stop him and search him and ask him for the documents. He will say, 'No, I don't have any, I'm from such-and-such a country, looking to feed myself, looking for a job.' Because he's black, we treat him like that. Black-on-black apartheid.

— **Inspector Rameama**

People from Mozambique are in South Africa; Lesotho people are in South Africa. Someone who comes from Mozambique is a foreigner. How can you be a foreigner in Africa? But the law promotes it and we have to serve the law. That brother of mine is a plumber, he's an electrician, he is a teacher – he has skills. He comes here because there's no money or food where he comes from. He comes here to work for his wife and children. When he gets here, we arrest him and tell him to go back. What about the wife and children and grandmother? For those three months before he is deported he is going to stay here. There will be no source of money at home. You are punishing that person. You are killing his family. Without knowing it, you are killing them. **– Inspector Moji**

They sting someone with one *stop* of dagga. Why would you let him lie in prison for the whole weekend? He may be a user of dagga, but he's got a family of eleven that he works for. Now you pick him up on a Friday with his salary. You lock him up. He doesn't book his money in because maybe he put it away somewhere so when you search you don't find it and he is put into the cells. It's his first time and he gets robbed. There are eleven people at home who don't have food just because of that one *stop* of dagga. So you need to look at alternatives. Let him pay that fine. Make an appointment for him. Make the family aware that he's been picked up. Make hell for him. But don't keep him locked up. I don't see anything wrong with that, because you're working towards a solution. It's also zero tolerance. You removed him from the street, although you didn't put him in the cells. He learnt his lesson. **– Inspector Lakay**

I've thought about it sometimes, whether my action is right or wrong, but I always make it clear to myself that one thing leads to another. If you allow someone to take bread, then next time it will be a pocket of potatoes. So I've never had a moral problem with policing. Maybe the only time I had a problem was when I really knew the guy was not a drunk; he was not fighting with his wife, and I had to arrest him for a *stop* of dagga. That's maybe the one thing that I feel uncomfortable about sometimes. It's nice to catch someone who's dealing or selling large amounts, but you get that situation where the oke is growing a tree in his garden and it's only for himself.

I've received a lot of negative criticism, especially from the white dagga-users in the Wilderness area – the hippies, the flower children. I like them, but they don't like the fact that I arrest people for dagga. I just tell them that everyone's got a job to do and there's a law that says it's wrong.

– Inspector Burger

We pick on fucked-up cars at roadblocks, where you are guaranteed of writing out tickets to poor old people. You let the guy in the brand-new BMW who is not wearing a seatbelt go, because you are scared he is connected to some or other person and you might get into shit.

– Constable van der Merwe

Some police misuse their powers. If a middle-class white person comes in to the police, they will be careful about how they present themselves and they won't look for any trouble because they know the person will report them. If they look at a drunk person, they will hit them. They look at a dirty person and they will beat them up.   – Constable Louw

We were driving around doing patrols. We spotted a group of men walking on the sidewalk. They kept on looking nervously over their shoulders at us. One of the men dropped something. I did not see this, but my crew alerted me to this. I then stopped and reversed to where my crew saw the object being dropped. We found a revolver. We got back into the vehicle and drove to the men, but they had already run away, leaving one of them behind. We searched him and found a butcher's knife on him. We ended up lying in our statements, saying we saw him dropping the firearm. We didn't mention the butcher's knife. So we actually planted the evidence. I felt guilty about that afterwards, and still do sometimes. But in the end, if all of them were carrying weapons like a butcher's knife or a firearm, then what was their intention? So you tend to justify your actions even though you've done the wrong thing.   – Constable van der Merwe

17

TORTURE

Some of what the security branch did was right. What some of the guys did was wrong. To have a farm where there's no law is wrong.* To have a farm where you take people to interrogate them in a reasonable fashion, to me, is right. To have a farm where you are the law is wrong. It's a difficult thing to explain. Some of the guys did overstep the boundaries, but not all of them. I don't care who says what, if you're not going to torture somebody, you're not going to get much information. That's just the way it is. Liberals hate to hear that. But they like the result. Like one of the famous security policemen said, 'People want to eat the sheep, but nobody wants to slaughter it.' We all want the biltong, but we don't want to shoot the buck. Everybody's quite happy to eat the biltong but when it comes to the fact that there was a buck killed they say, 'Oh, but we didn't know that; we were just enjoying the biltong.' They go into this absolute state of amnesia. That's very much like the politicians – they forget that in order to be in power, people had to get hurt. Some people overstepped the boundaries – that's not my call.   **– Inspector Stevens**

Torture did happen; I saw it. I remember the first time I saw it, it felt so degrading. I said to the guy, 'Look, I understand why you're doing it, but I don't agree with the methods.' To which he said something which I can't

---

* Reference to Vlakplaas, a farm used by the security branch for interrogation, torture and murder.

repeat! I heard about it many times. It happened. Can it be justified? Can you justify somebody being tortured for a particular reason, or is torture unjustifiable under any circumstances?

I've always had a problem with torture. There are other ways you can do your investigation, but it takes time. Are you after a quick fix, or are you after the truth? **– Director Grobler**

Torture techniques were just passed down from generation to generation. You just observe. There's a recipe which you just add to. There's a tube, for example, and you can decide if you want to suffocate for twenty seconds or thirty-five seconds, or whatever.

I think my first experience of torture was with the blanket. We used to take a wet blanket and roll the guy in it, and just rough him up a bit. We rolled the guy, a bit like a roti or a pancake. You stand on him and hit or smack him a bit. The blanket protects him from marks, so he goes to court quite normal.

As far as I can remember, that first incident was related to a farm attack. They killed a fifteen-year-old girl and shot the mother dead as well. We caught the one guy when he was fleeing to Lesotho, or coming back from Lesotho. We used 'encouragement' to get the people that were with him, and to find out where the weapons were that they had used.

Another technique was just the normal slap, the 'charge office slap', as we called it. I used to see some detectives – the '*maarfokkies*' – shock suspects. The name *maarfokkies* was from '*Maar fok die* docket, *kom ons praat*.' The *maarfokkies* worked at the housebreaking and theft unit. They used to use shocking as a torture technique – 'ET phone home'!

I wouldn't say these techniques seemed normal, but I knew that without using them, more people would be hurt. We dealt with some hard guys. They didn't speak. You literally had to beat it out of them.

– Inspector Stevens (1993)

The methods that were used in the old police force are still used in the new police force. Like tubing – you take the inner tube of a tyre and stretch it over his mouth from behind until he passes out or starts talking. Or if you're near the beach, you take him and put his head in the sand because there are no marks. *Jy werk met hom.*

It's only about solving the case, because if you don't solve the cases you don't get a promotion. Each time you don't close a case your promotion gets stopped until the case is solved.   **– Inspector Marais**

If you want to know more about a suspect, you must interrogate him. Sometimes we use illegal means to get information from the suspect. Sometimes you must *moer* him. Sometimes you must break the law to get the information. We use the tubing method sometimes, but it's very dangerous. We use a plastic hand glove and you put it over his head, up to his neck, so he can't breathe. You will see by his nose – it will be like a balloon; he is gasping for air but he can't breathe. Then after a little time you remove it. Then you put it back. After a while, he will tell you everything! It's quite dangerous if the person has asthma – he can die. I'm not encouraging it, but we do it sometimes.

The other method we use is that we assault them straight away, but make sure that there are not traces. We assault them under their feet so that there's no evidence. We remove their shoes and assault them with a tonfa. Sometimes what we do is we put toilet paper between each toe. Then we light it with a cigarette lighter. That's very painful. You leave that tissue paper to burn completely. Unfortunately there's no other way. Most of these people are hardened criminals. They are not afraid of police officers. They won't tell you anything unless you make them tell you.

– Constable Sibuyi

They're still beating and torturing people. You can do whatever you like. You get a bus in Standerton with a hundred and twenty-four bags of dagga with an average of ten to fifteen kilograms per bag. You've got seventy-seven people on the bus, but nobody knows whose dagga it is. So you have to use torture. What's happening in the movies is really happening in the world. I can't sit here and ask you, 'Did you steal that TV?'

'No, I didn't.'

'Okay, I believe you.'

So the police did use torture. Some of them can torture without leaving marks, some can't. It's skills. It's genuine. No nice stories; that's the truth. There were some who went overboard. There were some who could have questioned the suspects, but sometimes they just gave a little pinch. These days they still do it, but they do it in different ways. It's going on all over – you'll never wipe it out. Never ever. When you have to get information to prove something – I'll challenge the guy who says he can do that without a pinch.

— **Captain de Beer**

I was driving and I saw two men and a lady. The lady started waving, but I realised too late that she wanted us to stop. When I stopped and reversed, the two men had already run away. She told us that the guy had a firearm, so we called all our vehicles and we searched that area. We found the two guys next to the Golden Highway. We questioned one about the gun. We beat him a little bit but he didn't want to talk. Then we found out that he was HIV-positive. He had his medication with him. I threw his HIV medication into a ditch and even that didn't work. In the end, we locked them up for a case of kidnapping against the lady.

Sometimes afterwards you feel a bit guilty. I don't do it any more, but sometimes it did work; we did have a lot of success – mainly in drugs and firearms – with tactics like that. — **Constable van der Merwe (2007)**

If you work on a suspect – housebreaking, murder, robbery – he has been doing this for five or ten years. He makes his living from this – he won't just come out with it. They make it look easy on TV, all these American police series where it's half an hour and then the guy starts writing out a statement. It doesn't work like that in real life. So, you 'work' with him, but the secret is that there can't be any marks on him. If you've got marks on the guy and he goes to the doctor then you're going to be in shit.

In the end it was about getting the job finished and solving the case. It wasn't about hurting the guy; it was about getting the evidence. But when I got married I said, 'Now I've got to stop, else I'm going to go to jail.'

— **Inspector Marais**

One guy, his favourite tactic was taking a suspect to the toilet, putting his head down the toilet and flushing it a couple of times until the guy eventually talked. That tactic worked very, very well and we got a lot of information. Since I joined the detectives, I've stopped. I'm still young in the police; I can't lose my career over something like that. Nowadays when someone says 'no', you just take it as no. You speak a bit aggressively, but if that doesn't work then you leave it.   — **Constable van der Merwe**

It happens in the shifts *and* detectives. You work night shift, you get a housebreaking or assault and you've got six, seven, eight hours left and you go for it. You catch the guy red-handed with the stuff; the other guy got away. Now you want to get the other guy in before seven o'clock when you change shift. The guy you've got is not going to talk to you. So you say, 'Listen, let's take a hike.' He's going to talk in the end.

In the TRC, they talked about the hand exchange, electric shocks – it was still used in the '90s; I saw it being used. That's one of the fastest ways to get someone to talk. You've got three or four people on the shift – that stays with you. The machine is kept in the garden, definitely not in the station. In the end it was about solving the case – get your housebreakers, get the murder case, get the weapon, then you take it further in the court. It wasn't to hurt the guy; it was about closing the case. It's not like on TV where you bring him a cup of coffee and the guy's going to talk.

— **Inspector Marais**

We got a complaint of attempted murder. The lady said she was sleeping in her shack and she heard something that sounded like thunder and felt things hitting her bed. She realised someone was shooting at her. We got to the scene and found the bullets, but there were no cartridges so we thought it must be a revolver. She eventually said she suspected someone. Her husband had had a fight with someone, who made threats that he was going to kill the husband. So we went to one of the hostels and we found the guy. We searched him but we didn't find anything. One of the other constables, a black guy, took out a pocket knife and took the guy's testicle in his hand and he started chipping away at it with his pocket knife! Then the guy started shouting and said the firearm was in the TV. We found the firearm: it was a .38 revolver with five spent cartridges inside. Certain things were not mentioned in the statement, but the guy was convicted of attempted murder and illegal possession of a firearm. That was a torture tactic, but it worked!   **– Constable van der Merwe (2006)**

I've seen many people being tortured. The people in the murder and robbery units used to torture people. I was friends with them. Sometimes I went and helped them with arrests and things.

There was one incident I experienced which must really have affected the person being tortured. The person had murdered someone, and they took him to the mortuary and put him in the drawer where the dead person was lying. They made him lie on top of the body, and closed the drawer. He was lying with that dead person in the mortuary. Even in jail that suspect must still have imagined that dead person sleeping with him. It would affect that person in his mind.   **– Captain Ndlovu (1998)**

I used to beat people when I was working in the satellite station in Mamelodi. Three or four of us were working on a shift. I used to assault the ones who would come to us drunk and unruly. I managed to kick them hard and they left.

The one day I kicked a guy and he fell down. I thought maybe he was dead. I felt his pulse: it was weak. He wasn't breathing. I was frightened. Then I realised it's easy to kill a person, and I stopped.

The reason I kicked him was that we had been sleeping and he wanted to come inside, so I was angry. He was homeless. We chased him outside. Then he came back. We chased him again and he came back. Then the third time when I chased him, he pulled my head and tore my buttons. Then I started kicking him. It seems he hit the back of his head on the floor.

I started imagining that I'd killed a person for nothing. Luckily he got up. Then we put him inside and started giving him food, water, cigarettes. We were afraid he might open a case. But he was drunk. He didn't even realise he had been beaten. He said, 'Ai, I just fell!'

– Inspector Kekane (1999)

There have been times when there was more force used than was necessary. It's the frustration that builds up. Someone comes and says, 'Fuck you.' Then he gets a decent hiding. That happens at the police station, definitely. I've seen torture, but that was many years ago. I always made sure I wasn't part of it. I always believed in honesty, doing the right thing for the right reason. I could have been part of it; I've had the opportunity. I excused myself every time. But whatever they did, it worked. People confessed. If you follow up afterwards then the pieces come together; it's not just the confession without any evidence.

I know it still happens.   – Inspector Burger

I've been involved in the usual – a sack over the head and you throw water over him, or you tube him – but not any more. Although it still happens, I don't participate. I believe that it's sometimes still the right thing to do. For example, if someone has abducted a child and you don't know where it is, but he won't speak, then you've got to do what's necessary. But not for nonsense.

It happens a lot in organised crime. If I'm honest, often innocent people are tortured. The policeman thinks he's guilty, tortures him and then he offers a false confession just to stop the torture. Not everyone is guilty.

I think there are police who want to speak out about it, but we go and see them and make them keep quiet. There have been people who've spoken about it but we deny it; we lie. We say, 'Are you crazy? We wouldn't do that!'
                                                                – Inspector Kotze

I don't think people made false confessions to make it stop. A false confession won't work, because then you won't get the housebreaking things back. You do get to a point where you know if the guy was involved or not. If there were three guys in the room I'd work on the most scared one; from him I'd get the information.   – Inspector Marais

18

CORRUPTION

When I started in the police, the inspectors that I was working with were heavily involved in corruption. We would go to this location around Sebokeng. On our arrival there the inspectors would say to the illegal immigrants, 'You must pay your fee or we are taking you in.' Then those guys would pop out four hundred rand, five hundred rand. I didn't blame them. I know we are civil servants, but it's hard for us. It's hard to buy decent food.

I also took money from immigrants. You are surrounded by people who are doing it, so you find yourself doing it. If you don't do what they are doing, it means you might go and tell senior management. I can make about seven hundred rand on a shift taking money from immigrants. Seven hundred for myself. It's good; it's all right. Even the people who are working organised crime, the people who are investigating the police, they are taking *tsho-tsho* too. That's the problem. They are taking from the very same people we take from. With that money, you can survive. The police is so fucked up that the intelligence side goes there, the organised crime guys go there – everybody goes to the immigrants to get money. The booming business for the police is the immigrants.

The SAPS must give members decent salaries to survive. More importantly, though, we need a shelter. I can't provide for my family; that is a problem. I live with my wife and my child. My wife does not work. I have three children. The sad part of it all is that I live in a shack. It is hard for me. I've lived in the shack for three years – my whole police career. I spend my money just paying the rent.   **– Constable Shabangu (2007–2009)**

Corruption in the police service has become a culture – police culture. People don't give out information about other policemen and don't report them for fear of being sabotaged.

We have individual corruption, but it is not as common as when people are in groups. Sometimes you blame the police, but you can't blame them because everyone knows the police are underpaid.

I remember this scenario where these two policemen took a taxi, then the taxi man shot at them. When the investigation was conducted they found out that these policemen didn't have money for transport. That's why he shot at them. Some of them don't have money for lunch. That's when they start approaching people for corruption – to buy some rolls or cooldrink at least. **– Inspector Ramela**

We arrested a guy in the Northern Cape. Just me and an officer were in the room with him. He was involved in theft, huge theft. This suspect knew that he was being arrested – we did it all the proper way. He said, fine, he's arrested; he said he's cool, he accepts it, he's not going to go ballistic. He opened a safe in the bedroom and took out about a hundred and ten or a hundred and twenty thousand rand cash and stashed it on the bed.

While he was packing that money out, there was silence. He didn't say anything. He didn't say, 'I'll give you this.' He just packed the money out. The officer looked at me and I looked at him and I thought, don't even think of taking that money! I was worried he was going to say to me, 'Fuck, let's take it!' But luckily he was an upstanding chappie. He looked at me and I looked at him and I said, 'Listen here, I think there could be a bit of an investigation for the Receiver of Revenue here,' and he said, 'I agree with you,' and that was it. We phoned the Receiver of Revenue and then we had him for tax evasion as well.

There is a moment when you think, that's a lot of money. But it's not worth it. It's not worth losing the job and being branded. It didn't even cross my mind. Had it been two million bucks maybe it would've been a different story, you never know. I actually just had a good chuckle and thought, fuck it, not for me. Not for me. **– Inspector Stevens (1996)**

Many years ago, in Laingsburg, I caught a guy with two hundred and eighty-seven bags of dagga. He had a furniture-removal truck full of it. The driver opened a bag of money and said, 'You can count; I've got the whole night. It's especially for you.' It was the old fifty-rand notes with a white border around them. I remember he said it was seven hundred and fifty thousand rand. He told me, 'Constable, it's yours. I specially brought it with me in case I needed to give it to you.' But I arrested him, I didn't take it and I charged him for attempted bribery as well.

– Inspector Burger (1989)

I caught a guy in Standerton with a few bags of dagga and he wanted to give me ten rand. I laughed, 'You think I'm cheap, hey?'

– Captain de Beer (1989)

The biggest bribe I've been offered was a motor vehicle. He gave me a Valiant Regal, then they brought me a Chevrolet 4.1 street engine. He gave it to me as brothers and friends in crime: smuggling, beer selling, protection. That was in the early eighties, in apartheid. It was black *bafanas*. They took it from white men and they brought it to the locations. The police didn't want to take us from work to home. Even now you must buy your own car to get to work. But management are busy driving. They pass you on the way, from the same place.

I took the car to a chop shop because it was stolen. They gave me a second car, which I drove and then chop-chop-chopped. Then I used the money from those cars to buy a straight car. We have brothers who are crooks in the urban areas. They do it. We do it.

Corruption is still here and there. They won't stop it. They can't. You can't prove it in court. If all the police can get money then everything will be all right. How can I say no to a hundred rand? With a hundred rand I buy milk, mielie meal and chicken feet.

– Inspector Moji (early 1980s)

I've been involved in corruption, but not anything bad. In Khayelitsha we always struggled to get money before operations to catch the *smokkelhuise*.

We knew a certain house sold parcels of dagga, so what we did was we would go there and find a rasta with a parcel. We would take his parcel and say, '*Voertsek!*' Then we would take that parcel and go to another rasta and sell it to him at half-price. Then we would take that money and send our trap boy in with it to buy drugs. That's how we found out where the storehouses were. So we did that. It was wrong, but we had to do it.

– Inspector Kotze (mid-1990s)

When I started, because I was training under the seniors, I had to do what they were doing. Then I went to detectives and saw they were doing the very same thing, attending scenes, meddling with exhibits. You go to the scene – maybe there was a shooting. Instead of getting the photographer, you know what you have to do there. You collect whatever is on the scene and then when you interrogate the suspect and you find that the suspect has money, you start destroying those cartridges; you meddle with the firearm before you hand it in for analysis. Some of the policemen clean those firearms, they take a long time in taking them for analysis, then the prima residue disappears. Then they change the barrels or they swap the firearms. Terrible things happen.

– Inspector Ramela (1995–2000)

My colleague was working with exhibits, giving criminals firearms and uniforms to commit crimes. When they had finished the job they would bring the guns to him. One criminal was sleeping at that policeman's house and when the policeman went to work, he raped the wife. When the wife talked to her husband, he said, 'Hey, shut up, this is my friend!' When the policeman went to work, the criminal became the husband at home.

That police member was going home and was shot in the stomach and chest, through the windscreen. He lived but he had internal injuries and passed away. He was my junior and my respectable friend and my little brother and my colleague. That thing won't leave my mind. The policeman who was giving the crooks the guns was killed by those same criminals.

– Inspector Moji

My two younger brothers are constables in the police. My elder brother was also in the police – we were at the same rank: we were captains. He was working at the murder and robbery unit handling a cash-in-transit case and he was ambushed and killed together with his wife. I suspect that corrupt police officers who were working with him are the ones who sold him out. Hence I am very, very serious about corrupt police officers. They are very dangerous because they might sell you out, even if you are their colleague. It was bad; I became sick, emotionally sick. At least now I have healed.

They did it during the night. These were the people he was looking for. They phoned him and said, 'We've got information for you. Come to Magopane police station.' When you like your job and people phone to say they are at the police station, you go. His wife was knocking off from work at ten o'clock so he went to fetch her from work, then went to the Magopane police station. When he arrived there and asked if there was anybody waiting for him, nobody came out.

On his way back home, a car came up behind him. His car was shot with thirty-six rounds. They used a police firearm, an R5. The scene went on for a long time until he lost control of the car and crashed into the wall of a house. Those guys then alighted from the vehicle and shot him together with his wife, then they ran away.

He was a very strong person. Should he have survived, they would not have lived. So they got him, they knew. The car had thirty-six bullet holes. I don't know how many went through the windows. Corrupt police officers are the ones who sold him out. Hence I say, corruption in the police – we have to deal with it. We have to arrest them. They will sell their colleagues for nothing, for five rand or ten rand. The suspects were never arrested, the firearms were never recovered, but one day it will come out. I still believe that one day we will get them. Information will leak, somewhere, somehow. **– Superintendent Molebatsi (2001)**

With drunk driving accidents you would approach the suspect that you arrested and say, 'You are drunk; we're going to take your licence; you're going to lose your job.' The fact that there was an accident and the police came makes the civilians happy: 'Oh, the police came. They arrested the person.' But the police would just go somewhere with the suspect and wait for a long time. Then they would tell the person to drink milk, then wait, wait, wait. Then they take the person for a blood test much later. Then the blood is not going to come out all right. When the blood comes, they find out that it is below the minimum, then they pay the police. I was involved in those kind of things. I used to tamper with the blood of people. I have experience: I used to delay taking the person to draw blood because I saw that person had money.

There were cases where we worked in a team. Sometimes you didn't approve of things but you'd just do what other people were doing. There were cases where cocaine was involved. There's this thing which we call the continuous chain of evidence. It's not properly followed in the South African Police Service. In many cases investigating officers get approached by suspects. I was approached. What happened is there was cocaine. We had to fiddle with the evidence. The evidence is kept in a store. We approach the person at the SAP13 – the store in the police. In the police, they use these sealed bags. The members use a razor blade to slit the evidence bag. Then from there you can take that cocaine out and put crushed Grandpa tablets in its place. Then when it goes for analysis they'll say these policemen arrested the person incorrectly. Some members keep the cocaine and give it to others to sell; some throw it away. I did that at the time. It was very wrong.   **– Inspector Ramela**

I knew about my colleagues' involvement in corruption. They would just take favours in return for not proceeding with the charges. People give out money so that their guilt can be overlooked. It's common. If you see someone doing that, you can't stop him.   **– Inspector Kekane**

In Bellville, if you see a car stuck next to the road and you say to them, 'I'll phone a breakdown for you,' then you phone your friend who has a breakdown, he'll give you three hundred rand. If there is an accident and there are injuries, then you must first phone the ambulance and then phone the breakdown, but some guys phone the breakdown first.

Everyone does it. I did it three times. It was the end of the month, I didn't have much money, so I phoned. If there are two cars involved then it's five hundred rand. Lots of policemen have been doing it for a long time; it's good money. One of Bellville's best policemen, he probably makes a thousand five hundred a month from breakdowns, but he's also the one who catches the most *skollies*, so leave him.   – **Inspector Kotze**

Everyone in the police has phone numbers for lawyers – myself included. As a detective we charge people. After we charge the suspect, we start negotiating about the bail. There are cases where the bail is less than two thousand rand. The police can offer bail for minor cases. When the person is arrested, the detective sometimes reduces the crime. You'll find it's a serious crime but they try to turn it into something minor so that they can give police bail. They change the scene to favour the suspect so that they can exchange money.

There's a very good relationship between the lawyers and the police, especially the police who work in the cells and the detectives. They help the suspects get a lawyer. Then the lawyers exchange money with the police. There's also a good relationship between the prosecutor, the investigating officer and the lawyers. The lawyer gets money from the suspect for bail and then shares it with the policeman. The suspect just sees that the lawyer is there and he pays five thousand rand. I had numbers for lawyers. I knew that when I was on standby, I could call the lawyer and I would have a thousand rand when I left. This involved me; I did that.

The lawyers themselves would approach the policemen and say, 'Here's my card, you can make money.' They usually used to come to the station during the night and search for suspects. Then if there were suspects they would say, 'Who's the detective on standby?' and then they would call the person.

These were defence lawyers. The prosecutor was also involved, but he wouldn't get involved with the detective; he had a good relationship with the lawyer. It was a corrupt relationship. At night, he would say, 'Come and make an application for me – I'll buy you a drink.' A 'drink' in the police doesn't mean just a drink. If I say to a person, 'Buy me a drink,' I mean something of value.

It's simple to eliminate positive witnesses from the case, because the lawyer is your friend and you want him to win the case. Out of three hundred cases at a station, only one would be successful. I was a detective; I worked there; I know. All the cases were thrown out of court due to lack of evidence. This is being done on purpose; the policemen know what they are doing. They understand the procedures and because they know the evidential value of a certain item, they make sure that they mess it up so that the matter will fail. This doesn't mean to say there aren't good policemen out there – there are good policemen. But, out of a hundred per cent, I'd say twenty per cent are all right and the rest are corrupt.

– **Inspector Ramela (2000–2005)**

There's a saying that goes, 'When they beat you, join them.' So I joined them. I started taking *tsho-tsho* right from the beginning. Sometimes you could say it's *tsho-tsho*, but it's not really – it's just five rand for a cooldrink.

Since democracy, we don't ask for *tsho-tsho*. If the community feels they want to do something for us, then they do. We've been working well since 1994. Since then it's not *tsho-tsho* any more; it's a thank you, a protection fee. Taverns pay, taxis pay. It's not like we threaten with arrest and they give us money. If I don't ask for the gift, then it's not *tsho-tsho*; people just give.
– **Inspector Moji**

One night I found a guy in a Tazz; his tyre had burst. He asked me to drive to Mandalay and ask his dad if he could bring a spare. I said I could go and get the spare myself.

A few weeks later the dad phoned me and said he wanted to say thank you for helping his son. He came and gave me fifty rand and told me to go and buy cooldrink and chips. Fifty rand was a lot of money in '95. I don't think that's wrong. Nobody's been bribed. We just helped him and he thanked us afterwards.
– **Inspector Kotze**

In hindsight I've done things that could have been seen as corruption, but in practicality they weren't. Most police units at that stage would have an end-of-year party. They would go and solicit donations from people they had worked with. It's one thing I've never done personally, but I saw the effects of it.

I was called into a bottle store to attend a complaint of fraud. I interviewed the guy and he said, 'I know where the person is; I just want you to go and scare him so I can have my stuff back.' I said, 'No, sir, I need to investigate this. I can't actually do that.' I remember his words to this day: 'But I gave you guys a pocket of potatoes for your year-end function. You guys owe me.' That was like a shot in the gut and I realised that things we'd been doing as a common practice actually had ramifications.

It's lucky that that happened when I was still a detective constable, very early in my career. That's when I said to the guys I worked with, 'You can solicit whatever you want, but I won't have anything to do with this.' That was a big eye-opener for me in terms of what being part of the police really entailed. It made me realise that it literally is a slippery slope. You just start on it and then you're done. You wonder how many cops have been compromised because of something very innocent.

Luckily I realised it when I was a young cop. How many other cops realise it much later in their career when it's too late?

– **Sergeant Jordaan (early 1990s)**

When I was off duty at the bar, they would say, 'Hey my *bra*, take a hundred rand.' Even at the robot they would say, 'Oh, it's you – wait, wait! Take a hundred rand; put petrol in your car.' They do you favours so that next time something happens you should not be harsh.   – **Inspector Kekane**

When the anti-corruption unit was established in 1996, I knew the commander in Mpumalanga. He was a very strict and thorough person, someone you could learn a lot from, someone you could respect. I was at intelligence at that stage and they started with the restructuring process around 1998. I worked at the provincial office back then and, from the intelligence reports that I saw, there was starting to be a problem of corruption in the police. I put in for a transfer to the anti-corruption unit and I was interviewed. They had a very strict recruitment policy. It wasn't always followed, but in our province it was. They did a background study on you, then they had an interview with you. Eventually I succeeded and I was placed there. We had three offices. I was the commander of the Middelburg office for about a year and a half, then I became the acting provincial commander for about a year and a half. Then the anti-corruption unit was closed down.

When I was involved with the anti-corruption unit we dealt with four types of corruption. The old Corruption Act was still enforced back then. We had a lot of cases where police officers were involved in different types of criminal activities, like robberies, which were not classified as corruption. Our clients back then – if I can refer to them as clients – were basically the vehicle theft unit, the murder and robbery unit, and general detectives. They were our threats, although there were people from the uniform branch too. We were doing a lot of overt investigations but we also did covert operations.

When I had to go and arrest people, I would go to the station or to the Midrand murder and robbery unit with video coverage of the corrupt act so the whole unit would see. You would read the person's rights and arrest them. I wanted them to see that corruption is not something to play with. In a way I thought it would have some preventative value because it's not easy to go to a police officer's house and face his wife and children and to arrest him. It's also traumatising for me. Unfortunately I've been in a situation where I had to arrest colleagues that I knew from before I went to the anti-corruption unit. In some cases I worked with some of them. It's not easy; it's not nice. **– Senior Superintendent Boning (1998–2001)**

The biggest problem of working in an anti-corruption unit is the absolute hostility that you experience from your friends and colleagues. Absolute hostility. That is probably the most stressful situation that you could ever think of – to be ostracised, especially in small communities, and the policemen know who you are, and you're shunned.

The police organisation is a close-knit organisation. They are reliant on themselves. Your friends are your colleagues. And the wives and children of your colleagues spend time together. Now suddenly the children won't play with your children, the wives won't talk to your wife, your colleagues avoid you and you can't visit the police pub. The moment you walk in there, everybody keeps quiet; they don't want to know your troubles. Even if you do leave the unit and join another unit, they will always think of you as a spy. That's what makes the job so extremely difficult: you don't receive any kind of recognition or support from your colleagues.   **– Director Grobler**

We were at the anti-corruption unit for four years in Mpumalanga. Working with the anti-corruption unit you don't feel safe. People can come and kill you.   **– Captain Ndlovu**

I did special duties at Johannesburg International Airport, which is the crime and corruption Mecca of South Africa. We actually caught some police officers taking illegal immigrants through the border post. Unfortunately while following the guys we lost the police officers. But I arrested an illegal immigrant, a Nigerian. His brother phoned me and said he would offer me a price. I said, 'Okay.' I spoke to my partner and we decided that we were going to arrest the brother as well.

At the old terminals, the police station had a big glass window in front of it. My partner stood inside the police station and watched him bribe me. He offered me fifty dollars, standing in front of the police station. I was quite offended! Then my partner came out and promptly arrested him. I remember saying to my partner that it felt so bad; I felt like I was being arrested myself. I had the shakes!

We opened his wallet and found about four or five hundred dollars inside the wallet. I thought, such a cheapskate! So we took all his money and put it in the SAP13 and promptly arrested him for bribery and corruption.

I would arrest anyone for doing that. It's just unacceptable. There's no way you can justify being corrupt. I don't care if your children are starving; you can't justify being corrupt. There's another way to do everything. Corruption is not on the list.   **– Inspector (F) Kemp (2006)**

Corruption is a system in the police. When I worked for the uniform branch, we were the first to arrive at the scene of the crime. You arrive there and you find the suspect and he's kicking you and insulting you and there is a fight. You manage to arrest him, take him to the police station and write up your docket. The next morning at eight o'clock that guy is released. I started to think, how could I struggle so much to arrest that guy and then the next moment he is released? After releasing that guy I'd meet him and he'd say, 'Who do you think you are? Who can take me? I know so-and-so; I won't ever sleep in jail.'

I started getting angry because I had almost killed that man and he had almost killed me and then I arrested him and all of a sudden he's released. That is nonsense. I decided this guy had been released by the detectives. I thought, let me transfer to the detective unit. I went there as back-up for the uniform branch. I knew their frustration.

So I got a docket at the detectives. The case was for robbery of a firearm. He had robbed a security officer of his firearm. When they arrested him they found the gun in his possession, so it was two charges: robbery and possession. I interviewed him, and I was convinced this person was guilty. When I was charging him he hinted that he wanted to pay a bribe. He said, 'No, *bra*, can't we do something?' I was angry that this kind of thing had happened after I'd struggled to arrest the person before. I thought, ah, this is how it's working. I told him, 'Don't worry, we'll work it out,' and I sent the docket to court knowing that on the last day of the trial he would be found guilty.

I did everything that was required and took him to court. Then he got bail. It was okay; I was convinced I was going to get a conviction. I went to court twice but it was postponed. The third time the docket did not come back. Then I went to court and they said the docket was not there. So I reconstructed the docket. I went to the complainant, the witnesses, everything.

Maybe the docket was stolen and given to that guy and he paid. When he got to court, he was sure he would be released because the docket was missing and the case would be withdrawn. I had the new docket with me. I didn't take it through the procedures. I took it myself. I saw him there and he said, 'Bra, I thought we were going to talk, but don't worry, it's okay, some people will help me.' I said, 'Fine.'

When they called his name the prosecutor said the docket was not there and he decided to postpone the case. After they postponed the case I stood right in front of the prosecutor so that I could sign for the new docket myself and take it away. He said, 'No, I'm still going to check the docket.' I said, 'Okay, I want you to sign this for me.' So I wrote a little statement saying, 'I am Prosecutor So-and-So, I am taking this docket and I'm going to make sure that this docket is safe until the day of the trial. If the docket leaves the court it will go directly to the investigating officer.'

Then I started hearing rumours: people were saying that I thought I was clever and that I could be killed. A colleague was saying I didn't know the criminals in Mamelodi; they could kill me at any time. I came to understand that this cop was corrupt and had sold the docket. Two or three weeks later, the same cop was shot: the one who had been complaining that I had constructed the docket; the one who had been saying to people that I was going to get killed. I realised that it may have been that suspect who gave him money to steal the docket and that he knew that now the docket was back, he was going to court and could be convicted, so he needed revenge.

He went to court and was found guilty with the second docket.

It becomes difficult for one to work in that environment, undoing what someone else has done. After they shot him, I was frightened. I thought they might come and kill me because I had been the one driving the thing. I believe that he didn't have time to kill me before he was convicted. He was given eight years.   – **Inspector Kekane** (2002)

When the dockets are still fresh, the policemen will sell them straight back to the suspects and then say that the dockets disappeared. Sometimes they steal from one another. That's why it's important for detectives to lock their offices. If you don't lock them, other policemen will go and look at what dockets you have. Even if they don't know the people, at the back of that docket are the suspect's contact details. They need these heists and armed robberies – that's where they know there's money. After they get the docket they check the suspect is out on bail, they call them: 'Come, let's talk; here's the docket. You give me the money and we burn it now.'

I was never caught.

It's rotten in the South African Police Service. It's police culture: you don't report each other because he is doing it today and tomorrow it's your turn. You can't report somebody when you know you're going to do the same thing in turn.

I liked working in the South African Police Service; I liked to uphold the law, to help people. I resigned from the police because I didn't want to get fired. I was involved in corruption, but as time went on I decided, no, I won't get involved in these things because I'm serious about my post. I changed from detectives to the uniform branch. I was doing a good job.

– **Inspector Ramela (1995–2005)**

In Mamelodi most of the cases we dealt with involved family: a brother, a girlfriend, a friend, two friends fighting when they drink beer. Then the docket would come to me. I would go to the complainant and the witnesses. The witnesses would say, 'Those people are friends; they always fight.' I'd say, 'No, I need the statement so I can arrest that man.' Then they'd say, 'But why can't you talk with these guys? They are friends anyway.' I realised what I had to do.

In the docket the one is bereaved: he is the victim. The other one is the suspect: he doesn't want to go to jail. The victim needs some compensation or apology or something else. His main aim is not to get this person punished by going to prison. He just expects some kind of compensation.

I would start with the complainant because I knew that if I ever got involved in corruption where the complainant was not satisfied, then my action could be revealed. So the person who can protect me is the complainant. I talked to him. I said, 'Now that you've opened a case against that man who you see all the time, can't you think of anything that maybe that guy can do to satisfy you, maybe restore your friendship?' He said, 'Like what?' Now because I live in Mamelodi I often hear people say, 'If you assault me, you will pay me.' So I said to him, 'What if the guy pays you – will you cancel the case?' He said, 'I don't have any problem with that guy, but he must come and talk to me.' He wants the guy to apologise, to compensate him. He said, 'Since he assaulted me, he has never come back to me. I went to the doctor and he never cared how much I paid.' So I said, 'Okay, can I talk to him and find out what he can do for you? How much can he pay you?' He was afraid to say an amount so I said, 'If I tell him to pay five hundred will it be okay?' He said, 'Ja, ja, it's all right. In hospital I paid one hundred for the doctor.'

Then I went to the other guy. I said, 'Listen man, you will go to jail. That man is complaining that since you assaulted him, you haven't been to see him and he paid one hundred rand for the doctor. Why don't you go to him and give him five hundred rand?' He said, 'No, I can't go to him and give him the money, because then he'll go to the police station and say I'm harassing him.' I said, 'No, I can do that for you.' He said, 'Sure, if you do that I will give you something.' The complainant had also told me he would give me something. Now I'm in the middle. So he gave me the five hundred rand and I gave it to the complainant. The complainant gave me one-fifty for myself for cooldrinks. I gave him the withdrawal statement and he signed it. Then I went to the suspect and I said, 'I gave him the money and that guy is okay.' So he said, 'Take two hundred rand; do something.'

So that was that. I got three-fifty and I took the docket to court. The prosecutor read the docket; the complainant was satisfied so the case was withdrawn. It was the fifteenth or sixteenth of the month and I didn't have money, so at least I had that three hundred and fifty – it was something. That's how I did it.

I couldn't do it often. Usually the people who come to the police station are people who don't have money. If you ask him for a hundred rand, that is how some of us end up being arrested for corruption. Because we go to that poor guy and say, 'Okay, for me to cancel your case give me a thousand rand.' He doesn't have a thousand rand, so he reports you. You can't do this frequently.

I don't have any feelings about it being wrong. Sometimes when you do something that helps you, you become happy. I also helped those guys. I restored their relationship. The one did not go to jail and the other one was fine with it. **– Inspector Kekane (2004)**

We have a police warning system, but it gets abused by the detectives. You have a matter in front of you, like shoplifting. The policeman can offer bail, he can give a warning, or he can choose not to give a warning, and charge you a thousand rand. He tells you he will do you a favour: 'You give me a thousand rand,' and then he releases you on a warning and keeps the money.

I was involved in that. Somebody would get arrested for shoplifting and say, 'I don't have money,' and I would say, 'Okay, how much do you have?' They would say, 'No, I only have five hundred rand.'

'Okay, give me that five hundred rand then I can release you on a warning. But you mustn't go back to court with this slip saying you're looking for this five hundred rand – this is mine.'

You learn from the superiors. That is the police culture; that's how it is. You work in a group, you learn from them, you do what they do. Sometimes you go to the shebeens, confiscate liquor then share it among yourselves.

Then we have these things of policemen abusing power with building construction. There are policemen who are involved with the construction bosses. Those people employ illegal immigrants. They pay them every fortnight. When it's pay day the bosses don't pay, they call the policemen and then the police arrest those poor people. In turn, the bosses give those policemen money. They know they don't have passports. They just detain them and take them to Lindela.   **– Inspector Ramela**

Working in the riots in the eighties, beer was like water. When we were on patrol we took people's beers, but we didn't get drunk because we didn't sleep. We worked with the army. A soldier drinks like a fish, so we learnt from them. We drank while we worked; it was official. Even the chiefs. We would steal people's meat and make a braai. We did it all the time. We only took from black people.

We raped, we robbed. It was natural. It was functional, serious. I would say to someone's girlfriend, 'Let's go and sleep together,' and afterwards she would say, 'How much will you give me?' and I would say, 'Nothing,' and so she says, 'Okay, let's go to the police station and open a case of rape.'

It wasn't really rape. It wasn't forced. But there was a docket. The boyfriend would think his girlfriend was telling the truth, so he would say, 'Let's go to the police station and open a case.'

Robbery occurred in the shebeens. We would take the beer.

– **Inspector Moji (1985–1986)**

I've assaulted suspects for information and things like that. I have never taken bribes. Just free coffee from McDonald's and Sasol garages and free car washes at Total garage. — **Constable van der Merwe**

I had information about a chop shop in Harare. Every time I went there to look for a vehicle, there would be nothing in the yard. One night we went there and found a brand-new Toyota Hi-Ace GLX. It was flipping smart; it had just been hijacked. The one brown policeman who worked with me went and took the radio and two speakers out. His father had just bought a new car and he wanted to give them to him. He took it and put it in the police bakkie. We went to the station and booked the Hi-Ace into the pound. When we got to our car another policeman had stolen the radio from him! He was angry. — **Inspector Kotze**

White people were looking after their own. Black men were their tools. If there was a robbery at a shopping complex, you had to guard the premises until the next morning. But never a white person. Those places are huge. There was no security at that time. They would tell you, 'It's your brothers who did it, so you must guard it and wait for them to come back.' The people had stolen some things, but there were still things left there, so I would further the crime. I took some more things. That was the best we could do. It was cold; it was raining; I would go inside and take chocolates, cooldrinks, mielie meal, rice – whatever I didn't have at home. My wife knew. Where can you buy groceries at midnight? I didn't see it as a crime, but it was a crime. — **Inspector Moji (1980s)**

When I was in Joburg, I was stationed at Rosettenville detective services and then at Booysens. I was working with this sergeant. He said to me,

'I'm just going to visit my friend,' so I went along. His friend was a Chinese guy: 'Oh, hello Sergeant, how are you? Sergeant, you come for cigarettes today?' 'Yes,' he says. He says, 'Oh, you've got a packet of twenty?' He says, 'Listen here, you bloody Chinaman, you mustn't give me twenty; you must give me fifty, because twenty make me cough!'

Then we went there to this Chinese guy on a Friday. 'Oh, good morning!' says the Chinaman, 'Why you come Friday? Friday you know is for officers' day.' This has been entrenched; it's the done thing in some places. You go to the Chinese guy; he gives you your groceries for the week.

– **Director Grobler (1966)**

Four of the guys one night went to a *smokkel* house. They didn't find any drugs, but they took the guy's money – twelve thousand rand. They split it four ways. I heard about it; I knew about it, but when the internal investigators came and asked me if I would speak against them I said, 'I know nothing.' Those guys will kill you. Two weeks later they did it at another house; they stole fourteen or fifteen thousand. The guy opened a case and internal came to me and I said I knew nothing. But I knew.

– **Inspector Kotze**

We had corrupt guys at my station, but I could never prove it. Fortunately we put pressure on them and they left the police. I followed them around and they knew about it. I made it clear to them that I believed they were busy with something and I was going to catch them. It was tough. The fear – you know they are going to come after you, but at the end of the day you serve the community. This person who takes advantage, he's not just doing harm to himself, he's doing harm to the image of the whole police. You need to go and stand up in front of the community and they need to believe what you're saying. You can't tell them you're going to provide a good service and then you've got corruption there. It was difficult because nobody else in my station wanted to become involved. There was one guy who helped me. It was difficult, but at the end of the day it worked out. Even though we weren't able to punish him, we eliminated him: he resigned.

There was a lot of bad publicity when I was the station commissioner. I took it personally, so I went to a psychologist. It was in the mainstream papers. I went into the whole thing blindly; I didn't think it would hit the papers. — **Superintendent (F) January (2007)**

Sometimes you are trying to do your job faithfully, only to find out that your colleagues are selling you out behind your back. These suspects I arrested were working hand in hand with two inspectors at Parkview. All the state vehicles in Gauteng have trackers in them. The tracking system scans how many vehicles are in an area. The inspectors would log onto the system and tell the suspects where the vans were and what they were doing. They would sell the information to the suspects, then the suspects would go to a certain street and steal cars. When the suspect revealed that to me, I was shocked.

So unfortunately, I had to arrest two inspectors. It's bad. I can't trust anybody now. These are the people that I'm supposed to trust. Those kind of people can kill you. — **Constable Sibuyi**

I knew a policeman who was arrested for armed robbery. It went to court and it was thrown out. Now if you go to Mamelodi, everyone knows him. He's a constable and he's like a mafia boss, walking around the streets. I don't think they're winning the corruption war. — **Inspector (F) Kemp**

Life is a road full of choices. You make the wrong choice, take the wrong road, you'll end up on the wrong side. Luckily I haven't ever had to make the wrong choice. But I will always motivate in briefings and station forums, speak to the younger members about what lies ahead, because some of them can easily fall into traps. The way some of them are about cars and money – as soon as you see someone moving in that direction, you speak to them. But life is a road full of choices. At the end of the day, you didn't choose to be in the component or situation you're in, or to work under these circumstances. But you chose to be in the police, so the first choice you made was yours, and you need to adapt. Because there's two ways, you stay in or you buy out. Go and look for another security job, but don't make it unbearable for other people. With corruption, you're going to end up in prison. — **Inspector Lakay**

Corruption and extortion and bribery happen because of money: money and promotions. They don't promote older inspectors. We have a lot of experience; we know what we are doing but the state says we must study. How can I study when my children are still schooling? I can't afford to pay for a diploma or degree from UNISA. Always, in the third week of the month, we visit loan sharks. Then when my brother needs money, you say that it's bribery, it's corruption. Then promote me! — **Inspector Moji**

We used to go for illegal immigrants. People were abused. We used to lock up bakkies and trucks full of immigrants, and whoever had money would get out. If you had nothing you went to Lindela; if you had one hundred rand or upwards you put it in the hand. I don't know how they can try to stop that. Everyone was involved in that, working as a team – you can't say no. I was feeling shame for them: they come from so far, seeking shelter or food. I get paid at the end of the month, I have relatives here, I'm far better off than them, but I have to take their hundred rand.

It's a shame. There was a team of people; there was nothing I could do. I'm afraid of them. They work with guns. If you go and report them, then you start to become an enemy. Then when you do a raid, they can shoot you on purpose. They can make it look like an accident because you want to cost them their jobs. This is what we call 'police culture'. As long as you're in the same boat with them, it's very difficult for you to report them.

I started to pull myself out of there; I tried to be clean. If it's not in your blood, you can do it, but there's God in there; God is alive. Sometimes you have to have fear that God is there. What is God saying? Why am I taking this poor person's money? It's greediness. I felt very bad because I was abusing power. This is not good. I'm working; I get paid for what I do. They work very hard. You find they don't even have a shelter. They left families far, far, far from home. Some of the policemen even end up searching the people. That is robbery, common robbery.

I wanted to improve police integrity, but the thing is that there were too many people who only worried about salary. You must love what you are doing. I love the South African Police Service.

Corruption is killing us.   **– Inspector Ramela (1995–2000)**

I had a case of malicious damage to property. Every Friday when this guy got paid he broke the windows at his house. But the suspect was the one who was supporting the household. The family don't want you to arrest him; they want you to talk to him.

I took him on probation. I had the docket and I said to him, 'My *bra*, every time you get paid, give me a call and I will go home with you and you promise those people that you will not break any windows that weekend.' This guy's been paid so when I leave he will take fifty rand and say, 'Go and buy a cooldrink.' I wouldn't say that's corruption. I'm just concerned about making that family get along. If you arrest him he will lose his job and the family is going to suffer. They just needed someone to help them out.   **– Inspector Kekane (2004)**

I think corruption is getting worse. The guys are getting away with it. I worked at Komatipoort border post for three months in 1999 or 2000. There every police officer was driving a three-litre Camry, top of the range. The guys that were there before us told us to watch the vehicle theft unit. They were so corrupt that they only came there when there were cars going through. We arrested hundreds of people. Then about three months later they arrested almost the whole border post on tax evasion. One guy was arrested for three million rand. You've got to have a lot of money to be arrested for three million rand on tax evasion! None of those guys were ever arrested for corruption.   **– Inspector (F) Kemp**

Working in the anti-corruption unit was a very sad experience in a way. We were quite well known to the police officers and we received death threats on occasion, especially after I'd arrested four people from the murder and robbery unit in just over a week. After the arrest of the last two we received intelligence that a hit squad had been recruited to take us out.

What's heartsore about this is that murder and robbery work with murderers and robbers so they know them; they pay them; they get paid by them. The scary part of it is that if you had been killed in such an incident, the very same murder and robbery unit would have investigated it.

I changed my will at that stage to add a paragraph saying that if I died in such circumstances the case should be investigated by a specific superintendent and not by murder and robbery. If murder and robbery investigated my murder, what would be the chances of it being investigated successfully if they were the very same ones who had recruited the people to take me out? It's scary.

When I got that letter that the anti-corruption unit was closing down, I couldn't believe my eyes. At that stage corruption in the police was part of the national priority crimes. I thought to myself, the only possible reason behind this madness was that someone, somewhere was being protected.

– **Senior Superintendent Boning**

19

SEX AND POWER

It's easy to get sex when you're a policeman in uniform. Most police proposition ladies when they are in uniform or in a marked police car. Ladies like uniform. You see a car parked at the police station during the night and then you just talk to the woman and you go to the police car. We call it 'room service'. You do your job there. We don't do it any more because of AIDS.

When I worked on shifts, it was nice. Say it's you and me working. We would go and collect my girlfriend, go and collect your girlfriend, we work together the four of us. Then you leave me somewhere with my girlfriend and I do my thing and you do your thing and within some hours you come back and collect me and then we drop the girls off and continue to work. Shifts are like that. Even the detectives – when they take a suspect somewhere, they don't just go there. They go somewhere, sleep there, *jol*, arrest the suspect, detain them and then come back. It's nature; there's nothing you can do. They like us. Women like men, especially men in uniform.

When a woman is cross with her boyfriend and comes to make a case against him, we lock him up and then we further the crime. If the boyfriend assaulted her, then I take what was supposed to be taken by the boyfriend. I talk with her and then she gives me a thank you. The lady gives you her body because you arrested her boyfriend. If you push more than the boyfriend, then you are going to become her husband. She will say, 'Marry me.' Policemen divorce wives in the area that they come from and marry women in the area they work in.

Someone in our station has been suspended and fired for rape, but it was not rape. It was by mutual consent. The policeman's wife is a friend of the girl's mother. Then he goes with the police car and the girl comes out and they go and do their thing. The policeman's wife and the mother make a plan and open a rape case because she is sixteen years old and he is thirty-eight, so it's statutory rape. — **Inspector Moji**

Let's say a lady is selling dagga. She's running from the police in the veld. She will maybe ask for her freedom by offering sex. You are a police officer in uniform, so you will look around and then say, 'I can have this.' I've seen it happen to many of my colleagues – trying to arrest a lady and she starts to undress. — **Captain Ndlovu**

I saw many police propositioning suspects. When a person is arrested, they will do anything for their release because they are under duress. I know many cases where policemen were arrested for rape. Where women are arrested, especially for shoplifting, the policeman is then attracted to her and they start having sex in the police cells. Then you find that they don't deliver on whatever they promised to the suspect, so the suspect reports the matter and the policeman gets arrested. — **Inspector Ramela**

If you do a complaint in Plettenberg Bay and the lady is on her own, you can take it further if you want to. When you sit at the table, you feel if she's open to it or not; you see if they are flirting. It gets to a point where you realise this could go further. It's for you to decide. Some guys just take it further. If I had got involved with women I would never have done it with someone else there, with a partner, because that's when the shit comes out. When it comes out, it's not malicious. The guy makes a joke at a braai or a shift meeting – '*O, jy het lekker gekuier en by daai vrou goeie koffie gedrink*' – and then it's out. When you work in a small town, the guy that you work with is the guy who plays rugby with you and goes fishing with you. So your girlfriend and his wife work together, and that's where the problems arise. — **Inspector Marais**

Women liked us because of our uniform. White women never made moves on us. There was a white lady colleague who was very friendly – very, very friendly – when I was working at the security branch. Because this lady was so friendly, my friend who was new from the college thought maybe he could make a move on her. She got very angry and she reported him to our commander. They called that guy names and they beat him up. He was transferred from the security branch because of that. It was a warning for us to say, 'If you try this again …' But we never tried it, because we knew. **– Captain Mthembu (1991)**

One day we planned to do team building at Monwabisi Beach in Khayelitsha. We drove in a scout, a bulletproof vehicle. There on Baden Powell we found a brown man and woman whose car had broken down. The one policeman said he would quickly take the man to Tokai to go and fetch something to fix the car; we would wait with the woman. We went to braai and took the woman with us. Then this other policeman went with her in the back of the scout – quick-quick. The first policeman came back with her husband and it was as if nothing had happened, but it was in front of everyone. It's not difficult – it happens; it's there. **– Inspector Kotze**

Some colleagues get involved with women. We are human beings, but you must try to control yourself. In the 1980s, if you got involved with women you could easily get killed. If you were posted in a different province at a riot, those people knew there was a woman having an affair with a policeman. They would go to that woman and say to her, 'Because you are having an affair with the police and we don't like the police, you are going to pull him out so that we can find him. Otherwise, we're going to kill you.' She will do that; she will say to the policeman, 'Take me to the mall today.' They would wait at the clinic – you wouldn't know they were waiting for you – then when you came back they'd jump on you. At that time, in the 1980s, that's how most of the policemen were killed – beer and women.

You had to know you were there to work. If you wanted to drink, you should have bought your beer and drunk it where you knew you were safe.

Then after sleeping you could wake up and go and report on duty. If you went with the women and got liquor outside, then you knew your life was in danger. You had to control yourself. If you ran after those women, it would cost you financially; your family was going to suffer. Some of the police are divorced because of those things.

– **Inspector Mampuru (1980s)**

It is not difficult for a policeman to get a girlfriend. I used that kind of advantage for a period of time. But after I got married to my wife, I stopped. Also there are now diseases; you can't do that as much.

When I was a municipal police officer we were just doing guard duties. You could organise a girlfriend to come and do the guard duties with you. It was very easy. What made me stop was that most of my colleagues started having a lot of children. Because you had a post, you got a girlfriend and then all of a sudden she's pregnant. Then you change posts, you find another girlfriend and she's pregnant. All of a sudden you've got your wife who you left at home in Limpopo and you've got a lot of women. So I decided I didn't want to do that. I began gradually leaving that.

I would just initiate the relationship with them to prove that I could have sex with them. All of a sudden when I broke up with them, they would get hurt; they loved me very seriously. One of them even attempted to kill herself. That's when I came to realise the consequences of my actions. I became a one-woman person.   – **Inspector Kekane (1987–1989)**

When I arrived at Kameeldrift, no black members were allowed to drive a van, only white colleagues. This was 1995. I was the first to drive, but before that I would patrol with my white colleague. He'd go and stop at his girlfriend and I'd have to wait for him in the van. He'd stay there for five or six hours. You couldn't do anything; you couldn't leave. Then he would come back without even saying sorry and we'd drive to the police station or continue with our patrol.

That happened three or four times. I got very angry and I told another colleague, 'We are going out on a patrol, but this guy – if he does it today, you will hear me parking the van here at the door and I will leave him there with his girlfriend.' And I did that. His girlfriend had to bring him back. When he came in he tried to fight me. I told him, 'I can no longer tolerate this. If you want me to report this, then try to fight me.' He kept quiet.

– **Captain Mthembu (1995)**

When I was in Laingsburg, there was a woman who used to phone me when I was working night shift. She would phone for the simplest of reasons – a cat on the roof or a knock on the window. I knew she had ulterior motives. After a while I just didn't attend. She only wanted me there. I was one of those who – I don't know if it was through intelligence or stupidity – never took the opportunity. I know people who have done it, especially the men, but not most. – **Inspector Burger**

Most of these straight men, they're all so macho, saying, 'You gay person, go away,' but they are the ones who are screwing the gay people – look how they come on to me! It has happened – we went all the way.

It was after work. I hooked up with one of my colleagues. It happened with another policeman on another occasion as well. They were married and they are straight and they've got kids. So these straight people who think they're all so macho and biblically correct, they're the ones who are *steeking* the gays and the lesbians in the dark. Go to Steamers – what do you see there? Married guys making an excuse to their wives, 'I'm working late.' They're not working late; they're screwing the gay people! Then the next day in the office they're like, 'I don't want that gay man in the office.'

I've gone all the way with two policemen. The others flirt, saying things like 'sexy butt'. It starts out as a joke, because they want to see how you hold out. Then later you respond seriously and you say, 'Thank you, I appreciate it.' Then they become serious and they try their luck and you just tell them to piss off. They're just looking for a narrow hole to stick their dicks in. The lesbians are more out in the open; the gay men are more in the closet. – **Constable Louw**

I met my wife in the SAPS. She was my senior. Love is love; it's not a crime.

– **Captain Ndlovu**

There were lots of policemen and -women dating at the station and even getting married, divorcing and remarrying. This one guy divorced and his brother came and married his ex-wife – weird!

I think you understand each other when you both work for the police. It's very difficult to have a relationship with someone who's not in the police force and who doesn't know how it is when you work two night shifts and two day shifts. You spend a lot of time one on one with each other – two people in a vehicle. A lot of relationships start there. I mean, what do you talk about for twelve hours if you're with somebody else in a car? You do your duty but you get to talk to each other, get to know each other better; you don't just focus on your job.

– **Inspector (F) van Niekerk**

20

GENDER

You have to prove yourself much more than men have to. When I went for my first hostage negotiator interview there hadn't been females involved in this before. The first thing they said to me was, 'You're a woman; why on earth would we want you on the negotiator team?' They gave me so much trouble! 'But you're a woman; how can you do this if you're a woman?' It's much more difficult to prove yourself as a good police person. People just accept that the police*man* is good at what he does. You have to prove yourself more when you're a woman, definitely.   **– Inspector (F) van Niekerk**

When I started in the dog unit there was only one woman in the unit. We were not the most favoured people there. That's actually why it took so long to get in there – they didn't want us there. I actually applied to do task force training and they refused to take me because they didn't take women. That was quite a long time ago.

In the beginning it was difficult in the dog unit, but I've now been there for twelve years and you become one of them; you become one of the guys. I know I'm not as strong as them; I know that for a fact. You will never catch me working with another woman. I don't think it's safe for either of us. You need a man to help you. If you're arresting a suspect, you need that male to help you. That's it. I'll never take a woman as my crew because I believe that safety comes first and it's not safe for me and it's not safe for the other lady either.

But there's a lot of things that we do that the guys can't do. The narcotics guys phone me a lot of times and ask me to help them search women.

I've taken out narcotics in places where some people don't want to look! So it has its advantages and you work through the disadvantages.

I think that respect comes with time. You need to earn respect. I'm not in the dog unit because I'm a woman; I'm in the dog unit because I'm a dog handler. I don't care if you don't respect me as a woman, but respect me as a dog handler. That's what it's about. I'm a capable dog handler. If you are apprehensive of me because I'm a woman, I would hope that the way I do my work will prove that I'm worthy of your respect.

– **Inspector (F) Kemp**

The only time I experienced sexism was in 1993. We were the only two females in the detective branch of twenty to thirty members. We were both straight out of college. The fraud branch was looking for people and we were nominated to go. I think it was their way of getting rid of us. It was all men and we were the only women. – **Superintendent (F) January**

I wouldn't say sexual harassment doesn't happen, but each individual must handle the situation as he or she sees fit. I'm sure that if I had wanted to I could have made a dozen sexual harassment cases, but that's not the type of person I am. If I don't like the way you look at me or I don't like the way you touch me or I feel it's inappropriate, I'm going to tell you it's inappropriate and we're going to have a discussion and that's the end of it. Especially in the dog unit – making sexual harassment cases is not the way to go if you want to stay in the dog unit. There are better ways to handle inappropriate actions. If a discussion isn't enough, then I would probably go a different way, but I've never had to do that. – **Inspector (F) Kemp**

Sexual harassment happens all the time, especially at one of the bigger stations I worked at. Silly things: suggestive comments, things like that. Maybe it's my attitude towards it that helps – I either brush it aside or walk away. It came from seniors at the station. There were times when I considered taking action, but it didn't affect me that much. When I started at that station I was married already. There's never been a situation where I've been cornered, but I've always tried to avoid that, knowing how they are there.

So I've avoided being threatened. Most of the guys there are like that – not all, but the majority. I don't know if it's the culture or what.

– **Superintendent (F) January**

In Thembalethu, there was a brown woman. Everyone always joked with her. Her husband worked in another town and she wanted to get away. On my rest day she went and opened a case alleging that I had taken her into the computer room, turned off the lights and tried to embrace her. What really happened was we were all standing outside smoking and she went inside to get her lighter. I made a joke by turning the light off and slamming the door behind her. But I opened the door again immediately and I could see she was stressed. Then she thought, ah, here's my chance to get away, and she opened a case of sexual harassment. At the end of the day it came out that she had lied. She was in shit and they transferred her. But it was bad for me, all the stories about me.   – **Inspector Kotze (2005)**

When I started at the station nobody knew I was gay. I have no hang-ups with telling anybody I'm gay. I don't care what they think of me. I just think that what I believe in, I don't have to force it down on you. I won't go out and tell anybody, 'Hey, I'm gay!' If somebody asks me, 'Are you married?' I will say, 'Do you mean am I married to a man or a woman?' And they will look at me and say, 'Of course to a woman; who marries a man?' And I will say, 'But I'm gay.' That's when they get shocked and start with the Bible thing. Then my answer to them is, 'You're a Christian. I don't believe in God and I don't believe in the Bible, so piss off!'

I think because I've got this 'Never mind, fuck you!' attitude, I just don't care what people think any more. After I came out of the closet and told my mom I was gay, I've never had any hang-ups telling anyone. If somebody doesn't agree with me being gay, then it's his problem or her problem or the church's problem. They must sort it out for themselves. Every day people still come to me with their Bible stories saying, 'It's wrong – how are you going to have kids? What if everyone was gay? There wouldn't be a population!' And they say, 'Having intercourse isn't going to make anyone pregnant.' Well, as the one guy says in the movie *Milk*, I'll keep on trying! It's nice to try and it's lekker to do it. I'll do it and do it until I die!

With me, people accept it in the end. I think if you allow people to walk all over you, then they will walk all over you. Respect isn't forced down on people; you earn that, and I think I've earned that. But I see a lot of gay gangsters coming into courts or jail. Some of them are very 'fem'; they are queens. I see how policemen treat them, being very homophobic towards them. What I then do is I go up to the policeman in front of that gay person and I'll tell him, 'Do you do that to me?' And he'll tell me, 'No, but look at him – he's wearing women's clothes!' And I'll tell him, 'So, how do you know that I don't have panties under my uniform right now?' And he'll just look at me and say, 'Ja, but you're *gay*; he's a *moffie*!' So I'll say, 'Well, "gay" or "moffie", that's what I am too.' So I always try to stand up for my fellow gay people, whether they are prisoners or not.

I was once told that I should not kiss my partner when in uniform. I said to the inspector, 'Well, you kiss your wife goodbye and hello in your uniform, so what keeps me from kissing my partner?' Then I kissed my partner *again*!

I've worked with lesbians, mostly lesbians. The men are a bunch of women – they are very scared to come out. They are very scared to be discriminated against. But I haven't felt discriminated against, and if I do, I will do something about it; I will open a case. They know I will do that, so that's probably why they don't give me trouble. **– Constable Louw**

I was in the dogbox because I refused to wear a police dress when I worked outside. They were very strict. You had to wear your stockings with your police dress. I worked in a dress until about '94 or '95.

Once I had to jump over a barbed-wire fence and shoot a guy. Afterwards they had to take the rust out of my leg because it's not easy jumping over a fence in a dress. So then I just refused and they gave me a lot of problems. I told them I couldn't risk my life because I wasn't capable of moving around. How are you supposed to move around wearing a dress?

In those days if you were too fat you were taken out of uniform, women especially. You were a disgrace to the police force being so fat and being in uniform. But today, they just make all the uniforms bigger. A lot of things have changed.

– Inspector (F) van Niekerk

The hypocrisy that's going on! I'm gay. So here comes a prisoner. I would say to one of my close lady colleagues, 'Fuck, he's hot, you know!' And she would say, 'Yes, he is!' Some of the police guys would see this. They complained one day to my superior that I did this. I left it. Then Dina Rodrigues comes along. Dina Rodrigues, the baby killer, was a very beautiful woman. Policemen came from all over to come and see her. Senior officials came from all over to come and see Dina. 'She's a baby killer!' I said to them one morning in the parade, 'You people complain about me for saying a prisoner is sexy or well built. Look at you people, how you're treating Dina Rodrigues, and you want to tell me *I'm* the one making eyes at prisoners? You're insane!'

– Constable Louw

21

HUMOUR

It would take me ten years to write a book about the funny things we went
through.   **– Captain de Beer**

I laughed at myself on a number of occasions. The best was when we were
trying to search a person's house and I pushed my police ID card under the
door to convince the guy that we were police officers. He refused to open
the door or to return my card, and he called the police. When they arrived,
I couldn't identify myself, because I'd pushed my card under the door, and
I was seen as a housebreaker. After being pushed around a bit by these
police, the owner of the house opened the door and gave my ID card to the
cop. I received profuse apologies and promptly arrested the guy.

– Director Grobler (1978)

You get a complaint of a housebreaking in progress. The complaint is
dispatched by the alarm company to which the landowner subscribes.
Because we take housebreakings very seriously, you go there with sirens.
One member covers the front entrance of the house, another will cover the
back entrance of the house and another will scale the wall.

On one such occasion I decided to scale the wall, but when I jumped
I landed in the pool! And who was standing next to the pool? The owner
of the house! 'Excuse me, sir, what are you doing in my pool?'

'Sorry, madam, I'm Inspector Khan from the police. We had a burglar
alarm here and they said it was a housebreaking in progress.'

'*Ag*, the stupid alarm, how could they do such a thing? Look at you!'

The woman was so embarrassed that we had responded to a false call. She was overwhelmingly caring. She even wanted to give me a change of clothes, but her husband's clothes didn't fit!   – Inspector Khan

I was trying to kick a door down. They had converted an old garage. They had taken a steel frame and there was a prefabricated wall with a door set into it. My partner was shouting to me, 'It's coming down!' and I was saying, 'Yes, I want the bloody thing to come down!' Meanwhile, I'd actually kicked out the connectors of the steel frame and the whole front wall of the house fell into the house! So I was like, okay, I don't know how to explain this one. I had literally kicked the damn wall of the house in!   – Sergeant Jordaan

I did a deal and caught a guy from Vryheid. He was a truck driver and I met him at the Ultra City. He took out the dagga there at the Ultra City. I said to him, 'No, man, you can't take it out here; maybe there are policemen around here!' He said to me, 'Hey, I smell a *boer* seven miles away!'   – Captain de Beer

In the police, it's not funny: it's something real. We are working with serious things. There is no game. Maybe the game will be your life.

– Captain Ndlovu

There are a lot of things that happen in this job. Sometimes we laugh about them, but sometimes they can cost us our lives. It's part of the package. It becomes fun and it is serious at the same time.

We were doing a house penetration. One guy was supposed to kick the door in; the other was supposed to give back-up. He had to proceed and I had to proceed after him. We had to cover the house. So he kicks, he runs in. As he enters the passage, he comes running back out of the house. Without saying anything, he just came running out of the house. He came running out because it was dark inside!

Another time my partner went into a room and this guy was waiting there with a gun. My partner dropped his gun and dived for the guy! He tackled him onto the bed. I asked him, 'Why didn't you shoot the guy? It's much quicker to shoot the guy than to drop your gun and dive!' But it worked!

— **Inspector Lukhele**

We went through a period where me and the guys I was working with were receiving threats. It was very stressful. It was just before the '94 elections and we were all sitting in a Spur one day having a few beers, just trying to relax. There was a kid's party going on and the kid was squeezing a balloon. The balloon popped and of course, in the confined space, it sounded like a gunshot.

I remember the scene – me rolling out of the chair, drawing a gun; one guy jumping over the back of the chair, drawing a gun; another guy diving over the couch, drawing a gun. And the next thing I remember is the mother's eyes looking at these three armed men pointing guns in their direction.

It was a bit embarrassing, to say the least, but luckily she saw it in good humour when she realised the situation. — **Sergeant Jordaan (1994)**

We were on foot patrol in Manenberg Avenue. Then one of my colleagues said, 'Hey, I've been shot!' I said, 'But you're standing?' He felt under his arm and we saw blood. He fell to the floor and they started shooting at us with R5s.

We could just see the projectiles coming towards us. I picked him up and threw him over a fence, then went to lie in the gutter. This other constable was lying on the other side and he shouted, 'No, man, let's go and attack!' As he jumped out they shot his finger off and his gun fell. I crawled out to get his gun. I threw him his gun and he said, 'No, man, go look for my finger!' I said, 'Fuck your finger!' How could I go and look for his finger when they were shooting?

We called for back-up. The shooting died down for a couple of minutes. I loaded my colleague who had been shot in the chest into the van. I said, 'Straight to Jooste Hospital to stabilise him!' – Jooste is a government hospital in Manenberg. He took out his firearm and he said, 'My brother, although I might die, don't take me to Jooste; I want to go to N1!' He said he would shoot us if we took him to Jooste! Then we had to get the fast cars to close the road so that they could rush him to N1 City, a private hospital.

– **Inspector Lakay (1996)**

We got a complaint of a body lying in the veld somewhere. We rushed there with five or six of our vehicles and searched the veld, but didn't find anything. Then a drunk lady came out the house and she said, 'It was me that phoned the police; I just wanted someone to come and drink with me.' She had a couple of beers in her hand. We were upset at the time, but afterwards we all laughed about it. You get funny stuff sometimes.

– **Constable van der Merwe**

They give you a message on the radio that at house number such-and-such there is a problem. Then when you get there you find that actually there's no problem. It's only that this man is worried that they did not give him food, and he is not working and they did not take care of him. He is just creating a whole lot of nonsense. He just doesn't want them to close the door. He's the uncle, sleeping in the back shack. He's hungry and drunk.

So I asked him, 'What do you want?' He said, 'These people are undermining me. I am also part of this house.' I took him along to the police car and we started talking. He asked me for a cigarette and I gave him one. I could see he had cooled down. I had a packet of chips. He asked for them and I gave them to him. I said, 'You are hungry?'

'Ja, these people don't give me food; that is why I'm so pissed off.'

I said, 'Oh, you need food?'

'Yes.'

'Okay, let's take you to jail so that you can eat for free there.'

He said, 'What would you take me in for?'

'You can just go into your house and burn your bed and then we'll take you in.'

So we left him. Then they call us on the radio for a second time. That guy burnt his mattress! I was just joking with him, but he burnt the mattress! He dragged it out of his shack and put it on the street and burnt it! Fortunately, he did not burn his shack or the other houses. When I got there he said, 'You said you'd take me, so take me!' We left. That's how fun it is sometimes.   **– Inspector Kekane (2000)**

One day our detective vehicle broke down. So I borrowed a marked van. Me and my colleague were tracing a suspect in Soweto. This suspect was well known in that zone: they knew him and they hated him and they were afraid of him. We went to his house, but his wife told us he was not there. We said we wanted to come in and have a look. While we were talking to the wife, he was climbing out a small window at the back. We heard a noise and pushed through the door to find the window wide open. We chased him. He was jumping from yard to yard, so we lost him. We went back to the van and drove around.

In another yard there was a lady who was bathing herself in her shack. She was naked. The suspect opened the door to the shack and locked it behind himself. When he turned around, he saw this naked lady. She was shocked. The suspect looked at her and made the 'sshhh' sign and told her not to scream.

This lady was shocked, so she didn't listen to him. She screamed. When she screamed she didn't know who he was. She didn't know he was a well-known dangerous criminal. She took her high-heeled ladies' shoe and she started beating him up. She didn't know what she was doing; she wanted him out of there. The people next door heard her screaming. He opened the door and ran away, but people surrounded him and started beating him up. We didn't know what was going on; we were just driving slowly and looking for him. At one of the yards I told my colleague, 'People are running towards us.' I could see them in my mirror. There was this guy in front and it was obvious that these people were chasing him. So I stopped; I wanted to know what was going on. While I was standing there that person running in front just came and opened the door of the van and got inside! He climbed into the back of the van! Then we realised this was the same suspect we were looking for! It was funny.

He was injured – they had assaulted him badly. That's why he decided to come and sit in the back of the van – those people would have killed him.

                                                    – Constable Sibuyi (2007)

When I worked at a suburban station we had two local vagrants, Buddy and Sarah. One quiet Saturday, she was sleeping in a drunken state. My colleague and I passed and said to them if she was still lying there when we came back we would have to arrest her. So we left and when we came back Buddy had put Sarah in a shopping trolley and was pushing her along the road. She was just sleeping there. My colleague said, 'If this is not love, then I don't know what is!'

They were always fighting, but that day he didn't want her to be locked up. And there she was, sleeping in the trolley, oblivious to everything that was happening. — **Superintendent (F) January**

People in Sebokeng are still very cultural and stuff. You can still scare a person with things like the tokoloshe. Sometimes you can even threaten people with the tokoloshe.

This one lady, she woke up during the night and could hear things in the house. When she got up, things had moved around in the house. She got frightened that it was the tokoloshe. She wanted to serve a protection order on the tokoloshe to prevent him from entering her house. It's not very professional, but we all ended up laughing and she was actually quite upset with us. We explained to her, 'Listen, we deal with natural things, not unnatural or supernatural things. For the tokoloshe maybe you can go to the church and ask the priest to come and say a prayer in the house to make it leave you alone.' — **Constable van der Merwe (2007)**

One of the farmers in Laingsburg came to me one day and wanted to open a damage of property case. I asked him what was damaged and he said his ostrich! So I went there — it was quite far out of town. The ostrich was lying there, dead. I saw bicycle marks on the gravel road.

A day later, someone complained a couple of kilometres from there that his farm worker was missing. Two days later, I found the farm worker lying in a house, nearly dead, covered in pink marks. He had been riding on his bicycle when this ostrich came after him, kicked him off and they had a terrible fight. At one stage he grabbed a stone and hit it on the head and the ostrich died, so that's where the dead ostrich came from. I've still got the newspaper article. It was quite a story, especially afterwards when he described what had happened. He had told the ostrich to *fokof* and things like that. He was in hospital for quite a few days – he nearly died – but it was quite funny.   **– Inspector Burger (1991)**

When I was still working in Newlands, this guy was my senior. One day he was supposed to book on duty at ten o'clock at night. He was drunk, so when he put on his uniform he put on his shoes and jacket and shirt but on his legs he put on jeans – he forgot to put his work pants on. He had his police shoes and shirt and jacket and tie, but he didn't change his trousers!   **– Inspector Mampuru**

A colleague of mine arrested a guy and roughed him up a bit. They were looking for a video machine that had been stolen and they thought that this guy was the suspect because he'd been near the house at the time. So they took him and 'worked' him a bit. Then he showed them where a hidden gun was. They radioed back and said, 'Was there a weapon stolen from the house?' and they said, 'No, the owner didn't have a weapon.'

You pick up a guy, tell him he broke into a house, he tells you he didn't, you 'encourage' him to speak a bit and then he goes and shows you where there's an illegal weapon. That's quite weird! I laughed when I heard that – what are the chances?   **– Inspector Stevens (1994)**

I responded to an arson complaint. On my arrival I found a few sector vehicles already there. The house was engulfed in flames. The complainant told me that her husband was drunk and after a heated argument he had torched the house with petrol. We spoke for about fifteen minutes while waiting for the fire brigade. When she was done with her story, I asked her where her husband was and she told me that he was still inside the house.

I realised that he would burn to death if he did not get out immediately, so I ran into the house. There was burning electrical wire coming from the roof; the whole place was ablaze. I called the suspect's name, but he did not respond. Instead I heard someone going through the cutlery drawer in the kitchen. One of my colleagues standing outside the house told me that the suspect was in the kitchen and that he might have a knife.

Upon entering the kitchen, this short, skinny guy threw the whole kitchen cupboard at me, never mind a knife! It was one of those short metre-and-a-half high, half-a-metre-wide pressed-wood cupboards. He missed me and I got my chance to tackle him. I dragged him out kicking and screaming.

Afterwards I found out that he had used dagga as well, hence the strength.

That was one of the times that I realised that you don't mess with someone on dagga unless you have to. The guy was totally out of his mind!

— **Constable van der Merwe**

We had an informer, a white guy. I got the guy from Middelburg SANAB to come and assist me in Standerton. Now the informer would go and introduce this guy from SANAB Middelburg to coloureds in Standerton and then he would buy dagga there.

We visited the canteen first and we didn't realise it, but the informer was getting drunk. We decided we're going to knock them tonight, whether it's just a *zol* or whatever, because we wanted to use the guys to get more information on other guys. I gave the informer twenty rand of my money. At that stage it was a lot of money. I said, 'Listen here, we'll write down the number and everything; you buy whatever you can get.' He said, 'No, it's fine.' *Jis*, we were *kuiering lekker*.

It was about eight o'clock at night. This guy from Middelburg drove a Skyline. The sign they were going to give me was that they would put the hazards on when they were ready and I would come and knock them. So I was in the dark in my car. Then I saw the hazards were on! So I drove there and jumped out of my car. There I found the informer sleeping on the steering wheel – he'd accidently pushed the hazard lights – click, click, click.

I realised I couldn't turn around because it would look funny, so I went in there and I could see all these coloureds smoking with this policeman and I said, 'Hey, what are you doing here, whitey? Okay, I'm looking for someone but I don't see him here,' and I left. I went back to the police station and I was very cross with this informer: he had buggered up everything.

When my colleague came back, he said, 'Look at this little dog.' I said, 'Where did you get the dog?' He said, 'I bought it for twenty rand.' I said, 'That's *my* twenty rand!' He said, 'Ja, but look at the poor little thing; they didn't give him food or anything.' I said, 'You *bliksem*! You can't use my money to buy a dog; I sent you to buy dagga!' He never paid me back and in those days twenty rand was a lot of money!

Many times you could have applied for money for traps but if you lost it you would have to put in reports and stuff. So we *sommer* used our own money a lot. We lost a lot of money through that, but it was part of our life and part of our love for the chase. — **Captain de Beer** (1989)

I was in Montagu when a lady came to the station. She wanted to open an assault case but she didn't want to tell us what had happened. The woman's eyes were big and swollen and the man's face had scratches down the cheeks. You could see it had been a big fight. He had caught her with another man the previous night. When he caught her she and the other man were still lying there, and the husband used about twenty pins and he closed 'that thing' with the pins. She was so drunk that she didn't wake up. She wanted to make a case.

It sounds bad, but it was quite funny afterwards. It was as if he had stapled her closed. He said he was *gatvol* of her sleeping around with everybody, so he was going to close it now. There wasn't damage or anything; that's why it's easy to laugh about it. — **Inspector Burger** (1995)

Part of our job description in the crime room was to get the new dockets and if there were suspects, to go and arrest them. This case was for malicious damage to property. We had to go and wake up the complainant. We used signs; we used everything to wake her up, but it didn't work. The inspector picked up stones and he started throwing them on the roof. He saw it wasn't working, so he picked up quite a big stone. I don't know if he slipped or what, but as he threw it he lost his balance and it went straight through the living-room window. The neighbours woke up, the complainant came out and she was so upset that she withdrew the original case. She said she was going to open a case against *us* now. The inspector ended up having to come on his off-day and repair the window.

– **Constable van der Merwe**

My husband sometimes does very funny things to people. In the community service centre we have two material money bags that the bank gives you. In the one bag we put the fines and in the other bag we put the prisoners' money. Every time the shift changes, we must count that money and make sure it is correct.

Then one day he took a frog and put it in one of those bags. When the next shift came on duty the bag was on the counter. The guy wanted to pick up the bag, but the bag jumped onto the floor. Then he put the bag on the counter again and it jumped onto the floor again. Then he put his hand inside and he found the frog!   – **Inspector (F) Basson**

During the 2007 Rugby World Cup final – it was a Friday night, I think – I got on a motorbike, got to the police station and found I was the only one there. I think there were about fifteen people who were supposed to be there who had booked off sick!   – **Inspector Burger**

22

LESSONS

I didn't go to university. I was too busy learning. I learnt that life's not fair. Police taught me that. Somebody who looks guilty is not necessarily guilty. Somebody who looks innocent is not necessarily innocent. You need to be open-minded; you need to set all prejudice aside. Prejudice can jeopardise an investigation. I had to make those mistakes to learn. Not all black people steal cars; not all white farmers beat blacks up; not all people that live in the Free State are racist; not all people that live in Natal speak English. You've got to get that kind of shit out and then you start realising how wrong you could have been.

The old stereotypes – the minute you realise they're nonsense, you say to yourself, 'Everyone has the same wants and needs as the next one.' I realised that through experience, through different investigations – feeling sorry for black people and for white people, feeling a black and a white have been done in because of the colour of their skin, both ways. I experienced all of that: a white guy branded a racist because he happens to have an FS number plate and a black guy branded a criminal because he happens to be walking at eleven o'clock in that street. It's sad. It's facts. When you mature, when you realise that those stereotypes actually hinder your investigation, that they penalise you, then you grow a bit. You become a better detective; you become a better person. You realise that all people actually want the same thing.

– Inspector Stevens

The biggest thing I've learnt in the police is, racially, you don't judge a book by its cover. I started learning that when I went to the air force.

I'm an average white guy. Coming from school and with family and friends, you always heard blacks this, blacks that. The air force was the first time I was forced to interact with other races. The people helped one another a lot. When we had a PT session where you fell down, collapsed or vomited, it was mostly the black guys that came and picked you up and asked you if you were okay. The white guys were mostly snobby. So when I came to the police, I was already fine with it. It was at the police college where the other white guys suffered. My best friends were two coloured guys. I just told myself, I'm not going to struggle with those guys, because they're negative.

Some of my best friends are my black colleagues. You can't just say, 'Okay, he's black; he's bad.' Some of the black colleagues can really work; they're a lot like myself. One or two guys, if you wrote our personalities down on a piece of paper without our names, you might say we are family, we are brothers.   **– Constable van der Merwe**

I'm busy with a BSc degree in criminal justice through an American university. The irony is that learning American law enforcement and criminal justice has given me a unique perspective on my own country. Our investigations I think in general are better. I think our guys generally are better, simply by virtue of numbers: not a guy who is crunching dockets to close them, but we have exceptional investigating officers.

It's experience under fire. Think of a combat situation: if you go to war you're under pressure; the guys with a natural ability pick it up quicker – they have to deliver. Someone once said to me a detective is born – you either are one, or you aren't. You can take a born detective and train them and they will be a great detective, but if someone is not a born detective you can train them and they will only ever be an adequate detective. I think because of our environment and the volumes of cases our detectives handle, our natural detectives have a chance to thrive and excel and become exceptional detectives. The drawback is that in our environment our non-natural detectives don't even reach a level of adequacy.

A colleague of mine from the asset forfeiture unit and I went over to Scotland Yard and we sat down with the detectives in their public corruption unit, looking at methodologies – just a couple of cops sitting around the table, looking through their cases. One detective constable brought in this case and said, 'Look at this big case!' It involved Nigerians and it had to do with benefits fraud, similar to our social grant fraud. I asked if I could have a look at the docket and said, 'Have you looked at this? Have you looked at that?' And they said, 'Geez, no we never thought about things like that.' The guys said to me, 'We're realising that your experience in South Africa supersedes our own experience,' simply by virtue of the environment that we've grown up in.

Law enforcement guys in this country sometimes have a tendency to undersell themselves. They tend not to rate themselves highly. They say, 'But we're just cops.' That's a bullshit argument. Our cops should be proud to be cops. They shouldn't look at the money they earn, they should look at the skills sets they've got. Despite what people say, we do still have some really damn good guys.

One thing I can say, especially having worked with guys from Scotland Yard and the FBI, is that a South African detective doesn't have to stand back for anybody. I was on an anti-corruption course with the FBI. The guy that was the lead instructor of the course was a special agent who used to be the head of the FBI's public corruption unit. He was also an investigator on the Watergate investigation. This guy knows his stuff. He's kind of a legend. I went into a class presentation – I was the team leader – and we did a presentation on how we would do a particular investigation. He came up to me in the break and said to me, 'That's probably one of the best pieces of investigation planning I've ever seen.' And his exact words, something which will live with me, were, 'You would have made an amazing FBI agent.' I was like, wow! That is the dream. They are still something to aspire to.　　　　　 **– Sergeant Jordaan**

I have realised that it is so easy to become a convict, to go to jail, for something that you have not done. You will sit for twenty-three, -four, -five, -six years for something that you haven't done. But because you're connected to these people who did it, and they said that you were with them in the crime, and you're the only one saying you were not involved, you're going to go to jail with them until the court finds that you weren't involved. It's just so easy to be blamed for something that you have not done. There are so many people who have been convicted for things they have not done.

For instance, one lady came the one day and I overheard her saying to her friend outside the court, 'He didn't do it, but he deserves it. He didn't rape me, but now he's going to jail for thirteen years,' something like that. Maybe she was making a joke; I don't know.

It depends on how good one's lawyer is. I've seen some good lawyers and I've seen some bad lawyers. If your lawyer is good, even if you've done the deed, you will be set free. If your lawyer is bad and you haven't done the deed, you will go to jail. That's how fucked up our legal system is in South Africa.   **– Constable Louw**

I'm very grateful for what I've seen during my time in the police. It helps you understand people better. The public tell you things that you wouldn't hear if you weren't a police officer, because they trust you.

– Inspector Burger

I've learnt not to trust people. I don't have a middle point. You're either lying, or I'll believe a whole lot of crap. I'm very watchful of what people say to me because ninety per cent of the time they're probably lying. So I'm not very trusting and I think that comes from the type of job that I do.

– Inspector (F) Kemp

I do not trust people very much. This is something I learnt in the police. But on the other hand, I have learnt that sometimes I must trust people. I don't have another choice; I must trust people in my work. If I'm going into a house, I must trust that my colleague will not run away when there is a problem. He will protect me and I will protect him. It's still difficult for me to trust people, but I'm working on it.   **– Inspector (F) Basson**

I've learnt not to take things for granted, whether as a police official or when I'm off duty. That's one thing I've learnt in the police. When you drive you keep the doors locked, keep the windows up. Don't assume people at the robots are innocent passers-by. I always create a safe space for myself because when you least expect things to happen, they will happen.

I've also learnt to make use of my eyes. Use your eyes to the maximum. Take note of things around you, and don't take things for granted. It becomes part of your life. You don't have to worry about it; it doesn't cause fear. It costs you nothing just to move your eyes.   **– Inspector Lukhele**

This job has taught me that people are sick outside there. They are killing one another; they are stabbing one another; they are raping kids.

– Constable Shabangu

For a year and a half, I worked with street children. I manned an office in Woodstock. Schoolkids from different areas would come in. There I made food for them every day and gave them programmes like computers, sport activity, hygiene, safety on the road. We used to have social workers coming in to empower them. At the end of the year I did eight camps with sixty street children. It was hectic because before the end of the week they had eaten up half of the potatoes raw and half of the food. They would steal your stuff, so you needed to have a passion for working with them.

On the Friday you would cry with them. Especially on my fifth camp. The guys were from the Robertson–Paarl area. On the Thursday night they just started crying and it touched me. I lit some candles and made some juice and took out some biscuits, which I bought out of my own pocket because there's not that budget for street children, and I like my job. And as we sat, we discussed. The one boy started crying and another one started crying, and I could feel there was something wrong. And as I spoke to them, they said they didn't want to go home. They didn't want to go to their parents because most of them had been abused and there was no money. There's money on the streets.

On the corner where they slept in Paarl was an old bar. It was going to be demolished. By the time they got back on Friday, the building would be demolished and they didn't know where their clothes and blankets would be. I was crying with them.

I did a basic counselling course with Self-Help Manenberg. You learn to debrief yourself, but you won't get rid of all the pain when you see what people go through. You may think you sit with a problem, but at the end of the day you realise you don't have a problem. To you it's a problem, but if you weigh it against other people's problems, you've got nothing, only things that you brought upon yourself. Ninety per cent of the time it's stuff that you brought on yourself. — **Inspector Lakay (2005)**

We are all human. If you are human you must feel what the other person feels. If he is victimised, you must feel it because you are also human and that thing can happen to you. Respect other people. If you don't respect the person you don't know, then you are not a human. After dealing with a person, when they come to you and say, 'Thank you – you helped me; I'm over that problem,' then you know, I am human.

— **Inspector (F) Dlamini**

We applied through the police to join the peacekeeping mission in Sudan. I always like new experiences. I was there for seven months. You can't explain it. You have to be there. I got to learn some Arabic. Got to appreciate what I have in my country as well. I worked with other African police and exchanged ideas. We could see that we are really in front; we're tops compared with the other African police. The Gambians had to make their own uniforms – buy the material and make their uniforms!

There was a school in the desert, just outside Muhajariya in Sudan. It was just wooden poles with reeds as a roof. It was attacked and burnt down. We went there to negotiate with the rebels. I started a project where each one of us gave five dollars, then one of the guys went to Joburg to get books and pens and diaries and pencils and we rebuilt that school. They had been using slate boards before. So that was one of my proudest moments, just rebuilding that school, and what we meant to them for the seven months that we were there. I was proud that I could do something beyond what the normal police do.

I found it quite similar to South Africa. There were the privileged and underprivileged Arabs and there were the white Arabs and black Arabs, so it was similar to apartheid, but it was just more vicious. The way they went about killing – it was everyday life. There is no police structure; there's no law and order. There was a police station in the town I was in, but it was manned by the rebels.

I've applied to go back. I really want to take that process forward.

– Inspector Lakay (2006)

23

MESSAGES

I would like the people to know that police officials are also people. I know we have more authority and we can do a little more than the broader community, but sometimes people forget that we are also people and that if we get to a crime scene, we don't know who the perpetrator is either. We must also do an investigation to find out. Sometimes when you arrive at a crime scene the people say the police didn't catch the perpetrator yet. Sometimes the people know more than us, but they don't give us the information, and they want us to catch the perpetrators. We are still people; we are not superhuman. We cannot look through walls and see a rape happening inside a house or a thief inside a house.

– **Inspector (F) Basson**

Police are human. They feel what other people feel. The public must involve themselves in the community policing forums and do projects with the police and help the police out. The police can't work alone. We can't police without the community. Crime is not the responsibility of the police. It's the responsibility of the community and the police both.

– **Inspector (F) Dlamini**

South Africans must know that crime is not only a police responsibility; it's everybody's business. The police are there to facilitate so that the person can be put through the proper channels. But the community members themselves know the criminals; they can help us. We detectives come after the crime has been committed, then people are shying away. They are afraid of giving information to us, but if they could come and work with us we would have a ninety-nine per cent success rate. We need that relationship with the community; they mustn't see us as separate. We need them – without them we can't solve any cases.　　　　**– Superintendent Molebatsi**

Police are also human beings. South Africans should accept that and treat us like human beings. When it's their time for lunch, they go into Woolworths to buy a pie. You as a policeman go into that same Woolworths, but when you start eating, it's a problem. People think policemen don't get hungry, policemen don't get tired, because they're not part of society. But we're also part of a family. We're also fathers; we're also mothers; we've also got a need to lead a structured life. Sometimes the disgust that they throw at you – you don't deserve it. It might have been one of your colleagues, but not you. And going home every day, that stuff starts to have an effect on your life. If we stand together as one, communities and the police, we can conquer the world. We can conquer the world.　　　　**– Inspector Lakay**

Especially in white areas, most people still think, *ag*, the only reason you became a police official is because you couldn't find another job; you don't have matric – things like that. We've got people with master's and doctor's degrees who are working in the police. There are a lot of us who are studying and who are a little smarter than people think. You get people telling you these things. In the end the way I deal with it is when the person is locked up in the cells, I say, 'Okay, you with your university degrees, look where you are and look where I am now!' People think that we are still uneducated, when it's actually quite the opposite.　　　　**– Constable van der Merwe**

People must always respect the laws of the government of the country. They must abstain from crime. They must try to build a successful nation where we will respect each other. They must teach their children how to conduct themselves. They must look for things that will build their future. They must always trust in God and they must respect their elders. Their elders will teach them how to lead their lives.　　　　**– Inspector Mampuru**

I believe the citizens of South Africa should not cut the cops any slack. If they are treated badly, if the work is not done properly, they need to hold the police accountable. It doesn't help just to bitch and moan about bad police service or bad cops; they need to do something about it.

That being said, they mustn't be entirely negative towards the police. They need to support the police and be there for them because the police really do need the support of the public. There are a lot of good cops out there who are demoralised, who are run down, who believe that nobody believes in them, nobody supports them – and maybe in some instances they are right. But I honestly think the people of South Africa need to support their police. It sounds like a contradiction in terms, but by holding individual police officers accountable you are supporting the police, because you are supporting the cops who actually are doing their jobs.

If South Africa could weed out the cops that are there because they couldn't find something better to do, or they're just there to earn the money; if we had a force of police officers that were dedicated and committed to the country, we wouldn't have the crime problem that we have today. We have a situation today where they say, 'Sorry, I can't attend to that complaint because I have to drop my kids off at school,' or something ridiculous like that. We need to get rid of those cops: they dishonour the profession, they dishonour the badge they wear and they dishonour the memory of anybody who's ever worn the uniform.

We as law enforcement officers need to be held accountable. We need to be held to a higher standard and as members of the public we shouldn't tolerate anything less than a hundred per cent commitment and service. We need to create a culture where the police is a proud profession once again. Where it's not something you do because you couldn't find anything else to do. Where being a cop makes you proud: your community, your family and your friends should look up to you and say, 'Wow, that guy is a cop.' But cops also need to earn that respect, and they need to earn it by going that extra mile and doing their job well. I think the efforts of the good cops are being undermined by those bad apples that are hampering things for everyone else. We mustn't lose faith in them, but we can't tolerate incompetence or inefficiency or even poor service.   – **Sergeant Jordaan**

South Africans must just be patient with the police. We are getting there. We will fight crime, but we will fight crime with their assistance. They mustn't treat us like we are violent and brutal and corrupt. They must see police officers like their brothers and sisters who are there to fight crime. The image of the police has been damaged by the apartheid system and it will take years to fix. For many black people the police are still seen as the enemy. If you say, 'I am a cop,' you won't get all the answers you need. It shouldn't be like that. The South African citizen can change that.

– **Captain Ndlovu**

Black people have attached history to the police. The police are doing a lot in their job, fighting crime. If you are a Christian and there is one Christian who gets involved in crime or gets drunk, it doesn't mean all Christians are like that. You get police officials who are working very, very hard. Some have laid down their lives, lost their lives in the fight against criminal activity in South Africa. If black people could stop attaching history to the police I think we could have a better understanding.

– **Captain Mthembu**

It's not all bad. There are a lot of good people out there who are really putting their lives on the line for people they don't even know. You as the police will meet someone for the first time and that person's well-being is important to you. I don't think people realise that. They think we come to work and do our job to get our salary. But it's not always like that. You're going out there and you're doing things for people you might never get to meet again, but it's influencing their life in some way.

People ask how many people were murdered in a day. How many people were *not* murdered? I think we need to start looking at it like that, see the positive. I always try to look at it like that. Maybe there were five murders yesterday, but how many millions of people were not murdered? People don't look at it in that way. It's gotten better and it's going to get even better, definitely. – **Superintendent (F) January**

I'd say to South Africa that what messes the police up is not the policemen; it's the politics. Politicians mess the police up, really. Politicians use the police and misuse the police to achieve political goals, not to help the public. There's always three sides to a story: my side, your side and the truth.

– **Inspector Stevens**

People must know that we are there for them. On the other hand we are human and we need their support. We are given guns so we are better resourced than ordinary citizens, but for us to win the fight against crime we need their support. We are committed to fighting crime, despite our shortcomings. We are quite aware of those internal problems and some of our colleagues who do not take crime fighting seriously, but we would like to expose them. When communities are aware of them they must report it. – **Inspector Lukhele**

The average South African does not know of the dangers facing everyday officers. While most of us are at home, they are out on the streets trying to protect us – while their families are alone dreading a midnight telephone call from a kindly chaplain telling them that their loved one is not coming home, ever. – **Director Grobler**

The police don't have it easy; they really don't have it easy. Yes, I feel that everybody deserves the best they can get from a police service and they should get the best, but it's not the guy on the street's fault that he can't deliver the type of service that the people are entitled to. Sometimes we were working in a really big area and we were only one police vehicle, so even though you have two excellent policemen on that car, it's only one car. Even being great policemen they can't give the service that they are supposed to give. You've got two housebreakings at the same time; you can only be at one. So don't be too hard on the guy out there on the street. It's not easy for them. But we do need a better police force, we definitely do. – **Inspector (F) van Niekerk**

If you haven't been a police officer, you don't know what it's really like. People are quick to judge. There are a lot of good police officers who serve with pride and a lot of us do it because it's a calling for us, and that's why we stay. South Africans must see us for who we are and not judge us based on what the other twenty per cent are doing.　　　— **Inspector (F) Kemp**

Let South Africans love the police. It's the security of our nation. I'm your neighbour; I'm a policeman. You know nobody will break in. If you get broken into, then you don't go to the police station, you come to me. Then I take you to the police station and you open a docket and we arrest the suspect. Police are security. We are here to serve the people.

South Africa must love its country. The police are there for them. The world must know that when the World Cup comes, we are ready for them. We are just waiting. Nothing is impossible in South Africa. South Africa is a country of many possibilities.　　　— **Inspector Moji**

24

STAYING AND LEAVING

I enjoy my job. I cannot imagine doing anything else. When I am reporting for duty I know this is the only job I will enjoy doing. I used to build houses. I can put a roof on a sixteen-roomed house; I can do everything, but I don't enjoy it. The only thing I enjoy is policing. Every morning when I wake up I know I am going to meet different people and face different challenges. It makes you stronger.

Detective work is about problem solving. Sometimes when I have a docket, when I sleep, especially if I am looking for a suspect, I think, tomorrow, what should I do to track down this suspect? Sometimes I even have dreams about my job. I enjoy it.

Very few people will do this job because they really like it. Some of them just join because they couldn't find a job anywhere else. It was different for me. I had a job and I quit that job for this one, because I really love this.

When I was alone the salary was okay for me alone. I could afford this and that, buy a car, sell it, buy another one. But ever since I had a son things are different. I have to put money aside for him. I don't want him to end up joining the police service because he couldn't go to school and can't find another job somewhere; join the police as a last resort. I don't want him to do that like other people do. So I'm saving for him so that he can go to whatever varsity he likes. I will help him become educated. Then he must choose a job that he likes. When he needs something, I must pay, but my salary is still the same. I'm not concerned about it. The main thing is that I enjoy my work.

— **Constable Sibuyi**

It got to the point where, *waba*! That's me. I knew it was game over. You don't just resign from the police. It's not like it's Monday and Tuesday you resign. You have relapses and then you go back and you convince yourself that it's not that bad and you tell yourself, 'Maybe I will get promoted, maybe I will.' It's a whole emotional rollercoaster until the day you leave. Then you can't believe you've left and there's a piece of you that hates the police and another piece that loves it. It's the weirdest thing to explain, but it's an absolute emotional rollercoaster. It's the security you had which is gone and it's a fear of the unknown and a whole mixture of stuff just being slammed into you at once.

My fondest memories are of just being a policeman. It was an awesome experience. I'm glad it's over; I'm glad I made it out physically and mentally. I didn't come out too bad; I could have been much worse off. I know a lot of my friends are not well. Their minds are warped. For them, things are hard. It's sad; they're a product of the system.

I was very proud of being a cop because it was an upstanding thing to do. I didn't do it for the money, obviously, I couldn't. Anybody who says he's a cop because of the money is an idiot. I did it because I thought it was the right thing to do and I enjoyed it. — **Inspector Stevens**

I stay because I love this job. Sometimes I look at the jobs in the newspaper. I tell my wife, 'Hey, I saw a post at salary-level twelve somewhere, but not in the police.' I'm at level ten. She says, 'Hey, man, you must go outside and check other jobs!' and I say, 'No, I would rather stay in the police. I'm not going anywhere!'

I joined the police as a calling. You can't work for money, but I am satisfied with what I get. I tell myself the most important thing for me is to serve the community, to give the community a quality service.

— Superintendent Molebatsi

It's who I am. It's what I do. I've thought seriously of leaving, but at the end of the day it's what I do and I believe I make a difference. After you've been overlooked for promotion you get a bit pissed and you think, 'I need to find another job,' and then a week or two go by and you start settling down and you carry on; you come to your senses and you carry on doing what you're supposed to be doing.

If I look back, there are some times when it's not always been sunshine and roses, but I believe it's what we make of it. I have fond memories of the police. It's not fun when you have to carry your friend's coffin, but you get past it. It's gone and you carry on. I have fond memories of the things I've done and achieved. It's been great.   **– Inspector (F) Kemp**

I stopped enjoying the police five or six years ago. Affirmative action and the *boetie-boetie* nepotism – there's a lot of that. When I worked in Khayelitsha in 1994 there was a special constable who worked with me. They're no longer specials; they're all permanent. He became a sergeant, then an inspector. Then in 2002, he became a captain. He worked under me. I was his boss. He never arrested anyone, he didn't catch anyone, he slept every night – but he became a captain. I earned my police diploma in 1998. I didn't even bother to fetch it. It's useless in the police. I've applied for promotion seven or eight times. I'm *gatvol*. It's nepotism. Unfortunately there are many black and brown and Indian policemen and -women, who have studied and worked, but they are not getting the jobs. It's all the people who are friends with whoever. There are too many people in big posts who are incompetent. He came to the police long ago but has done nothing, now he wants to tell you how to do the job.

It's not lekker. It's not what it was. I want to work. I'm not keen for office politics. Everything's changed, unfortunately. If I hear today that I got a security job and can fly to the Middle East tomorrow, I'll go.

   – Inspector Kotze

I've never thought about leaving. According to me this job is a call of God. I don't think it's a good idea to leave. Let me work until it's time to retire.

   – Inspector Mampuru

I believe some members are there just to get a salary. Some of them are really stupid. It comes from the top as well. If I leave the police, that will be the reason. I can't see myself working with people like that – commanders who were special constables a while ago, people with blue overalls and a shotgun who used to guard the gates, Standard 2 or 3 qualification. With respect, maybe it's not their fault, I don't know. But some of them are now commanders and unfortunately they believe that when they get pips on their shoulders they get brains as well. I don't see myself working with those people. Unfortunately, promotion goes the same way. People who get promoted are not the suitable candidates for certain posts. One guy told me the other day, 'No, man, look here,' tapping the pips on his shoulder. 'You don't know, man, I know.' I said, 'You don't know shit.' That's too much for me.

But our intake at college were nice guys. One guy told me the other day, 'The real shit is going to happen when all of that old batch is out.' All the time I see people who were with me in the police or college – now he works for an insurance company or something like that. We put a lot of effort in but it's just easier for some to get promoted. I'm not talking politics; it's not only black or coloured members, but white members too. They get somewhere but are not supposed to be there, especially the butt kissers.

The majority of people who are leaving are white, because they are not getting promoted. I was one of the younger warrant officers in the police when I was promoted. That was sixteen years ago and I'm still here. I've got a clean record. I don't even have a warning against me. I've done everything from station commissioner to mortuary work. And people who were still in school at the time, special constables, they are the big officers now. That pisses you off.   – **Inspector Burger**

Some people survive on the basis that for them it's just money. For me this work is not just any other employment. It's more than that.

We can't run away from the fact that for some of our colleagues, policing is just a job. They will tell you that if they're not in uniform they will not behave like a policeman. But people are watching. People always see you as a policeman. Some people do not understand the importance of the integrity of the organisation at all times. That makes our job very difficult.

When I joined the permanent force I wanted to prove a point, to say, 'Look, we can do things better. There are solutions for things.' In 2008, I won the award for the Western Cape detective of the year. I had twenty-eight murder cases that I was investigating and I was able to solve twenty-six of them. I recovered about twelve or fifteen firearms. If you stay focused, anything is possible.

— **Inspector Lukhele**

I attended a scene. A man said to me, 'You know, your job, even if they gave me a hundred thousand rand per week, I wouldn't do it. I don't know how you people survive.'

Only when you get promoted do you feel proud. I also felt proud when I managed to solve a case. I thought, at least I contributed something or helped a victim of crime; I did something for somebody's life. When I was successful, I felt very proud of myself.

An old lady came to the station to get an affidavit. The policeman who helped her, the way he rose from that chair to fetch the paper for her, that old lady said, 'Ja, the South African Police Service, they are hungry.' They are very weak. Weak, weak. There's no self-motivation.

I left because I foresaw that I would not improve. I wanted to make some changes in the SAPS. I wanted to be in management one day, but I was demotivated.

— **Inspector Ramela**

I left the SAPS after many years of exposure to life-threatening and gruesome incidents which adversely affected my health so that I could not continue with my career.

I also realised that all my efforts in trying to build and contribute to the police image were in vain. I started units such as Anti-Corruption Middelburg, which was closed after we became very successful. I was also very frustrated with the fact that several top managers and senior managers are appointed without formal police or legal qualifications or police experience.

I have legal degrees and am still striving to assist members who were unfairly dismissed. I also have empathy for members who developed post-traumatic stress disorder. I assist members who become seriously ill to apply for incapacity leave or ill-health retirement as well as with claims.

I had a great career. I will always have a caring heart for the SAPS, especially for members who do more than expected, who go beyond the call of duty. — **Senior Superintendent Boning**

Sometimes after I have arrested someone I feel like justice has been done. Just to see that community member satisfied – sometimes that keeps me going. But I stay in the police because the family has got to eat. I must provide for myself and for my family. Most of the people – even senior management – if you ask them why they joined the police they will tell you it's so their family can survive, nothing more.

— **Constable Shabangu**

I loved the police force so much, but it wasn't such a difficult decision for me to leave. I knew I couldn't be a good mother and a good policewoman as well. I just felt somewhere along the line I'd be neglecting one of them. I could leave the police force but I couldn't leave my children, so that made the decision for me much easier.

Sometimes when I hear the sirens and I see the speed they are coming at, I miss the adrenalin. But what I miss, I can never go back to. I don't think it even exists any more – specifically that period in the early '90s. The type of police I see in the charge office now; I don't want to be associated with that. At that stage I was proud of what I was doing. I know the salary wasn't good, but as I've said many times, at that stage it didn't bother me. How it made me feel, how I enjoyed it – that made up for much more than the salary.

But now, you won't be proud of what you are doing if you go back. You'll just try to uplift all these people and try to make them be more positive, and do things the way we did them in those days.

— **Inspector (F) van Niekerk**

If I could have been in a different line of work, as a social worker or something like that, it would have been better for me because I think I'm more of a social worker than a police official. But if I change now I cannot start again, start at the bottom. Maybe one day when my children are bigger, maybe then I will start to study as a social worker. But I think I will stay in the police. I've been here too long to stop. And I love my job. I can also be a social worker in the police. I can also do social things here. It was the police who let me recognise that I like to give people advice and to help people where I can. The police is the place where I can live my dreams.

— **Inspector (F) Basson**

I've been out of the police now for two and a half years, but I can never say I won't go back. I enjoyed it. But you come to a point where you want to look after your wife and your children and you're going to work until you're sixty-five, and I must just get out of here now. If you want to work organised crime or detectives, you must be available at all times. If you're not available at all times, get an office job.

When I talk to the guys, across the board most of the guys with thirteen or fifteen years are leaving the police. But the guys with twenty-two, twenty-five years, they're staying 'cause it's not worth it to leave now. They've only got a few years to work it out.

It's more the white members, but also across the board, brown or black. First white, then brown, because of affirmative action. If you're a white male in correctional services or the police service you won't get a promotion. They'd rather bring in a black guy from the Eastern Cape. That's a big reason. A guy at Thembalethu was promoted after I investigated him for corruption. That same year I thought, it's not worth it. They said they would investigate him, but he's still there as a captain.

I've got no complaints. I just came to a point where I realised I wasn't going to get any higher than where I was. I could stay where I was, or I could go to the Eastern Cape or something like that where I could become a captain. But I enjoyed the police, I really did; the adventure – especially organised crime. You can be in Cape Town for four days, then Gauteng, then George. The friendship – you connect with three or four guys. And doing the work behind walls, places where normal people can't get. It wasn't the braais or the liquor; it was the partnerships and seeing a purpose in your work – that was the best. — **Inspector Marais**

I've applied for promotions several times, but I'm not getting them. When I joined the police I found lots of sergeants and inspectors who are very experienced and dedicated, but due to the financial situation in the police they were forced to resign and go to the private companies, just to support their family. That's the problem – we are losing lots of experienced members because of money. So not everyone resorts to corruption when they are looking for money: others leave. Those ones who leave the police are dedicated and experienced and not corrupt. Those who are doing corruption, they are lazy – they are not dedicated; they are always off sick. Whenever they are at work, it's corruption for twelve hours.

So my main aim for staying in this job is that I have a dream that one day I will get a top post, a post from which I will be able to make decisions that might be able to change these things in the police, especially financially. In the police, promotion is not an issue. But if you don't promote someone who's doing a good job, you must at least give him something to show that you appreciate his good work. So, the more years you have in the police, the more you should earn. That's the only way the police service can keep the skilled members in the service.

I worked with a white inspector in the house robbery task team. He was the best cop I ever worked with. He worked with all the top detectives in South Africa. He has resigned now and is working for an insurance company. He tells me that he doesn't enjoy what he is currently doing, but he gets a lot of money. He's just doing it for the love of money. He was an inspector for eighteen years – not eighteen years in the police, eighteen years as an inspector! He has never been involved in corruption and he was making a lot of serious arrests. If you can't promote people like him in the police, why can't you give them money for their years in the service, just to keep the expertise in the police? **– Constable Sibuyi**

I never thought of the downside of being a police officer; I always thought of the positive. The downsides came with the job. If I think back over the forty years that I served, I still think of the good things. The bad things were there – so what? You dealt with them. Had I been given a choice, I would have done the same thing, made all the same mistakes. **– Director Grobler**

The saddest part of my career was when I had to leave the police in 2004. I had to think very carefully. I just thought I had served enough. For me it was about timing. I was offered a post at the NIA. I just needed something new.

– Captain Mthembu

I can't go back to the police because if I do I'm going to be corrupt; what can I say? Because there is no money.

– Inspector Ramela

I'm all for justice and pro-justice and stuff like that. There is corruption in the police and the police have always got a bad name. If one person messes up, then everybody gets a bad name. But where I am now at detectives, I can see the good that I am doing in the convictions I am getting, and in the faces of the complainants, even though they are dissatisfied sometimes. I can see that I am making a difference. Instead of complaining about how shit the country is like some other people, I'm actually out there doing something, and that's what gives me pride in my job.

I stay in the police to give hope to other people. I love the SAPS. I always wanted to be a cop and I will probably die or retire from the police one day. This is not my job; this is my career.

– Constable van der Merwe

I literally was a cop 24/7. I wasn't your typical commercial branch detective. There were weekends when I would go and work with the flying squad. I would put my bulletproof vest and my marked police jacket on and I would work complaints, housebreakings and rapes. I literally lived for the job. Ironically I still live for the job. People laugh at me. I don't read novels; I read law books and academic books on criminal justice and forensics. I am one hundred per cent law enforcement – it's who I am.

I won't lie and say money wasn't a factor in my decision to leave. Money was a huge factor. And I'd been waiting for promotion: equity was coming into play and I'd been waiting for two years to get a promotion to inspector. But if I got inspector by some miracle I'd probably be an inspector until the day that I died. That was what was going through my head and I'm a little too ambitious for that kind of scenario. Secondly, the resourcing in my unit was atrocious. I was using my own car every day to go on investigations. I would go on call with my own car because there was never a car available. I'd also had somewhat of an ugly run-in with my provincial commander. We just never saw eye to eye. The SIU approached me. They were busy with an investigation and needed my expertise. I would be doing the same work I was doing in the police with the only difference being I wouldn't have powers of arrest.

It was an easy decision to make, but I didn't anticipate the reaction that I'd get from other cops when I did it. I literally went from being one of the boys to being a traitor to the brotherhood overnight, which was very sad. I still am close to the police today. I take an active role in helping guys in the police's computer crime unit with issues. Once a cop, always a cop.

– **Sergeant Jordaan**

I love this job. I joined because I'd lost family members in a way that could have been prevented. I heard that my mom and dad used to fight all the time, then they went to report it to the police and were told that they had to solve their problems themselves. But if my dad had been arrested before he killed my mom, this whole thing could have been prevented. I would have both my parents today. It was a traumatising experience for me to learn that my parents were no longer there. I decided that if somebody else could lose their parents or a breadwinner because of crime, it should be prevented. I must be part of the solution. I don't want anybody to go through what I went through. I've been through a lot, something which could have been prevented. I want to prevent that, to help somebody else. That's why I joined the police. That's why I stay in the police.

– **Constable Sibuyi**

ABOUT THE CONTRIBUTORS

Below is a summary of basic information relating to the contributors to this book at the time of going to press in 2010. 'Race' and gender are indicated using terminology in line with SAPS equity policy. Names indicated with an asterisk have been changed and are false. Names are listed alphabetically.

Wilna Basson
White female, 34
Service: 1994–
Highest rank: Inspector
Uniform/shifts, human resources, social crime prevention, court orderly, supply chain management
Served at Groblershoop (Northern Cape)
Pages 15–16, 26, 34, 75–76, 126–127, 169–170, 191–192, 250, 254, 258, 269–270

Johan Boning
White male, 44
Service: 1982–2009 (resigned after interview)
Highest rank: Senior Superintendent
Uniform/shifts, detectives, security branch, crime intelligence, anti-corruption, national evaluation service, inspectorate, serious and violent crime unit, internal security investigation unit, riot-related crime and violence unit
Served at Bethal, Middelburg, Witbank, head office (Mpumalanga, Gauteng)
Pages 4, 26, 39, 44–45, 47, 56, 106, 140, 143, 155, 158, 168, 177–178, 216–217, 228–229, 268–269

Tiaan Burger*
White male, 40
Service: 1988–2009 (resigned after interview)
Highest rank: Inspector
Uniform/shifts, detectives, flying squad
Served at Laingsburg, Montagu, George, Wilderness (Western Cape, Gauteng)
Pages 8, 59, 104–105, 131–132, 133, 142, 147–148, 160–161, 167–168, 178–179,
    193–194, 195, 199–200, 207, 210, 234, 246–247, 249, 250, 254, 266–267

Bere de Beer
White male, 50
Service: 1977–2009
Highest rank: Captain
Uniform/shifts, security branch, South African Narcotics Bureau, human resource
    management
Served at Ermelo, Middelburg (Mpumalanga)
Pages 2, 25, 43–44, 71–72, 88–89, 137–138, 142, 144, 146, 149–152, 165–166,
    203–204, 210, 241, 242, 248–249

Vuyiswa Dlamini*
African female, 43
Service: 1991–
Highest rank: Inspector
Uniform/shifts
Served at Ladysmith (KwaZulu-Natal)
Pages 11, 29–30, 48, 96, 127, 160, 176, 177, 256, 258

Stef Grobler
White male, 64
Service: 1963–2003
Highest rank: Director
Uniform/shifts, detectives, planning & research, housebreaking,
    national head of anti-corruption unit, fraud unit, narcotics unit, commercial branch
Served at Sunnyside, Pretoria Central, head office, Durban Central (Smith Street)
    (Gauteng, KwaZulu-Natal)
Pages 1–2, 23, 40–41, 42–43, 45, 53, 54, 75, 103, 108–109, 132–133, 162–163, 171,
    201–202, 217–218, 224–225, 241, 262, 271

Wendy January* (some details withheld)
Coloured female
Service: 1991–
Highest rank: Superintendent
Uniform/shifts, detectives, fraud unit (Western Cape)
Pages 13–14, 32–33, 61, 64, 78, 95, 139–140, 142, 176, 225–226, 237–238, 246, 261

Jason Jordaan
White male, 37
Service: 1991–1998
Highest rank: Sergeant
Commercial branch (Eastern Cape, Free State)
Pages 1, 12–13, 30–31, 61, 68, 100–101, 111–112, 134, 135, 157–158, 159, 166,
    168–169, 181, 216, 242, 243, 252–253, 260, 272–273

Peter Kekane
African male, 43
Service: 1987–1989 (municipal police); 1989–2006 (SAP/S)
Highest rank: Inspector
Uniform/shifts, detectives
Served at Mamelodi East (Gauteng)
Pages 7–8, 28, 59, 67–68, 69, 96, 98–100, 122–124, 206, 213, 216, 219–220,
    221–222, 228, 233, 244–245

Jenny Kemp
White female, 38
Service: 1991–
Highest rank: Inspector
Uniform/shifts, detectives, head office, dog unit
Served at Pretoria Central (Gauteng)
Pages 12–13, 31–32, 77, 112–113, 117–118, 140–141, 173–174, 176–177, 195–196,
    218, 226, 228, 236–237, 254, 263, 265–266

Gert Khan
Coloured male, 49
Service: 1981–
Highest rank: Inspector

Uniform/shifts, detectives, serious and violent crime unit, public violence unit,
   fleet management
Served at Stanford, Protea, Cape Town Central, Bishop Lavis, Mitchell's Plain, Langa,
   Mowbray, Bellville South, Wynberg, Rondebosch (Western Cape, Gauteng)
Pages 3–4, 25–26, 57–59, 70–71, 76–77, 144–145, 167, 175–176, 195, 241–242

Kobus Kotze*
White male, 34
Service: 1994–
Highest rank: Inspector
Uniform/shifts, detectives, PAGAD unit, armed robbery task team, organised crime
Served at Khayelitsha, Bellville, Thembalethu (Western Cape)
Pages 16, 34, 97–98, 106–107, 109, 110–111, 113–114, 115–116, 130, 185, 194, 196,
   207, 210–211, 213–214, 215, 224, 225, 232, 238, 266

Llewellyn Lakay
Coloured male, 47
Service: 1992–
Highest rank: Inspector
Uniform/shifts
Served at Manenberg (Western Cape, with special duties in Gauteng)
Pages 14–15, 72, 108, 121, 134, 141–142, 146–147, 166, 170, 187, 199, 226–227,
   243–244, 255–256, 256–257, 259

Huram Louw
Coloured male, 32
Service: 2004–
Highest rank: Constable
Uniform/shifts, courts
Served at Table Bay Harbour, Cape High Court (Western Cape)
Pages 20–21, 36–37, 38, 94, 168, 200, 234, 238–239, 240, 253–254

Sipho Lukhele
African male, 40
Service 1995–2001 (reserves); 2002– (permanent)
Highest rank: Inspector
Uniform/shifts, detectives, tracing unit, reaction unit, serious and violent crime unit,
   commuter services unit (railway)

Served at Gugulethu, Nyanga (Western Cape)
Pages 16–17, 83–85, 114–115, 116–117, 119–120, 126, 139, 147, 182, 186, 188–189, 190–191, 192–193, 243, 254–255, 262, 267–268

Mpho Mampuru*
African male, 54
Service: 1975–
Highest rank: Inspector
Uniform/shifts, riot unit
Served at Protea riot unit, Newlands (Parktown), Pretoria riot unit, Mamelodi East (Gauteng)
Pages 2, 23–25, 40, 41–42, 45–47, 55, 56–57, 77–78, 120–121, 157, 181, 198, 232–233, 247, 259, 266

Jan Marais*
White male, 41
Service: 1991–2006
Highest rank: Inspector
Uniform/shifts, detectives, organised crime, liquor task team, unrest unit
Served at Plettenberg Bay, George (Western Cape, North West)
Pages 13, 48–49, 69, 73, 76, 95, 109–110, 127–128, 159–160, 180, 202–203, 204, 205, 207, 231, 270

Bokang Moji*
African male, 50
Service: 1983–
Highest rank: Inspector
Uniform/shifts, riot unit, detectives
Zwide, Witbank, Pretoria Central, Mamelodi East (Gauteng, with special duties in Western Cape and former Transkei)
Pages 5–6, 26–27, 57, 62–63, 103–104, 129–130, 163, 170, 198–199, 210, 211, 215, 223–224, 227, 230–231, 263

Thabo Molebatsi*
African male, 41
Service: 1989–
Highest rank: Superintendent

Detectives, family violence, child protection and sexual offences unit
Served at Atteridgeville, Everton, Pretoria Central, Pretoria Central cluster,
   Mamelodi East (Gauteng)
Pages 9, 86–87, 127, 172, 185, 212, 258–259, 265

Ayanda Mthembu*
African male, 41
Service: 1987–2004
Highest rank: Captain
Detectives, security branch/crime intelligence/counter-intelligence
Served at Kameeldrift, Pretoria Central, Witbank (Gauteng, Mpumalanga)
Pages 6–7, 27–28, 49–52, 53, 59–60, 61–62, 66–67, 73, 128–129, 142–143, 148–149,
   171, 179, 232, 233–234, 261, 272

Bheka Ndlovu*
African male, 44
Service: 1991–
Highest rank: Captain
Crime intelligence, anti-corruption unit
Served at head office, Witbank, Middelburg, Vosman (Mpumalanga, Gauteng)
Pages 14, 33–34, 49, 92, 101–102, 105, 182–183, 187, 206, 218, 231, 234, 242, 261

Tale Rameama*
African male, 48
Service: 1982–
Highest rank: Inspector
Uniform/shifts, riot unit, tracing unit
Served at Sandton, Zustershoek, Pretoria Central, Pretoria Moot, Silverton,
   Mamelodi East (Gauteng)
Pages 4–5, 26, 42, 55, 104, 141, 198

Tshepo Ramela*
African male, 39
Service: 1995–2006
Highest rank: Inspector
Uniform/shifts, detectives, firearms and ammunition unit
Served at Linden, Douglasdale, Randburg, Sandton, Honeydew (Gauteng)

Pages 16, 35, 69–70, 114, 119, 121, 143–144, 145, 165, 179, 180–181, 184–185, 209, 211, 212–213, 214–215, 220–221, 223, 227–228, 231, 268, 272

Mandla Shabangu*
African male, 25
Service: 2007–
Highest rank: Constable
Uniform/shifts, detectives
Served at Sebokeng (Gauteng)
Pages 21–22, 37–38, 117, 155–156, 184, 208, 255, 269

Xolani Sibuyi*
African male, 33
Service: 2000–
Highest rank: Constable
Uniform/shifts, detectives, serious and violent crime unit, house robbery task team, cluster trio crime unit
Served at Parkview, Cleveland, Hillbrow, Linden, Sandringham, Johannesburg Central (Gauteng)
Pages 17–18, 35, 80–82, 85–86, 89–90, 130–131, 135–137, 163, 164, 175, 189–190, 194, 203, 226, 245, 264, 271, 273

Shaun Stevens*
White male, 39
Service: 1991–2006
Highest rank: Inspector
Security branch/crime intelligence (Free State)
Pages 11, 29, 52, 53, 60, 64–66, 74, 87–88, 92–94, 94–95, 124–125, 135, 172, 186–187, 201, 202, 209, 247, 251, 262, 265

Gert van der Merwe*
White male, 26
Service: 2003–
Highest rank: Constable
Uniform/shifts, detectives
Served at Sebokeng (Gauteng)
Pages 18–20, 35–36, 77, 78–79, 102, 117, 124, 153–154, 173, 178, 183–184, 197, 200, 204, 205–206, 224, 244, 246, 247–248, 249–250, 251–252, 259, 272

Nelleke van Niekerk*
White female, 37
Service: 1990–2002
Highest rank: Inspector
Uniform/shifts, hostage negotiator
Served at Lyttelton, Adriaan Vlok, George (Gauteng, Western Cape)
Pages 9–10, 28–29, 67, 72–73, 87, 88, 90–91, 98, 107–108, 109, 121–122, 128, 129,
138, 163–164, 173, 178, 191, 197, 235, 236, 239–240, 262, 269

RANK STRUCTURE IN THE SAP/S

RANKS POST–1 DECEMBER 1995*	RANKS PRE–1 DECEMBER 1995
NON-COMMISSIONED OFFICERS	
Student Constable	
Constable	Constable
	(Lance Sergeant)†
Sergeant	Sergeant
	(Senior Sergeant)‡
	(Senior Chief Sergeant)‡
Inspector	Warrant Officer
COMMISSIONED OFFICERS	
	Lieutenant
Captain	Captain
	Major
Superintendent	Lieutenant-Colonel
Senior Superintendent	Colonel
Director	Brigadier
Assistant Commissioner	Major-General
Divisional/Provincial Commissioner	Lieutenant-General
Deputy-National Commissioner	
National Commissioner	General

*   Shortly before going to press, the SAPS announced a return to the pre-1995 military rank
    structure due to take effect on 1 April 2010. The new system would mirror the old but would
    exclude the ranks of lance sergeant, senior sergeant and senior chief sergeant.
†   Ranks reserved for training institutions and stations without full sergeants.
‡   Ranks reserved for non-white members only, abolished late 1970s.

TIMELINE

1910: Founding of the Union of South Africa.

1913: Formation of the South African Police force (SAP).

1948: Formal institution of apartheid in South Africa.

1960: African National Congress (ANC) and Pan Africanist Congress (PAC) banned.
Sharpeville Massacre takes place on 21 March: police fire on protesters demonstrating against pass laws, killing sixty-nine people. State of emergency declared.

1960–1978: The letters 'B', 'C' and 'I' precede the ranks of non-white members to indicate the racial categories of 'black', 'coloured' and 'Indian'. Prior to 1960 the letter 'N' had been used to indicate 'native'.

1961: Umkhonto we Sizwe formed by ANC as a vehicle to wage armed struggle against apartheid regime.

1962: Nelson Mandela is arrested, sentenced to five years' imprisonment for incitement to strike and for leaving the country without a passport.

1963: Senior leadership of ANC arrested – Rivonia Trial commences. The accused are charged with sabotage and attempting a violent overthrow of the state.

1964: Nelson Mandela and the other accused, apart from Rusty Bernstein, are found guilty of sabotage and sentenced to life imprisonment.

1966: South African Border War/Namibian War of Independence begins in South West Africa and Angola. SAP members periodically rotated to the Border. Later the SAP deploys counter-insurgency members in Rhodesia and Mozambique.

1970s: Black members first armed with firearms. Formerly they were issued only with sticks, sjamboks, knobkieries and assegais.

1970: First black commissioned officer is appointed.

1972: First 102 women enter the SAP.

1975: First female commissioned officer is appointed.

1976: Soweto Uprising: police fire at children protesting Afrikaans Education policy. Later that year it becomes mandatory for all police to undergo crowd-control and counter-insurgency training.

1980: Race-specific police uniforms abolished in favour of one uniform for all members.

1980s: The SAP becomes increasingly militarised.

Black members given authority over whites.

1984: P.W. Botha becomes state president of South Africa.

1985–1989: ANC calls on South Africans to make townships 'ungovernable', Congress of South African Trade Unions (COSATU) established. State of emergency declared in South Africa, characterised by frequent political violence and sweeping powers granted to the police and military.

1986: *Kitskonstabels* introduced.

1987: Strikes led by 300 000 mine workers cripple the economy.

1988: COSATU banned from conducting 'political work'.

1989: F.W. de Klerk replaces P.W. Botha as state president.

South African Border War/Namibian War of Independence ends.

Trousers introduced as part of uniform for female members, with members no longer restricted to wearing skirts.

1990: Nelson Mandela released from prison: political parties unbanned. *Kitskonstabels* become full police members and municipal police absorbed into the SAP.

1992: In a whites-only referendum, 68 per cent vote to dismantle apartheid. Convention for a Democratic South Africa (CODESA) negotiations commence towards an inclusive and democratic constitution.

SAP Basic Training becomes multiracial.

Boipatong Massacre takes place on 17 June: Inkatha Freedom Party (IFP) members kill forty-six Boipatong residents in revenge for attacks by members of the ANC. The attackers are mainly Zulu hostel-dwellers. The Truth and Reconciliation Commission (TRC) later finds that the attack was planned with the help of police – a finding subsequently rejected by the Amnesty Committee. The event is the most infamous example of political violence relatively common between ANC and IFP members during the 1991–1994 period.

1993: Interim Constitution enacted.

Clashes between members of the IFP, ANC and the National Peacekeeping Force result in the death of 1 800 people in Thokoza and Katlehong, south-east of Johannesburg.

1994: First all-inclusive democratic election in South Africa; Nelson Mandela elected president in a sweeping ANC victory.

Community policing introduced in South Africa together with the first community-policing forums.

1995: The TRC begins work and testimony is given on torture and murder committed by SAP members under apartheid.

South Africa's murder rate peaks at 67.9 per 100 000 citizens, following years of escalating political violence. It declines year-on-year to a low of 37.3 per 100 000 citizens in 2008/09. However, numerous other categories of violent crime increase into the early 2000s, making crime a central issue affecting the national discourse and psyche.

The SAP merges with ten homeland police agencies to form the South African Police Service (SAPS). Civilian ranks are introduced in favour of the military rank structure.

1996: Final Constitution and Bill of Rights enacted by Parliament.

1999: Second democratic election; Thabo Mbeki becomes president.

2004: Third democratic election; Mbeki remains president.

South Africa begins to experience a rapid increase in what become known as the 'trio crimes': house robberies, business robberies and car hijackings, often characterised by gratuitous violence.

2009: Following the fourth democratic election and swearing in of President Jacob Zuma, the Ministry of Safety and Security is renamed the Ministry of Police. Political discourse suggests a possible shift back to a police 'force', readopting the military rank system and amending Section 49 of the Criminal Procedure Act to give police greater clarity regarding their right to use lethal force.

2010: High levels of violent crime mean that fear of criminal victimisation remains a dominant feature in the lives of many South Africans. Return to a military rank system appears imminent.

A draft amendment bill for Section 49 of the Criminal Procedure Act is released for public comment but is criticised for being inadequate.

TRANSLATION OF AFRIKAANS DIALOGUE

p. 36 *Ag nee, nog dieper in die kak.*
Oh no, even deeper in the shit.

p. 61 *Daar sal nooit 'n Engelsman in bevel wees van die eenheid solank ek lewe nie.*
There will never be an Englishman in charge of this unit as long as I live.

p. 90 *Dit reën en dit is flippin' koud. Gee my die* gun *en laat ons ry.*
It's raining and it's flippin' cold. Give me the gun and let's go.

p. 202 *Maar fok die* docket, *kom ons praat.*
But fuck the docket, let's talk.

p. 203 *Jy werk met hom.*
You work with him.

p. 231 *O, jy het lekker gekuier en by daai vrou goeie koffie gedrink.*
Oh, you had a nice visit and drank good coffee with that woman.

p. 248 *Jis,* we were *kuiering lekker.*
Jeez, we had a good time.

GLOSSARY

9mm: a pistol with a nine-millimetre calibre (Z88 9mm being the standard SAPS issue)

37mm stopper: lightweight anti-riot control gun used by the SAP in the 1980s

.38: a pistol chambered for the .38 automatic Colt pistol cartridge

.45: a pistol chambered for the .45 automatic Colt pistol cartridge

ag: expression of indifference or irritation

agent: a police official working undercover, often infiltrating criminal syndicates in order to get information on their operations

aggro: aggressive

AK-47: 7.62mm assault rifle, generally remnants of Soviet support for the anti-apartheid resistance

ANC: African National Congress

APLA: Azanian People's Liberation Army, the military wing of the Pan Africanist Congress

Article 49: see Section 49

bafana: literally 'boys'

bakkie: a pickup truck, a light vehicle with an open-rear cargo area

berede (eenheid): mounted (unit)

bliksem: an insult, implying a scoundrel or good-for-nothing

blougat: literally 'blue arse', a rookie

boer: literally 'farmer', an Afrikaner

boet: brother

book on/off: reporting on or off duty at the start or end of a shift

Bophuthatswana: homeland created for Tswana people under apartheid, located in the present-day North West province

bossies: crazy

bra: brother

braai: barbecue

Buffel: mine-protected personnel carrier used by the South African

Defence Force,
introduced in 1978

Canter: type of truck used to
transport prisoners

cash-in-transit (robbery/heist):
crime of robbery committed
against a vehicle transporting
cash, and its occupants

Casspir: mine-protected personnel
carrier accommodating fourteen
people, specifically designed for
South Africa's Border War but
later deployed in townships

CCU: crime combating unit

charge office: apartheid-era term
for community service centre

COIN: counter-insurgency

community service centre (CSC):
the civilian walk-in area of a
police station where civilians
typically report crime and engage
with police at the station

control: central radio control
through which all radio
communication is rooted

crew: passenger(s) in a police vehicle,
typically one driver and one crew
are posted to a vehicle

CSC: community service centre

dagga: marijuana

EAS: Employee Assistance Services,
a section consisting of social
workers, psychologists and
spiritual advisors, formed
to provide emotional and
psychological support to
police members

eish: expression of surprise,
exasperation or disbelief

FCS: family violence,
child protection and sexual
offences unit

fokof: fuck off

gatvol: fed up

GBH: grievous bodily harm (assault
with intent to do)

geregverdigde skietvoorval: justified
shooting incident

haasman (plural **hase**): literally
'rabbit man', a civilian.
Commonly used pre-1994.
The term equates civilians with
rabbits, suggesting they are guilty,
fearful and running, and reflects
a psychological division between
the lives of police and civilians

handler: an undercover
agent's contact in the police,
responsible for the collection
of the information received as
a result of the operation

Hippo: a mine-protected armoured
personnel carrier used by the
South African Defence Force,

produced from 1974–1978; prototype of the Casspir

hokkie vensters: garden-shed-quality windows

ICD: Independent Complaints Directorate. A government body mandated to investigate deaths in police custody and other serious allegations against police

IFP: Inkatha Freedom Party

impimpi: informer or spy, usually working for the apartheid police

informer: a civilian with whom a police official has an information-sharing relationship. Often informers receive monetary rewards for information provided

Inkatha: see IFP

IO: investigating officer, the detective assigned to a particular case

J534: fine issued by police

jis: abbreviation of '*jislaaik*', an expression of surprise

jol: party

kak out: to shit on somebody, i.e. lash out angrily at somebody

kitskonstabel: literally 'instant constable'. Afrikaans slang term for special constables, a reference to the short period of training they received

klaar out: to finish one's military service

Koevoet: a police counter-insurgency unit in South West Africa during the 1970s and 1980s infamous for its brutal effectiveness

Kombi: Volkswagen minivan

KwaNdebele: a former apartheid homeland created for the Ndebele. Located in present-day Mpumalanga

laaitie: a younger person, most often a young male

lekker: nice

leerling bestuurder: learner driver

Lindela: a centralised detention facility for undocumented migrants awaiting determination of their legal status in South Africa and/or deportation. Located in Krugersdorp, it is the only such facility in South Africa designed specifically for this purpose

matric: the final year of high school

medically boarded: compelled to resign due to medical reasons

member: an appointee under the South African Police Service Act. The term is colloquially used by police to refer to colleagues

MK: Umkhonto we Sizwe, literally

'spear of the nation', the military wing of the ANC during the anti-apartheid struggle

moer: to beat, assault

moffie: derogatory term for a gay person

municipal police: police employed by the municipality to enforce by-laws, not part of the SAP

muti: traditional medicine in southern Africa, includes spiritual components

NIA: National Intelligence Agency

Nyala: a multi-purpose mine-protected armoured personnel carrier accommodating ten

OB: occurrence book, the main register in the charge office/ community service centre in which events are recorded

Officer: term applied to commissioned officers above the rank of inspector/warrant officer

Okapi knife: a type of pocketknife, usually with a wooden handle

oke: guy, man, bloke

one up: describes a firearm that has been cocked so that a bullet sits in the chamber. Police in South Africa increasingly work with cocked firearms to allow for a faster response time should they need to fire their weapon

open unit: crime intelligence unit falling under the detective services

ou, outjie: guy

Ovamboland: name given to the area in northern Namibia and southern Angola occupied by the Ovambo people, and site of conflict during the South African Border War/Namibian War of Independence

PAGAD: People Against Gangsterism and Drugs, a community group formed on the Cape Flats in 1996. PAGAD has been perceived by some as a vigilante group. Its members were implicated in a spree of bombings between 1998 and 2002, among other alleged criminal acts

panga: machete

parade: a formal meeting and inspection at the beginning and end of every shift, during which messages are communicated and members are 'posted' or given instructions for the coming shift, or are debriefed

parcel (of dagga): equivalent of between five and ten bank bags of marijuana, most commonly wrapped in newspaper (around 150–300 grams)

passing-out parade: ceremony to mark the occasion of graduating from police college

pass out: to graduate from police college

poepdronk: literally 'shit drunk', extremely drunk

poephol: arsehole

police bail: bail issued by police rather than the court, in the case of certain lesser offences

PTS: post-traumatic stress

R1, R4 & R5: 7.62mm and 5.56mm calibre assault rifles issued to police and national defence force members since the 1970s and 1980s respectively

recruiting: identifying and negotiating with civilians or criminals to become informers to the police

SANAB: South African Narcotics and Drugs Bureau, a specialised unit in the SAP/S

SAP: South African Police (force)

SAP5: investigation diary, a log of all work done in a case docket

SAP13: the secure police store at each police station into which exhibits are booked

SAP135: incident report completed by supervisors when commenting on work done by an investigator

SAPS: South African Police Service

Section 29: the section of the Internal Security Act of 1982 that provided for a detainee to be held in solitary confinement with access only to state officials, for the purpose of interrogation. There was no prescribed limit to the period of detention

Section 49: the section of the Criminal Procedure Act governing police use of lethal force. The section was amended in 1996, before which police could shoot at individuals suspected of involvement in a range of crimes, from malicious damage to property to public violence, theft, fraud, arson, rape and murder, among others

Section 205: the section of the Criminal Procedure Act that compels an individual to disclose information pertaining to a crime

security branch: intelligence branch of the SAP (now 'crime intelligence')

sinya ngo-one: literally 'we shit with one hole', an injury to one is an injury to all. Police terminology particular to training college in the 1980s

SIU: special investigating unit

sjambok: short leather whip

sjoe: expression of relief or amazement

skelms: rascals, thieves

skollie: offensive term referring to a young man involved in petty crime, a gangster

smokkelhuis (smokkelhouse): literally 'smuggling house', an illegal shebeen or house out of which alcohol or drugs are sold

sommer: just, used to describe a spontaneous action

special constable: a constable recruited during the final years of apartheid to address a critical shortage of manpower. Applicants for this post did not have to meet the standard requirements for SAP recruits, nor did they receive very much training

spring: to jump

Standard: the term formerly used to describe levels of schooling, now replaced by 'Grade'

stasiebevelvoerder: station commissioner

Station Strangler: the name given to a serial killer who terrorised the Cape Flats from 1986 to 1994, sodomising and killing twenty-two boys and burying them in shallow graves. He would lure the boys to train stations

steek: literally 'to poke', to have sex with

stop: small quantity (about 3–5 grams) of marijuana wrapped in newspaper, the size of one or two thumbs

Supt.: abbreviation for the rank of superintendent, pronounced 'soup'

swart gevaar: literally 'black threat', a term used to refer to the perceived threat the black population represented to national security under apartheid

takkies: sneakers

test: to supply a vehicle's registration details to radio control to check its particulars, such as whether it has been stolen and who it belongs to

tjommie: friend

Tokarev: 7.62mm pistol of Russian origin

tokoloshe: a mischievous, dwarf-like evil spirit in Zulu tradition

tonfa: police baton based on a traditional Japanese weapon

Transkei: a former apartheid homeland created for Xhosas. Located in the present-day Eastern Cape

TRC: Truth and Reconciliation Commission, assembled after the abolition of apartheid. Victims of gross human rights violations under apartheid were given the opportunity to place their

experiences on record, while
perpetrators could give testimony
and request amnesty from both
civil and criminal prosecution

trommel: literally 'drum', metal
storage box

tsho-tsho: police term for 'petty'
corruption

varsity: university

veld: an open, grassy plain

Vista: clinic in Pretoria treating

sufferers of emotional and
psychological disorders

voertsek: literally 'go away',
an offensive expression
of dismissal

werk met: see work on

work on (a suspect): police
innuendo suggesting torture
or beatings

zol: marijuana cigarette, a joint

Do you have any comments, suggestions or
feedback about this book or any other Zebra Press titles?
Contact us at **talkback@zebrapress.co.za**

To contact the author, email **faull.andrew@gmail.com**

For Ryan,
with love, Lyds
xxx